Assessment G

Grade 1

INCLUDES:

- Prerequisite Skills Inventory
- Beginning-of-Year, Middle-of-Year, and End-of-Year Benchmark Tests
- Diagnostic Interview Assessments
- Chapter Tests in Multiple Choice and Mixed Response Formats
- Performance Assessments
- Getting Ready for Grade 2 Tests
- Individual and Class Record Forms
- Correlation to Lesson Objectives

Printed in the U.S.A.

ISBN 978-0-547-58678-6

13 14 15 0982 20 19 18 17 16 15 14

4500492622 B C D E F G

Contents

Tests and Management Forms

Overview of *Go Math!* Assessment

How Assessment Can Help Individualize Instruction

The *Assessment Guide* contains several types of assessment for use throughout the school year. Assessment pacing can also be found in the *Go Math! Teacher Edition*. The following pages will explain how these assessments can be utilized to diagnose children's understanding of the Common Core State Standards and to guide instructional choices, improve children's performance, and to help facilitate their mastery of this year's objectives.

Diagnostic Assessment

Prerequisite Skills Inventory in the *Assessment Guide* should be given at the beginning of the year or when a new child arrives. This short answer test yields insight regarding understanding of prerequisite skills. Test results provide information about the review or intervention that children may need in order to be successful in the coming year. Suggestions for intervention are provided for this inventory.

Beginning-of-Year Test in the *Assessment Guide*, is multiple-choice format and should be utilized early in the year to establish on-grade level skills that children may already understand. This benchmark test will allow customization of instructional content to optimize the time spent teaching specific objectives. Suggestions for intervention are provided for this test.

Show What You Know in the *Student Edition* is provided for each chapter. It assesses prior knowledge from previous grades as well as content taught earlier in the current grade. Teachers can customize instructional content using the intervention options provided. The assessment should be scheduled at the beginning of each chapter to determine if children have the prerequisite skills.

Diagnostic Interview Assessment in the *Assessment Guide* is designed to provide an optional instrument to evaluate each child's level of accomplishment for the chapter's prerequisite skills on the **Show What You Know**. The interview task items test children at the concrete or pictorial level where appropriate.

Formative Assessment

Lesson Quick Check in every lesson of the *Student Edition* monitors children's understanding of the skills and concepts being presented.

Mid-Chapter Checkpoint in the *Student Edition* provides monitoring of children's progress to permit instructional adjustments, and when required, to facilitate children's mastery of the objectives.

Middle-of-Year Test in the *Assessment Guide* assesses the same skills as the Beginning-of-Year Test, allowing monitoring of children's progress to permit instructional adjustments, when required.

Portfolios encourage children to collect work samples throughout the chapter as a reinforcement of their progress and achievements.

Summative Assessment

Chapter Review/Test in the *Student Edition* determines whether additional instruction or practice is necessary for the children's mastery of the concepts and skills in the chapter. The test includes items in free response and multiple-choice formats and a performance task.

Chapter Test in the *Assessment Guide* measures children's mastery of concepts and skills taught in the chapter. This test is available in two forms. Both forms assess the mastery of the Common Core State Standards taught in the chapter. Form A is a multiple-choice format test. Form B is a mixed-response format test comprised of multiple choice, short answer, and extended constructed response items. The extended constructed response items, with a Depth of Knowledge (DOK) level, can also be used with Form A.

Performance Assessment in the *Assessment Guide* provides assessment of each grade level's Critical Areas. Each assessment contains four tasks to assess children's ability to use what they have learned and provides an opportunity for children to display their thinking strategies. Correlations to the Common Core State Standards and performance indicators are provided. Use the 3-point scoring rubric on page xi in the *Assessment Guide* to score these assessments.

End-of-Year Test in the *Assessment Guide* documents each child's level of mastery of the concepts and skills for the current grade level and mirrors the Beginning and Middle-of-Year Tests. Used together, these multiple choice tests allow for monitoring of growth throughout the year.

Getting Ready for Grade 2

Getting Ready Tests in the *Assessment Guide* evaluate the children's understanding of concepts and skills taught as readiness for the next grade level. These tests are available in two forms. Form A is a multiple-choice format test. Form B is a mixed-response format test comprised of multiple choice, short answer, and extended constructed response items. The extended constructed response items, with a Depth of Knowledge (DOK) level provided, can also be used with Form A.

Assessment Technology

Online Assessment System offers assessment flexibility to individualize assessment for each child. It provides the option to print, electronically assign tests, or easily build your own test using a bank of questions displayed by standard. Upon completion of a multiple-choice test, items are automatically scored, providing instant feedback. Additionally, prescriptive suggestions are given to indicate follow-up instruction that may be necessary.

Data-Driven Decision Making

Go Math! allows for quick and accurate data-driven decision making so you can spend more instructional time tailoring to children's needs. The **Data-Driven Decision Making** chart with Diagnostic, Formative, and Summative Assessments provides prescribed interventions so children have a greater opportunity for success with the Common Core State Standards.

Intervention and Review Resources

For skills that children have not yet mastered, the *Reteach Book*, Tier 1 and Tier 2 RtI Activities in the *Teacher Edition*, or *Soar to Success Math* provide additional instruction and practice on concepts and skills in the chapter.

Using Individual Record Forms

Individual Record Forms provided for the Beginning, Middle, and End-of-Year Tests and Chapter Tests in the *Go Math! Assessment Guide* correlate each test item to the lesson or lessons the item assesses and identify intervention options. Keep a copy of each child's form and use it to:

- Follow progress throughout the year.
- Identify strengths, weaknesses, and provide follow-up instruction.
- Make assignments based on the intervention options provided.

Prerequisite Skills Inventory

This Individual Record Form correlates prerequisite skills items to previous grade level Common Core State Standards and to *Soar to Success Math* intervention options.

Beginning, Middle, and End-of-Year Tests

There is one combined Individual Record Form for these tests. Improvements from the beginning of the year can be tracked through to the end of the year. Intervention options are provided.

You may want to provide enrichment for skills where children show mastery. Independent enrich activities are provided in the *Teacher Edition* for each lesson. Activities are also available in the Enrich Book.

Chapter Tests

There is one Individual Record Form for both forms of each chapter test. Intervention options are provided to reteach or practice.

Performance Assessment

Performance Assessment, together with other types of assessment, can supply the missing information not provided in standard multiple-choice tests and balance your assessment program. Performance Assessments, in particular, help reveal the thinking strategies students use to work through a problem.

Performance Assessment is provided in many places in *Go Math!*

- Diagnostic Interview Assessments in the *Assessment Guide* provide one-to-one interview assessments for each chapter.
- A Performance Task for each chapter is provided in the Chapter Review/Test in the *Student Edition*.
- Extended Constructed Response items are provided in the Chapter Tests in the *Assessment Guide*.
- Performance Assessments with multiple tasks for each Critical Area are provided in the *Assessment Guide*.

Each *Go Math!* assessment has four tasks that target specific math concepts, skills, and strategies. These tasks can help assess children's ability to use what they have learned to solve everyday problems. Each assessment focuses on a theme. Teachers can plan for children to complete one task at a time or use an extended amount of time to complete the entire assessment.

Teacher Observation Checklists and scoring rubrics are available. (Use with Diagnostic Interview Assessments and Performance Assessments.)

- Checklists with performance indicators aid in evaluating children's thinking processes.
- A 3-point scoring rubric is provided on page xi of the *Assessment Guide*.

Depth of Knowledge

There are four Mathematics Depth of Knowledge, or DOK, levels. Level 1 *(Recall)* includes the recall of information such as a fact, definition, term, or a simple procedure. Level 2 *(Skill/Concept)* includes the engagement of some mental processing beyond a habitual response. Level 3 *(Strategic Thinking)* requires reasoning, planning, using evidence, and a higher level of thinking than the previous two levels. Level 4 *(Extended Thinking)* requires complex reasoning, planning, developing, and thinking most likely over an extended period of time.

Depth-of-Knowledge Levels for Four Content Areas, Norman L. Webb, March 28, 2002

Scoring Rubrics

Go Math! provides a 3-point scoring rubric to help teachers evaluate the quality of a child's work and level of understanding. In scoring a child's task, the teacher should ask two questions: How well did the child use math conventions to arrive at a solution? and How well did the child communicate the solution?

Poor sentence structure, word choice, usage, grammar, and spelling should not affect the scoring unless communication of ideas is impossible to determine.

3-Point Scoring Rubric	
Levels of Performance	
2	**Generally accurate, complete, and clear:** All of the parts of the task are successfully completed. There is evidence of clear understanding of the key concepts and procedures. Child's work shows that all answers are correct or reasonable.
1	**Partially accurate:** Some parts of the task are successfully completed: other parts are attempted and their intent addressed, but they are not completed.
0	**Not accurate, complete, and clear:** No part of the task is completed with any success. There is little, if any, evidence that the child understands key concepts and procedures.

Use for the Performance Task in the Chapter Review/Test in the *Student Edition* (SE) and the Extended Constructed Response item in the Chapter Test in the *Assessment Guide* (AG).

Portfolio Assessment

A portfolio is a collection of each child's work gathered over an extended period of time.

A portfolio illustrates the growth, talents, achievements, and reflections of the learner and provides a means for you and the child to assess performance and progress.

Building a Portfolio

There are many opportunities to collect children's work throughout the year as you use *Go Math!* Give children the opportunity to select some work samples to be included in the portfolio.

- Provide a folder for each child with the child's name clearly marked.
- Explain to children that throughout the year they will save some of their work in the folder. Sometimes it will be their individual work; sometimes it will be group reports and projects or completed checklists.
- Have children complete "A Guide to My Math Portfolio" several times during the year.

Evaluating a Portfolio

The following points made with regular portfolio evaluation will encourage growth in self-evaluation:

- Discuss the contents of the portfolio as you examine it with each child.
- Encourage and reward each child by emphasizing growth, original thinking, and completion of tasks.
- Reinforce and adjust instruction of the broad goals you want to accomplish as you evaluate the portfolios.
- Examine each portfolio on the basis of individual growth rather than in comparison with other portfolios.
- Use the Portfolio Evaluation sheet for your comments.
- Share the portfolio with family during conferences or send the portfolio, including the Family Response form, home with the child.

Name _______________________________ Date ___________

A Guide to My Math Portfolio

What Is in My Portfolio	What I Learned
1.	
2.	
3.	
4.	
5.	

I organized my portfolio in this way because ______________________

____

____

Name ______________________ Date __________

Teacher Portfolio Evaluation

Evaluating Performance	Evidence and Comments
1. What mathematical understandings are demonstrated?	
2. What skills are demonstrated?	
3. What approaches to problem solving and critical thinking are evident?	
4. What work habits and attitudes are demonstrated?	

Summary of Portfolio Assessment					
For This Review			**Since Last Review**		
Excellent	Good	Fair	Improving	About the Same	Not as Good

Date ________________

Dear Family,

This is your child's math portfolio. It contains work samples that your child and I have selected to show how their abilities in math have grown. Your child can explain what each sample shows.

Please look over the portfolio with your child and write a few comments in the blank space at the bottom of this sheet about what you have seen. Your child has been asked to bring the portfolio with your comments back to school.

Thank you for helping your child evaluate their portfolio and for taking pride in the work they have done. Your interest and support are important to your child's work in school.

Sincerely,

____
(Teacher)

Response to Portfolio:

____
(Family Member)

Name ______________________

1.

○ 4 + 2 ○ 5 + 2

○ 4 + 3 ○ 5 + 3

2.

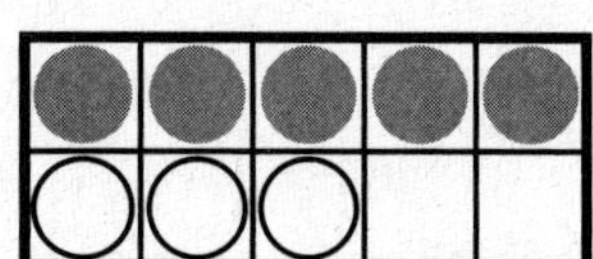

○ 7 − 3 ○ 8 − 3

○ 7 − 2 ○ 8 − 5

3.

○ 2 ○ 4

○ 3 ○ 8

4.

6 + 4 = ____

○ 10 ○ 4

○ 6 ○ 1

DIRECTIONS **1.** There are 4 flowers in the vase. Eva puts 3 more flowers in the vase. Mark beside the addition that shows how many flowers there are now. **2.** Jamie has 8 counters. 3 counters are white. Mark beside the subtraction that shows how many counters are gray. **3.** There are 6 frogs at a pond. 2 hop away. How many frogs are left? Mark beside the number. **4.** There are 4 ducks at the pond. 6 ducks join them. How many ducks are there altogether? Mark beside the number.

Name ______________________

5.

☆☆☆☆☆ + ______ = 10

- ○ 6
- ○ 4
- ○ 5
- ○ 3

6.

9 + ______ = 10

- ○ 3
- ○ 1
- ○ 2
- ○ 0

7.

71	72	73	74	75	76	77	78	79	80
81	82	83	84	85	86	87	88	89	90
91	92	93	94	95	96	97	98	99	__

- ○ 100
- ○ 89
- ○ 90
- ○ 80

8.

- ○ 20
- ○ 18
- ○ 19
- ○ 17

DIRECTIONS **5.** Count the stars. How many more stars are needed to make 10? Mark beside the number. **6.** What number is being added to the set? Mark beside the number. **7.** Point to the numbers as you count. Mark beside the number that completes the counting order. **8.** Count the baseballs. Mark beside the number that shows how many.

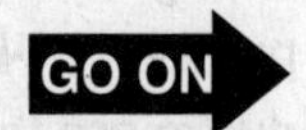

Name ______________________________

9.

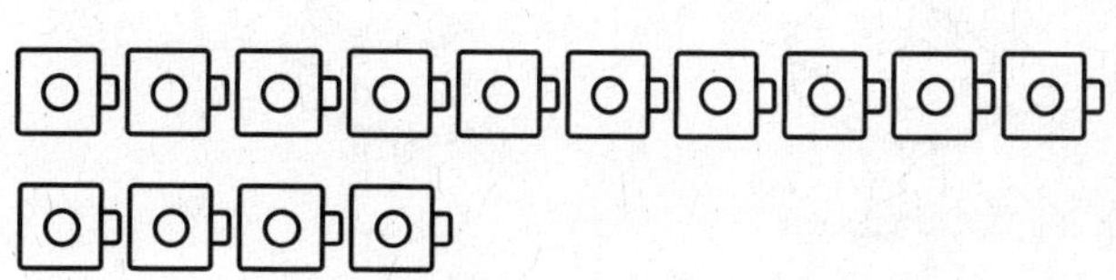

○ 5
○ 15
○ 14
○ 24

10.

5

○ 7
○ 3
○ 4
○ 1

11.

7

○ 2
○ 9
○ 7
○ 10

12.

○ 5 = 1 + 4
○ 3 = 2 + 1
○ 5 = 3 + 2
○ 4 = 3 + 1

DIRECTIONS **9.** Count the cubes. Mark beside the number that shows how many. **10.** Mark beside the number that is greater than the number at the beginning of the row. **11.** Mark beside the number that is less than the number at the beginning of the row. **12.** Mark beside the addition sentence that shows the number pair that matches the picture.

GO ON

13.

○ ○ ○ ○

14.

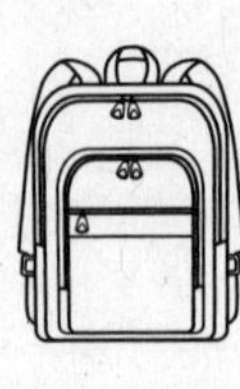

○ ○ ○ ○

15.

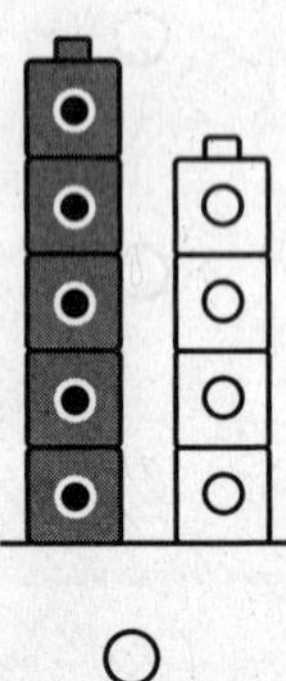
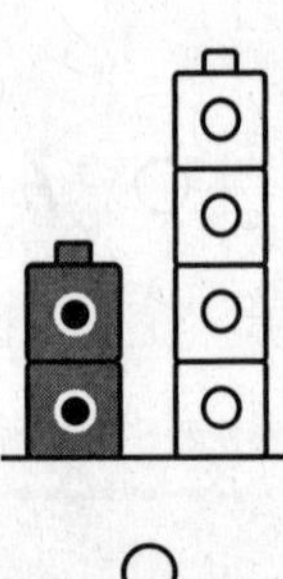
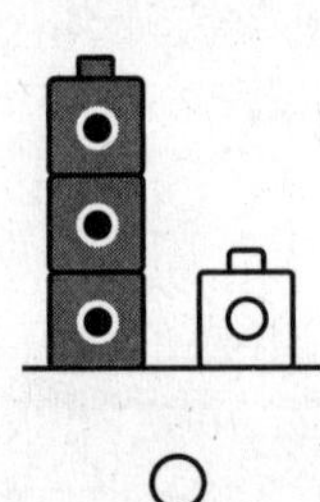
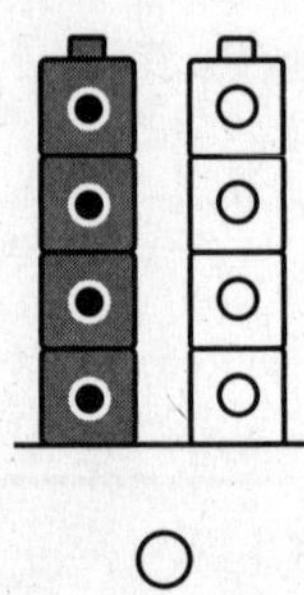

○ ○ ○ ○

16.

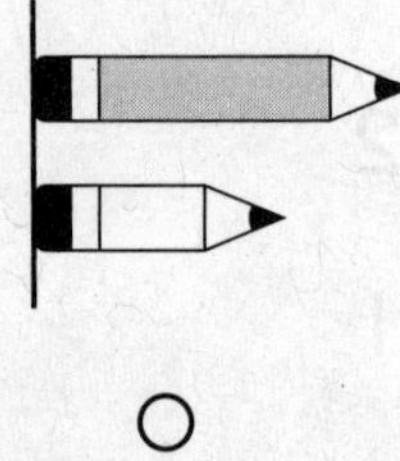
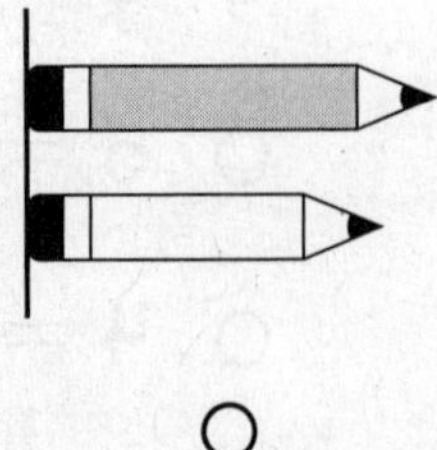
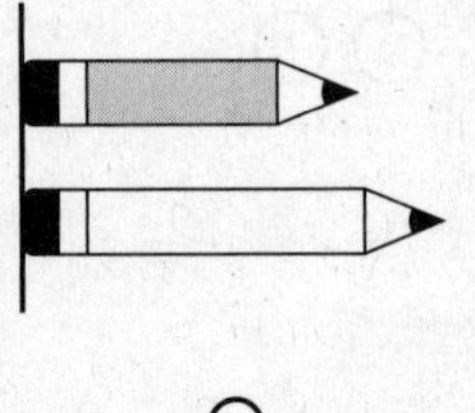
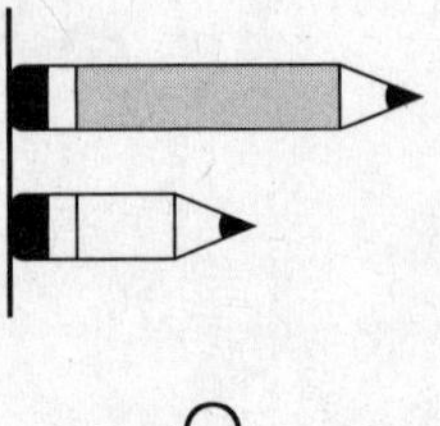

○ ○ ○ ○

DIRECTIONS **13.** Which tree is taller? Mark below the picture. **14.** Mark below the object that is lighter than a book. **15.** Mark under the set that shows that the gray cube tower is shorter than the white cube tower. **16.** Mark below the set that shows that the gray pencil is shorter than the white pencil.

17.

○ 5 ○ 3

○ 4 ○ 2

18.

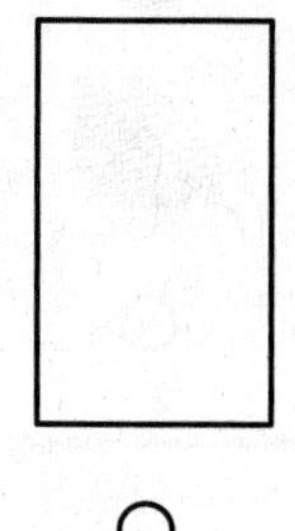

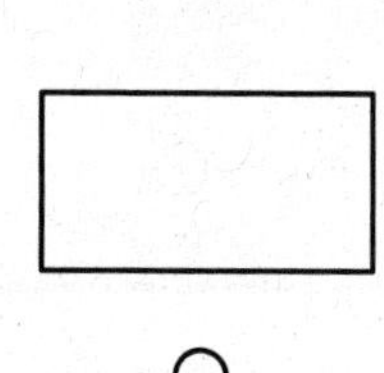

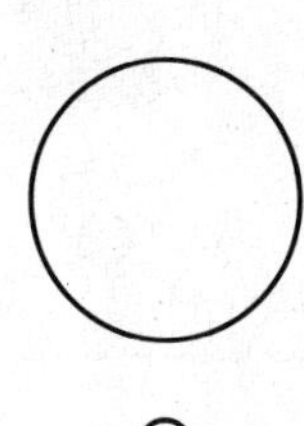

○ ○ ○ ○

19.

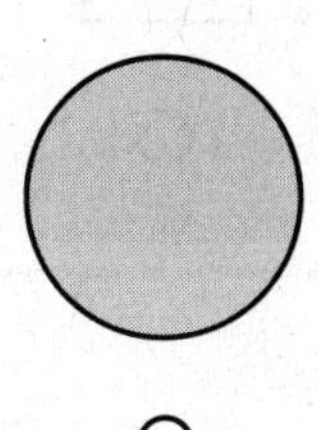

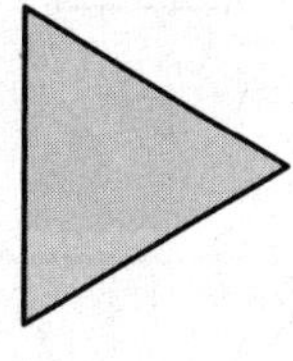

○ ○ ○ ○

20.

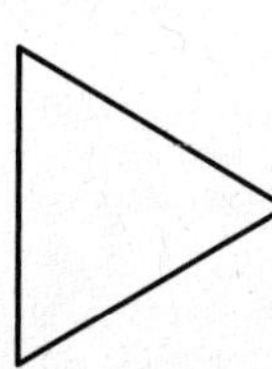

○ 2 ○ 4

○ 3 ○ 5

DIRECTIONS **17.** How many sides does a square have? Mark beside the number. **18.** Mark under the shape that does not belong. **19.** Mark under the size shape that does not belong. **20.** Mark beside the number that shows how many corners or vertices the triangle has.

GO ON

Name ______________________________

21.

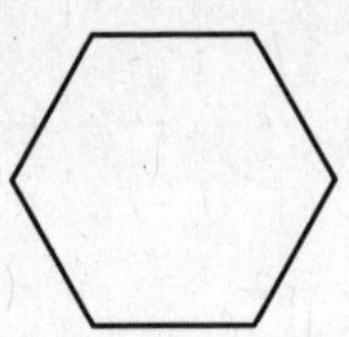

○ 10 ○ 8

○ 9 ○ 6

22.

 ○

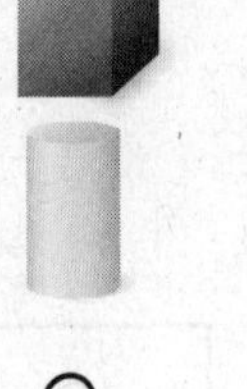 ○

 ○

 ○

23.

 ○

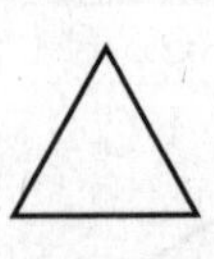 ○

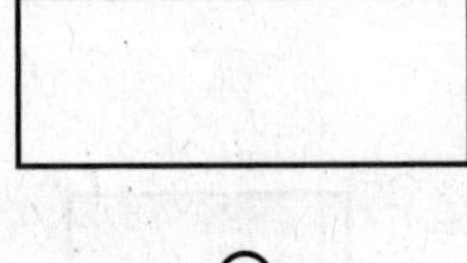 ○

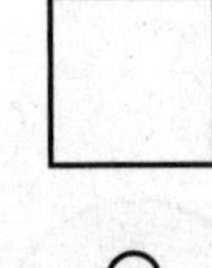 ○

24.

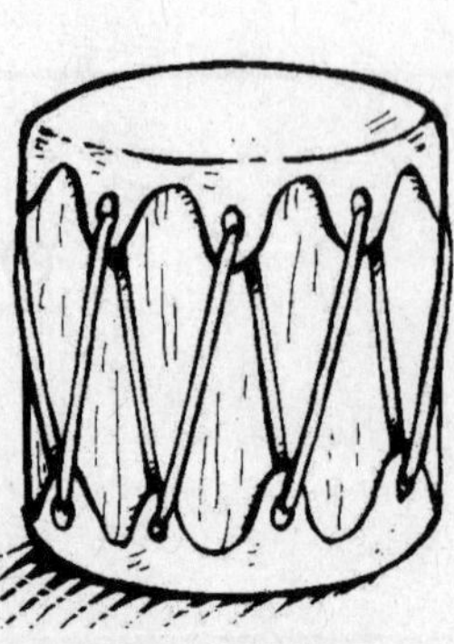

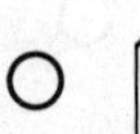
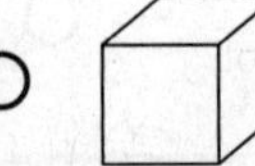
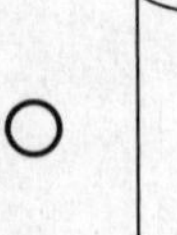
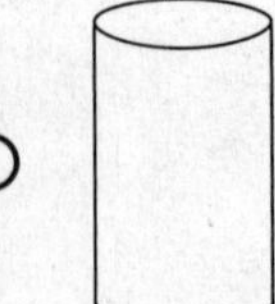

DIRECTIONS **21.** Mark beside the number that shows how many corners or vertices the hexagon has. **22.** Mark under the set that shows a cube beside a cylinder. **23.** Mark below the triangle. **24.** Mark beside the shape that is the same shape as the drum.

Choose the correct answer.

1. Josie has 5 apples. She eats 1. How many apples does Josie have now?

○ 6 ○ 4
○ 5 ○ 3

2. Which addition fact can help you solve 13 − 6?

○ 7 + 6 = 13
○ 6 + 8 = 14
○ 4 + 9 = 13
○ 3 + 6 = 9

3. Which shows how to make a ten to solve 15 − 7?

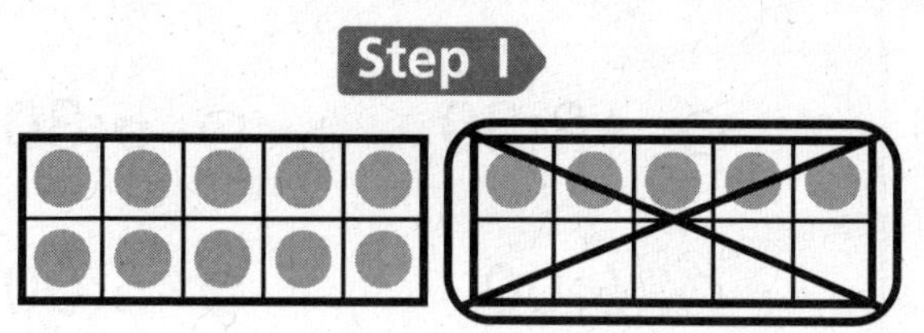

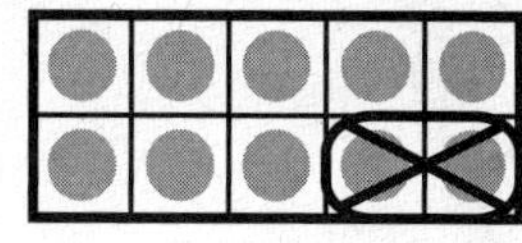

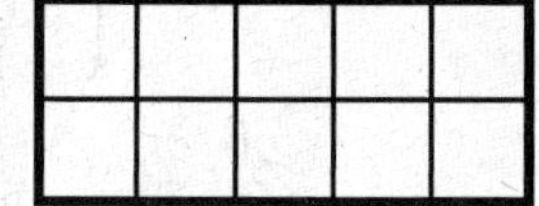

○ 10 − 2 ○ 10 − 5 − 2
○ 15 − 5 ○ 15 − 5 − 2

4. Which shows the pencils in order from **shortest** to **longest**?

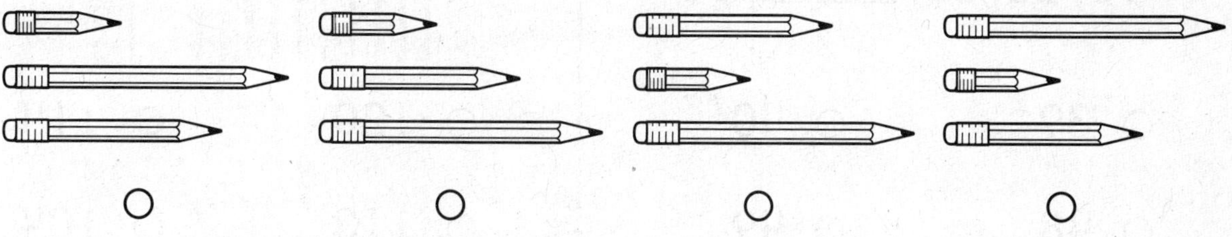

○ ○ ○ ○

GO ON

5. Ben measures a crayon with ■. About how long is the crayon?

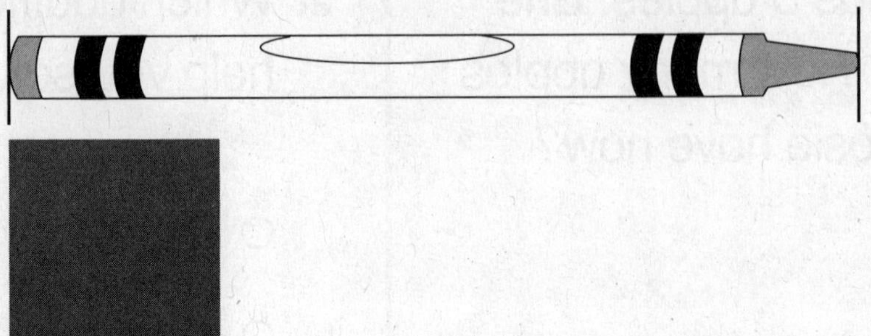

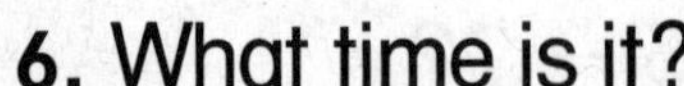

○ about 5 ■

○ about 3 ■

○ about 4 ■

○ about 2 ■

6. What time is it?

○ 12:30

○ 5:30

○ 6:00

○ 5:00

7. Count by tens. What number is missing?

18, 28, 38, ____, 58

○ 39

○ 40

○ 48

○ 49

8. What number does the model show?

○ 120

○ 114

○ 113

○ 104

GO ON

9. How many tens and ones are shown?

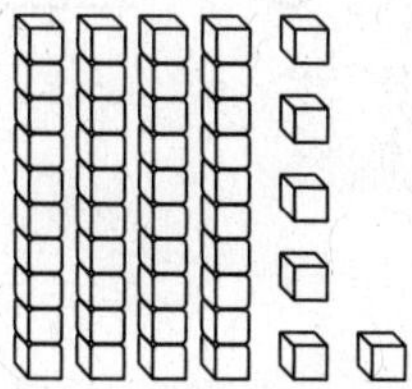

- ○ 3 tens 6 ones
- ○ 4 tens 6 ones
- ○ 5 tens 1 one
- ○ 6 tens 4 ones

10. How many flat surfaces does a cylinder have?

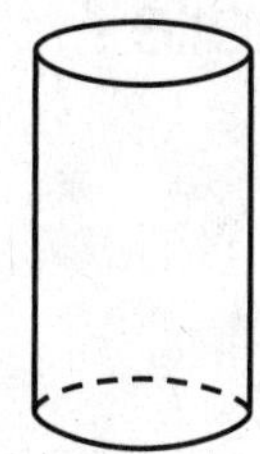

- ○ 0
- ○ 1
- ○ 2
- ○ 6

11. Sue combines these shapes.

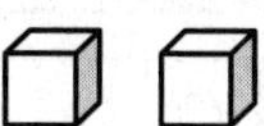

What new shape can Sue make?

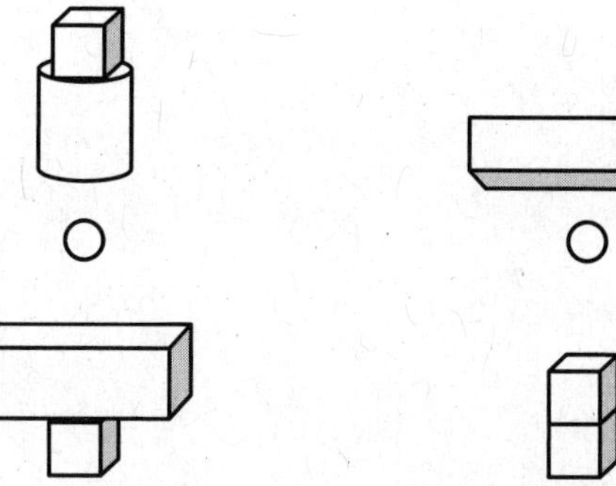

12. Which flat surface does a cone have?

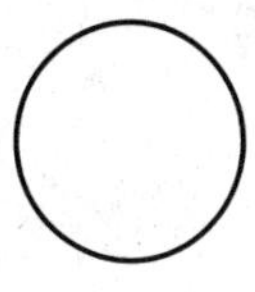

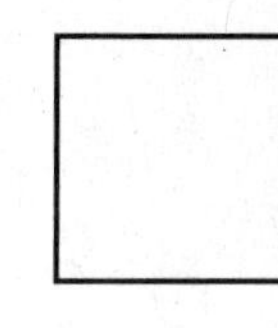

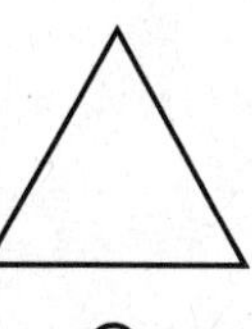

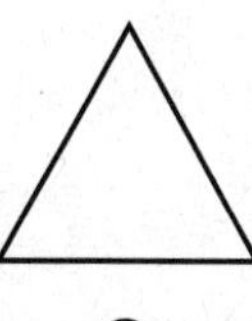

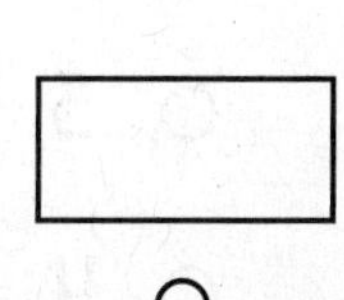

GO ON

Name ______________________

13. There are 2 red cups and 5 yellow cups. How many cups are there?

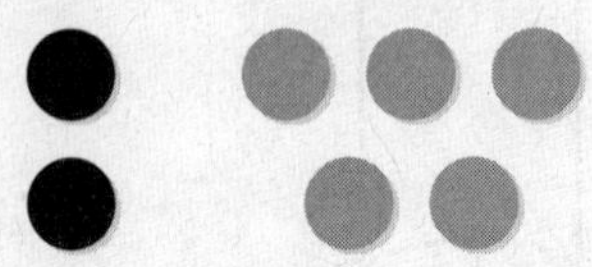

2 + 5 = ____

○ 8
○ 6
○ 7
○ 5

14. What is the sum?

0 + 3 = ____

○ 0
○ 1
○ 2
○ 3

15. Which shows the same addends in a different order?

1 + 4 = 5

○ 3 + 1 = 4
○ 1 + 4 = 5
○ 5 + 4 = 9
○ 4 + 1 = 5

16. Which shows a way to make 6?

GO ON

17. What completes the related facts?

$5 + 9 = 14$

$9 + 5 = 14$

$14 - 5 = 9$

- ○ $5 + 4 = 9$
- ○ $9 - 5 = 4$
- ○ $14 - 5 = 9$
- ○ $14 - 9 = 5$

18. Sean and Lana eat 8 crackers in all. Sean eats 5 crackers. Which number sentence shows how to find the number of crackers Lana eats?

- ○ $8 - 5 = 3$
- ○ $8 + 5 = 13$
- ○ $5 - 3 = 2$
- ○ $4 + 4 = 8$

19. What is the missing number?

$12 - 8 = \square$

$8 + \square = 12$

- ○ 8
- ○ 3
- ○ 4
- ○ 2

20. Which makes the statement true?

$11 - 2 = 5 + \square$

- ○ 2
- ○ 4
- ○ 5
- ○ 6

GO ON

21. What is the difference?

50 − 20 = ______

- ○ 20
- ○ 30
- ○ 40
- ○ 70

22. What is the sum?

28 + 6 = ______

- ○ 22
- ○ 24
- ○ 34
- ○ 88

23. How many tens and ones are in the sum?

$$\begin{array}{r} 45 \\ +\ 31 \\ \hline \end{array}$$

- ○ 1 ten and 4 ones
- ○ 6 tens and 7 ones
- ○ 7 tens and 6 ones
- ○ 8 tens and 6 ones

24. How many vertices does a triangle have?

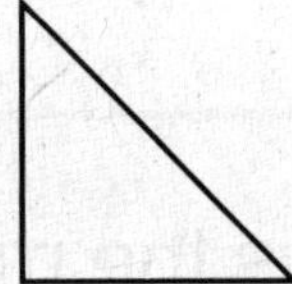

- ○ 3
- ○ 4
- ○ 5
- ○ 6

GO ON

25. Look at the picture. What are the parts?

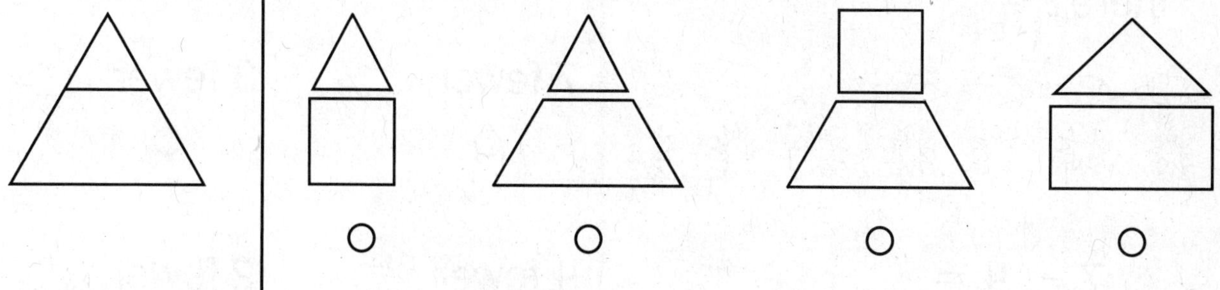

○ ○ ○ ○

26. Which shows fourths?

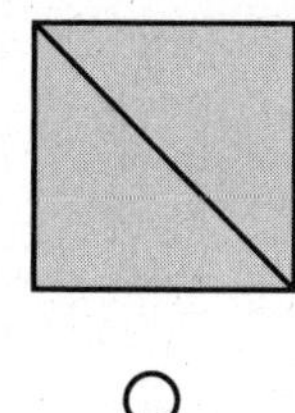
○

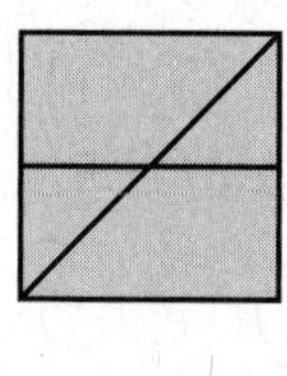
○

○

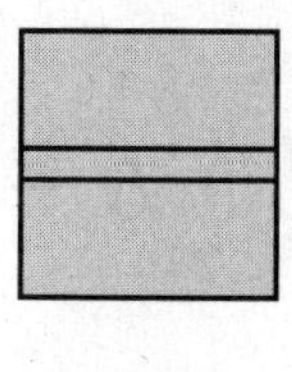
○

27. There are 5 trucks. 3 trucks are blue. The rest are red. Which number sentence can you use to find the number of red trucks?

○ $3 - 2 = 1$

○ $5 - 3 = 2$

○ $5 - 4 = 1$

○ $8 - 3 = 5$

28. There are 8 owls. 2 owls fly away. How many owls are there now?

8	
2	____

○ 10 ○ 8

○ 6 ○ 4

GO ON

29. How many fewer are there?

7 − 4 = ___

○ 7 fewer
○ 3 fewer
○ 4 fewer
○ 2 fewer

30. What is the difference?

6 − 0 = ___

○ 0 ○ 1 ○ 6 ○ 9

Use the bar graph for questions 31 and 32.

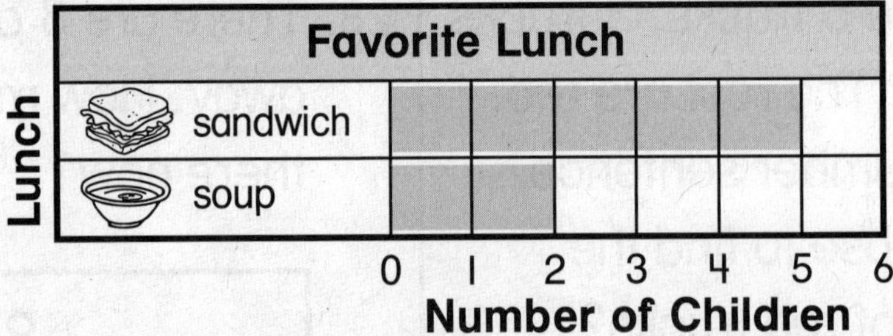

31. How many more children chose than ?

○ 7 ○ 3
○ 5 ○ 2

32. 1 more child chooses 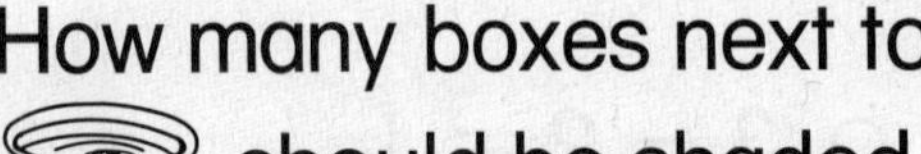. How many boxes next to  should be shaded now?

○ 6 ○ 4
○ 5 ○ 3

GO ON

33. How many children like apple?

Fruit We Like		Total
apple	IIII	
banana	II	2

○ 2

○ 3

○ 4

○ 5

34. Tino crosses out the numbers that are less than 68 and greater than 73. What number is left?

56 

80

○ 63

○ 71

○ 74

○ 80

35. Which is true?

○ $43 > 48$

○ $43 < 48$

○ $48 < 43$

○ $48 = 43$

36. What number is 10 less than 37?

○ 27

○ 36

○ 47

○ 73

GO ON

Name ____________________

37. Count on. What is the sum?

$6 + 3 = \square$

○ 6

○ 7

○ 8

○ 9

38. Which doubles fact helps you solve $3 + 4 = 7$?

○ $7 + 7 = 14$

○ $5 + 5 = 10$

○ $3 + 3 = 6$

○ $2 + 2 = 4$

39. Which shows a way to make a ten to solve $9 + 4$?

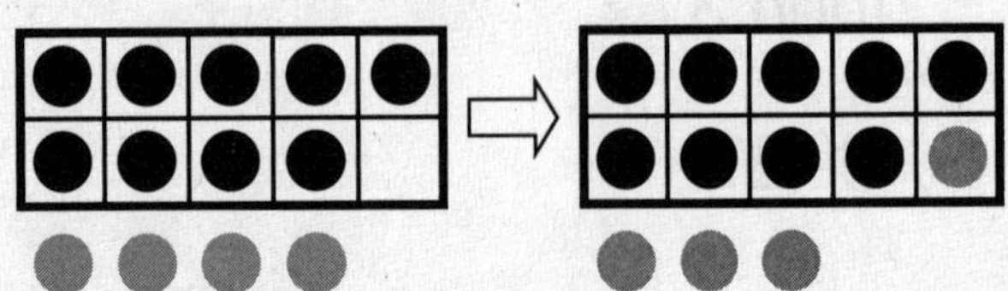

○ $9 + 1 + 4$

○ $9 + 1 + 3$

○ $5 + 5 + 4$

○ $4 + 6 + 5$

40. What is the sum?

$2 + 8 + 2 = \square$

○ 12

○ 10

○ 8

○ 4

STOP

1. Paco had 7 pencils. He gave 2 away. How many pencils does Paco have now?

○ 9 ○ 6
○ 7 ○ 5

2. Which addition fact can help you solve 11 − 7?

○ 8 + 3 = 11
○ 7 + 5 = 12
○ 7 + 4 = 11
○ 3 + 4 = 7

3. Which shows how to make a ten to solve 13 − 6?

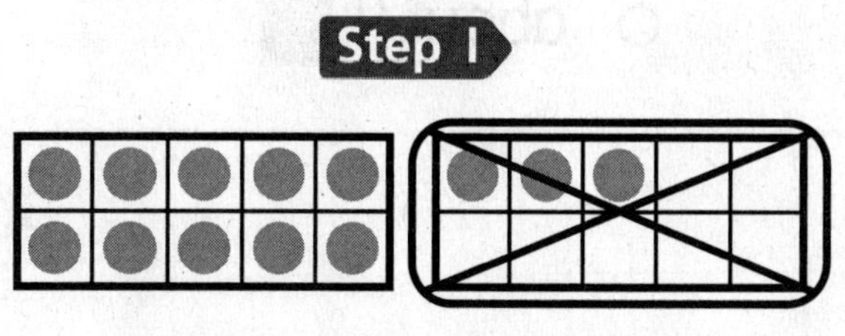

○ 13 − 3
○ 10 − 4
○ 13 − 3 − 3
○ 10 − 3 − 3

4. Which shows the arrows in order from **shortest** to **longest**?

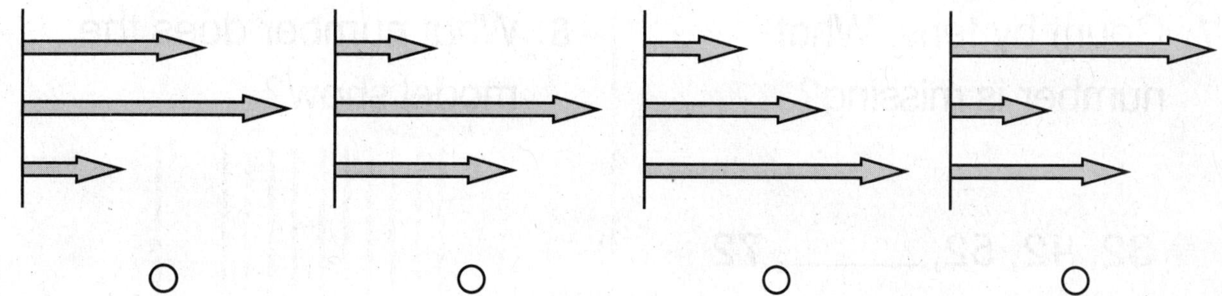

○ ○ ○ ○

GO ON

5. Ali measures a paperclip with ■. About how long is the paperclip?

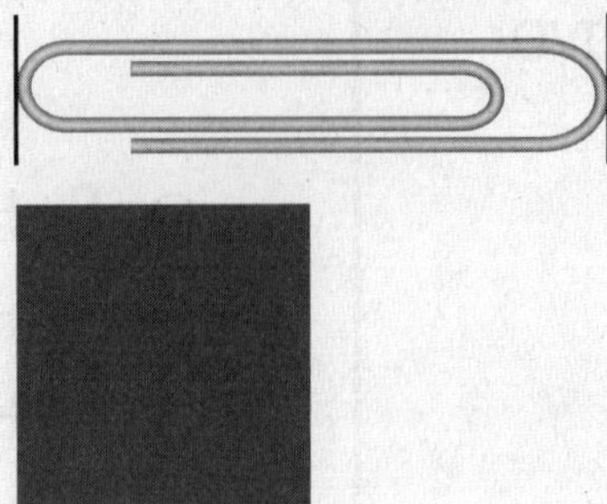

○ about 1 ■

○ about 2 ■

○ about 3 ■

○ about 4 ■

6. What time is it?

○ 1:00

○ 1:30

○ 12:30

○ 6:30

7. Count by tens. What number is missing?

32, 42, 52, ______, 72

○ 53

○ 55

○ 60

○ 62

8. What number does the model show?

○ 111

○ 110

○ 101

○ 100

GO ON

9. How many tens and ones are shown?

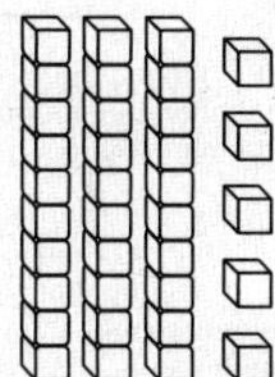

- ○ 2 tens 5 ones
- ○ 3 tens 4 ones
- ○ 3 tens 5 ones
- ○ 5 tens 3 ones

10. How many flat surfaces does a rectangular prism have?

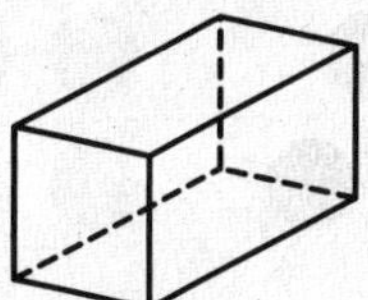

- ○ 0
- ○ 1
- ○ 2
- ○ 6

11. Jay combines these shapes.

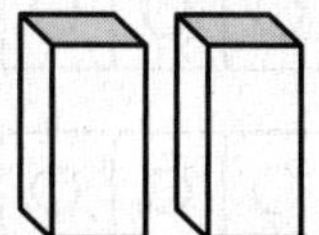

What new shape can Jay make?

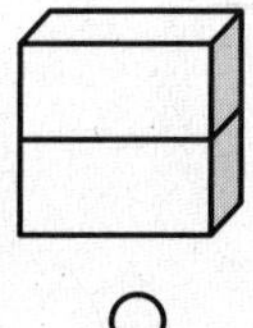 ○

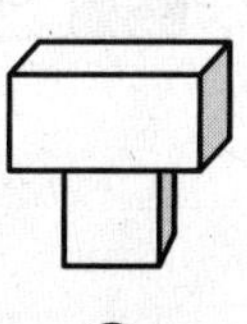 ○

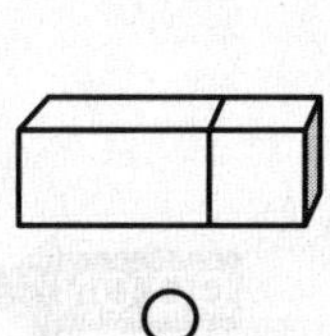 ○

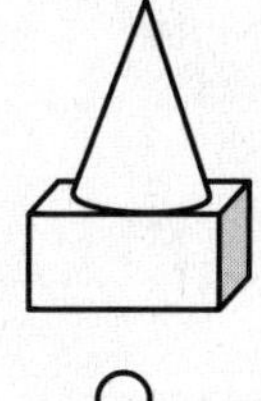 ○

12. Which flat surface does a cube have?

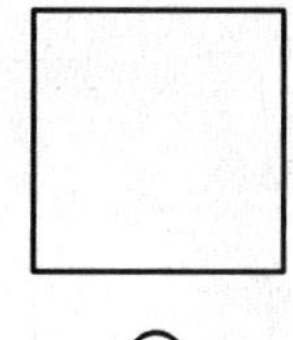

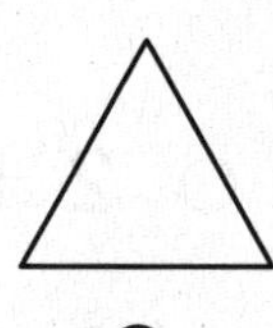

○

Name ______________________________

13. There are 3 large shells and 6 small shells. How many shells are there?

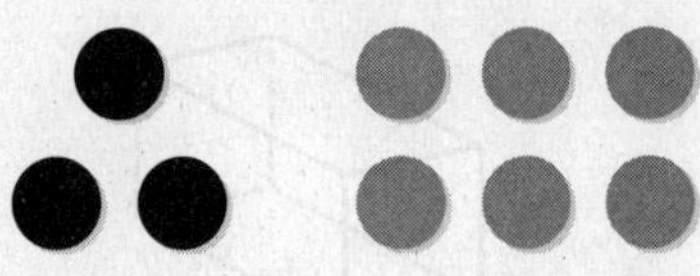

3 + 6 = _____

○ 10
○ 8
○ 9
○ 7

14. What is the sum?

8 + 0 = _____

○ 0
○ 1
○ 8
○ 9

15. Which shows the same addends in a different order?

5 + 2 = 7

○ 2 + 5 = 7
○ 3 + 2 = 5
○ 2 + 7 = 9
○ 5 + 2 = 7

16. Which shows a way to make 6?

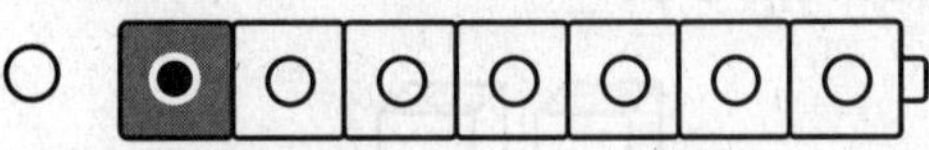

GO ON

17. What completes the related facts?

$4 + 8 = 12$
$8 + 4 = 12$
$12 - 4 = 8$

- ○ $12 - 4 = 8$
- ○ $12 - 8 = 4$
- ○ $8 - 4 = 4$
- ○ $8 + 2 = 10$

18. Sam sees 5 ducks. Tara sees 6 more ducks than Sam. Which number sentence shows how to find the number of ducks Tara sees?

- ○ $5 + 6 = 11$
- ○ $6 - 5 = 1$
- ○ $12 - 6 = 6$
- ○ $5 + 5 = 10$

19. What is the missing number?

$13 - 7 = \square$
$7 + \square = 13$

- ○ 4
- ○ 5
- ○ 6
- ○ 7

20. Which makes the sentence true?

$5 + 3 = 10 -$ ______

- ○ 8
- ○ 5
- ○ 3
- ○ 2

GO ON

21. What is the difference?

80 − 30 = ______

- ○ 20
- ○ 30
- ○ 40
- ○ 50

22. What is the sum?

39 + 2 = ______

- ○ 31
- ○ 37
- ○ 41
- ○ 59

23. How many tens and ones are in the sum?

$$\begin{array}{r} 53 \\ +\ 26 \\ \hline \end{array}$$

- ○ 3 tens and 3 ones
- ○ 7 tens and 6 ones
- ○ 7 tens and 9 ones
- ○ 12 tens and 7 ones

24. How many vertices does a hexagon have?

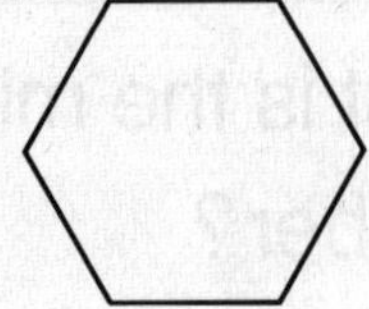

- ○ 6
- ○ 5
- ○ 4
- ○ 3

GO ON

25. Look at the picture. What are the parts?

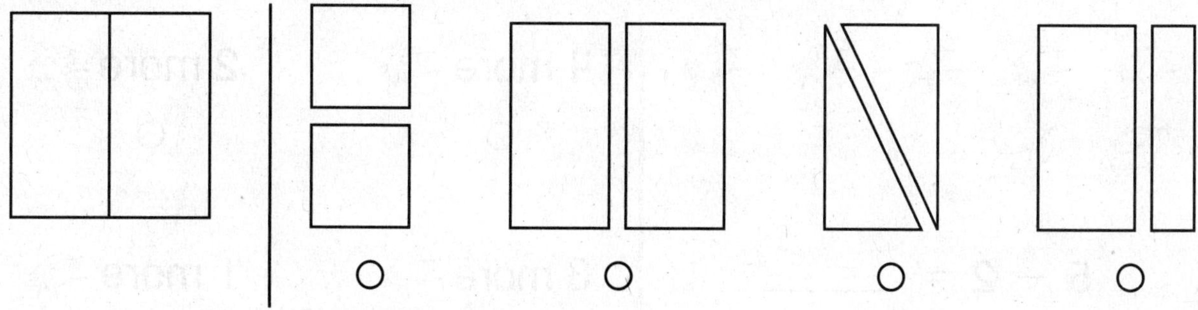

26. Which shows fourths?

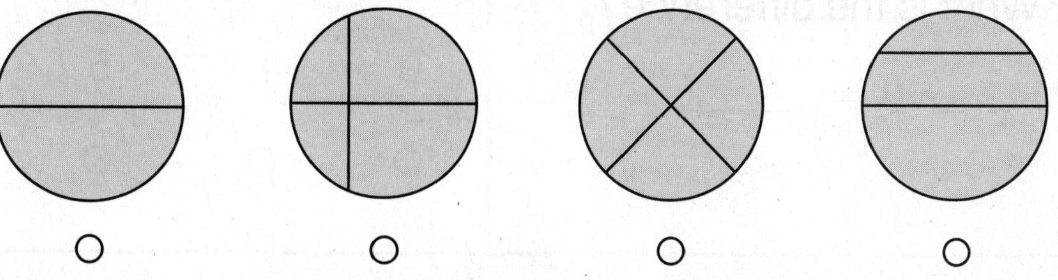

27. There are 6 beads. 5 beads are pink. The rest are blue. How many beads are blue?

○ 5 − 1 = 4

○ 6 − 3 = 3

○ 6 − 5 = 1

○ 11 − 6 = 5

28. There were 7 seals. Some swam away. Then there were 4 seals. How many seals swam away?

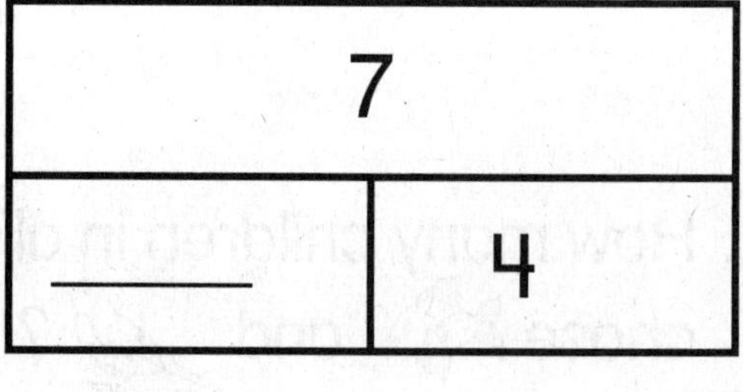

○ 11 ○ 4

○ 7 ○ 3

GO ON

29. How many more are there?

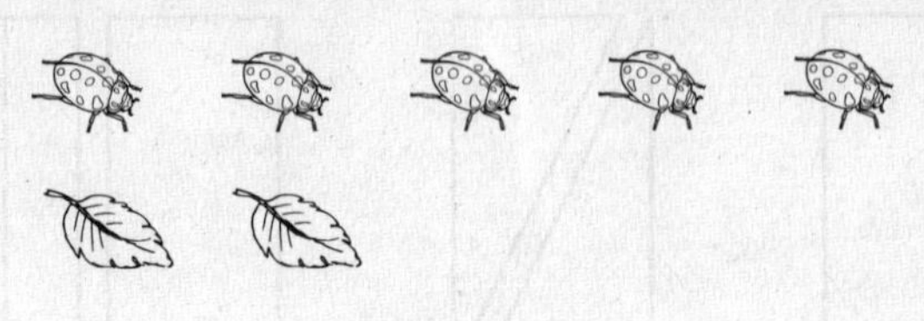

5 − 2 = ______

4 more ○

2 more ○

3 more ○

1 more ○

30. What is the difference?

7 − 0 = ______

0 ○ 1 ○ 5 ○ 7 ○

Use the bar graph for questions 31 and 32.

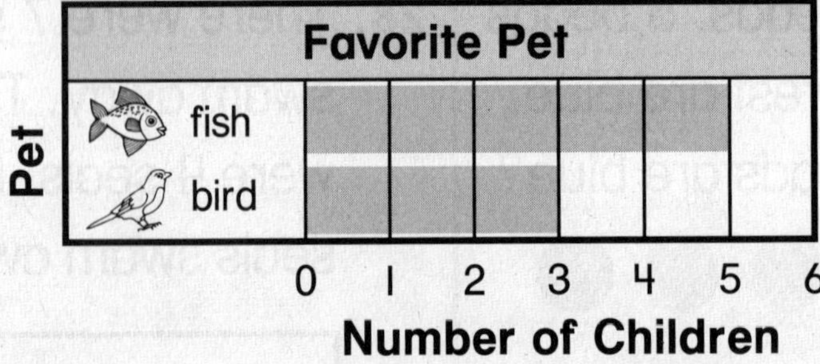

31. How many children in all chose and ?

○ 2 ○ 5

○ 3 ○ 8

32. 1 more child chooses .

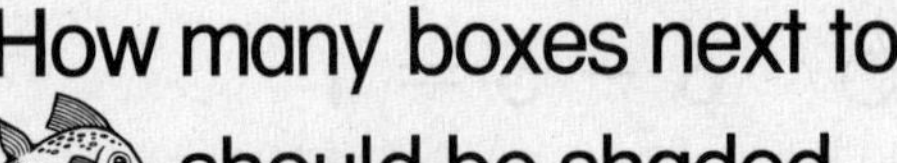

How many boxes next to

should be shaded now?

○ 6 ○ 3

○ 4 ○ 2

GO ON

33. How many children play soccer?

Sports We Play		Total
soccer	~~||||~~ |	
baseball	|||	3

- ○ 1
- ○ 5
- ○ 3
- ○ 6

34. Lita crosses out the numbers that are less than 55 and greater than 58. What number is left?

49	50	52	56	60

- ○ 60
- ○ 52
- ○ 56
- ○ 49

35. Which is true?

- ○ $81 > 87$
- ○ $87 < 81$
- ○ $87 > 81$
- ○ $81 = 87$

36. What number is 10 more than 24?

- ○ 14
- ○ 25
- ○ 30
- ○ 34

GO ON

37. Count on. What is the sum?

$5 + 3 = \square$

○ 5

○ 6

○ 7

○ 8

38. Which doubles fact helps you solve $8 + 7 = 15$?

○ $9 + 9 = 18$

○ $7 + 7 = 14$

○ $6 + 6 = 12$

○ $4 + 4 = 8$

39. Which shows a way to make a ten to solve $8 + 5$?

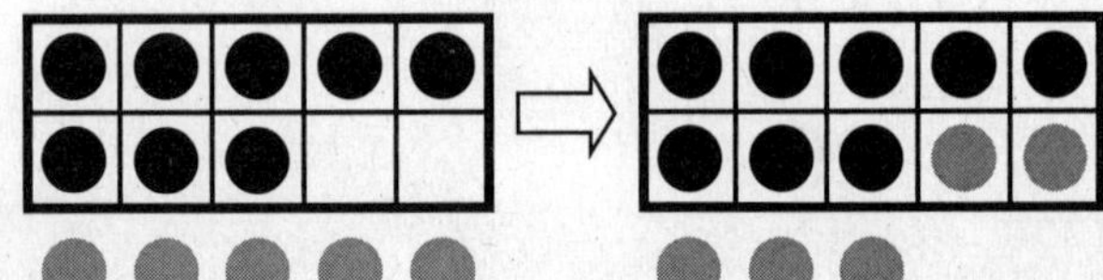

○ $8 + 2 + 3$

○ $8 + 2 + 5$

○ $5 + 5 + 4$

○ $3 + 7 + 2$

40. What is the sum?

$6 + 3 + 3 = \square$

○ 15

○ 12

○ 9

○ 6

STOP

1. Kim has 4 grapes. She eats 3. How many grapes does Kim have now?

○ 7 ○ 2
○ 3 ○ 1

2. Which addition fact can help you solve $17 - 9$?

○ $7 + 2 = 9$
○ $8 + 7 = 15$
○ $9 + 1 = 10$
○ $9 + 8 = 17$

3. Which shows how to make a ten to solve $13 - 4$?

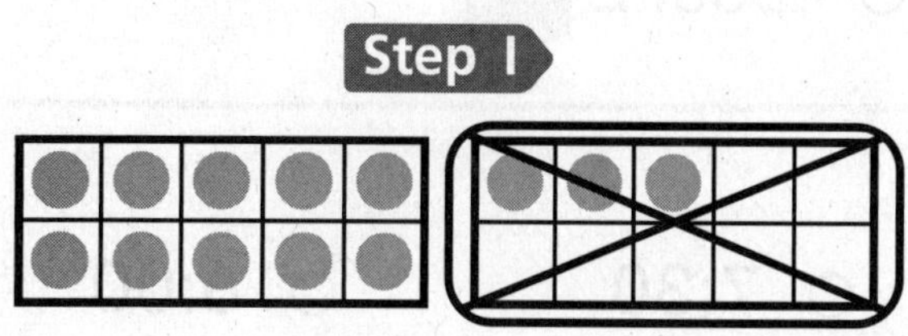

○ $13 - 3$ ○ $13 - 3 - 3$
○ $10 - 3$ ○ $13 - 3 - 1$

4. Which shows the strings in order from **longest** to **shortest**?

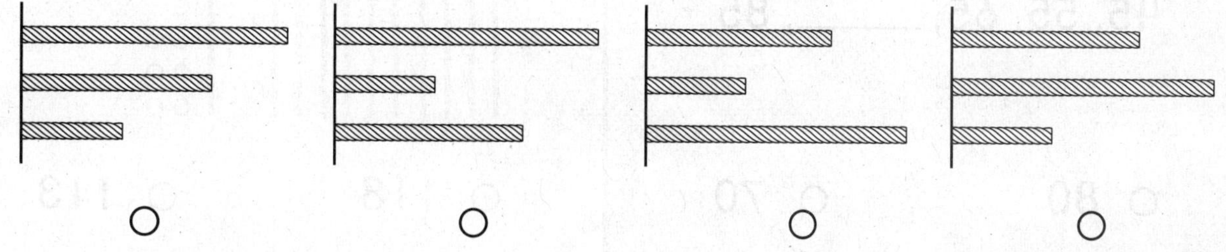

○ ○ ○ ○

GO ON

Name ____________________

5. Carmen measures a pen with . About how long is the pen?

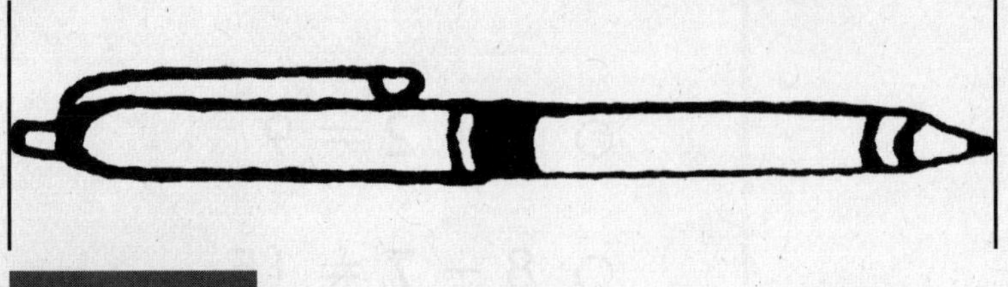

○ about 5 ■ ○ about 3 ■

○ about 4 ■ ○ about 2 ■

6. What time is it?

○ 7:30 ○ 6:00

○ 6:30 ○ 5:30

7. Count by tens. What number is missing?

45, 55, 65, _____, 85

○ 80 ○ 70

○ 75 ○ 66

8. What number does the model show ?

○ 118 ○ 113

○ 117 ○ 108

GO ON

9. How many tens and ones are shown?

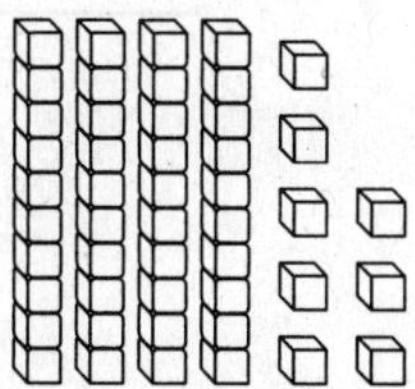

- ○ 4 tens 3 ones
- ○ 4 tens 8 ones
- ○ 5 tens 3 ones
- ○ 8 tens 4 ones

10. How many flat surfaces does a sphere have?

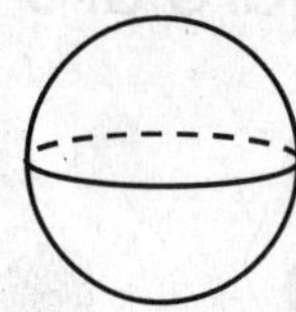

- ○ 0
- ○ 1
- ○ 2
- ○ 6

11. Jen combines these shapes.

What new shape can Jen make?

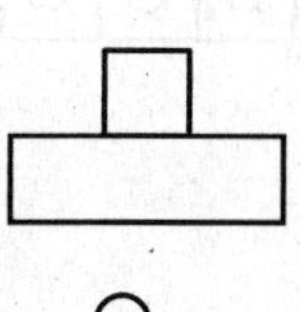 ○

 ○

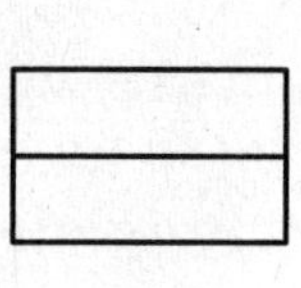 ○

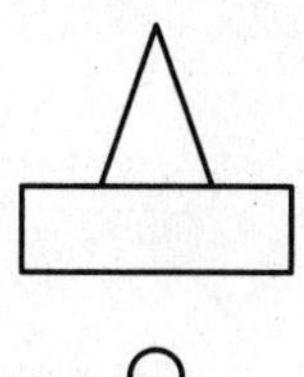 ○

12. Which flat surface could a rectangular prism have?

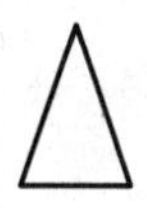 ○

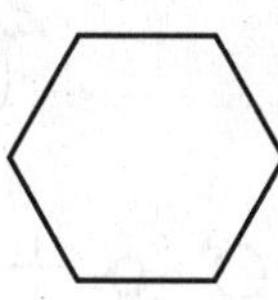 ○

 ○

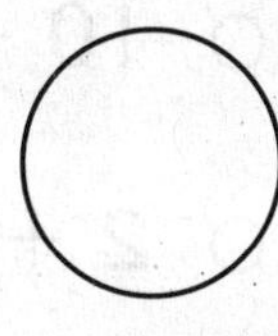 ○

GO ON

Name ______________________________

13. There are 4 brown bears and 5 black bears. How many bears are there?

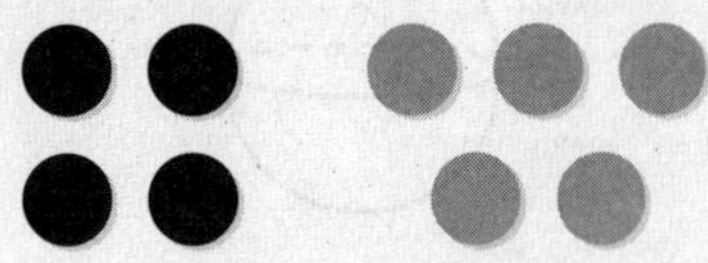

4 + 5 = _____

○ 10 ○ 9

○ 8 ○ 7

14. What is the sum?

0 + 7 = _____

○ 0

○ 1

○ 7

○ 8

15. Which shows the same addends in a different order?

2 + 8 = 10

○ 6 + 2 = 8

○ 8 + 2 = 10

○ 10 + 2 = 12

○ 2 + 8 = 10

16. Which shows a way to make 8?

○

○

○ 

○

GO ON

Name ______________________________

17. What completes the related facts?

$$7 + 5 = 12$$
$$5 + 7 = 12$$
$$12 - 5 = 7$$

- ○ $12 - 7 = 5$
- ○ $12 - 5 = 7$
- ○ $7 + 4 = 11$
- ○ $6 + 6 = 12$

18. Owen and Ana find 9 shells in all. Owen finds 5 shells. Which number sentence shows how to find the number of shells Ana finds?

- ○ $9 + 5 = 14$
- ○ $9 - 5 = 4$
- ○ $9 + 3 = 12$
- ○ $14 - 5 = 9$

19. What is the missing number?

$$11 - 4 = \square$$
$$4 + \square = 11$$

- ○ 8
- ○ 6
- ○ 7
- ○ 3

20. Which makes the number sentence true?

$$12 - 3 = 7 + \_\_\_\_$$

- ○ 1
- ○ 2
- ○ 4
- ○ 12

GO ON

21. What is the difference?

$90 - 50 =$ ______

- ○ 20
- ○ 30
- ○ 40
- ○ 50

22. What is the sum?

$49 + 3 =$ ______

- ○ 79
- ○ 52
- ○ 36
- ○ 42

23. How many tens and ones are in the sum?

$$\begin{array}{r} 45 \\ +\ 22 \\ \hline \end{array}$$

- ○ 2 tens and 7 ones
- ○ 6 tens and 3 ones
- ○ 6 tens and 7 ones
- ○ 7 tens and 6 ones

24. How many vertices does a trapezoid have?

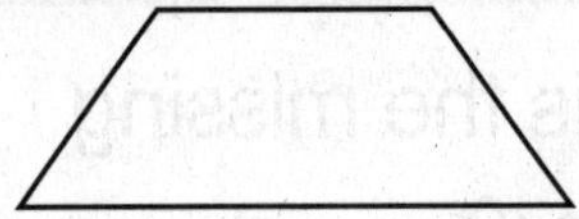

- ○ 3
- ○ 4
- ○ 5
- ○ 6

GO ON

Name ______________________________

25. Look at the picture. What are the parts?

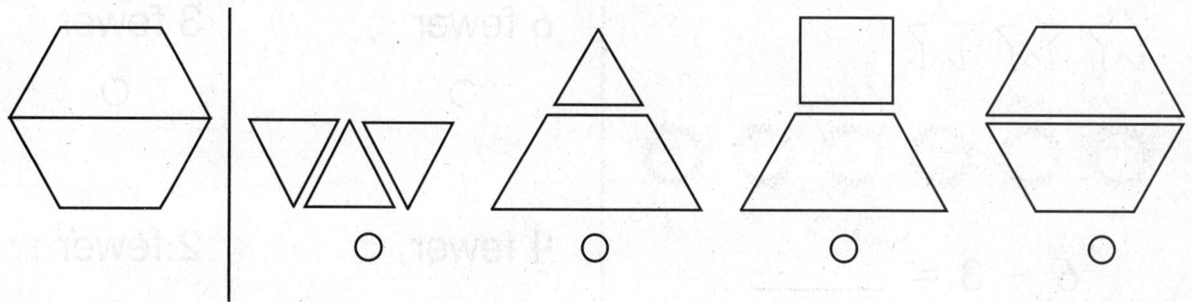

26. Which shows fourths?

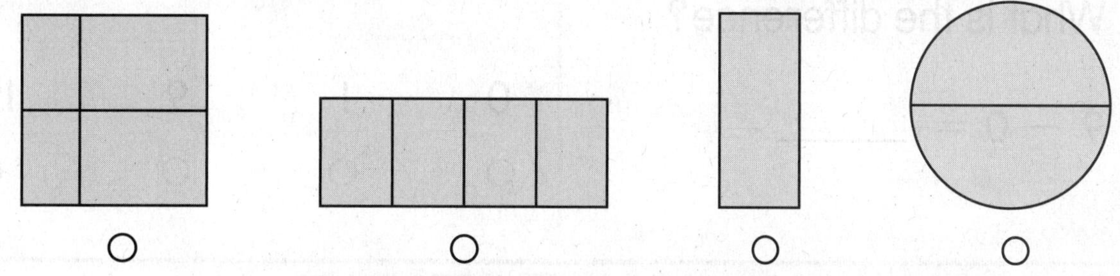

27. There are 9 dogs. 2 dogs are large. The rest are small. Which number sentence can you use to find the number of small dogs?

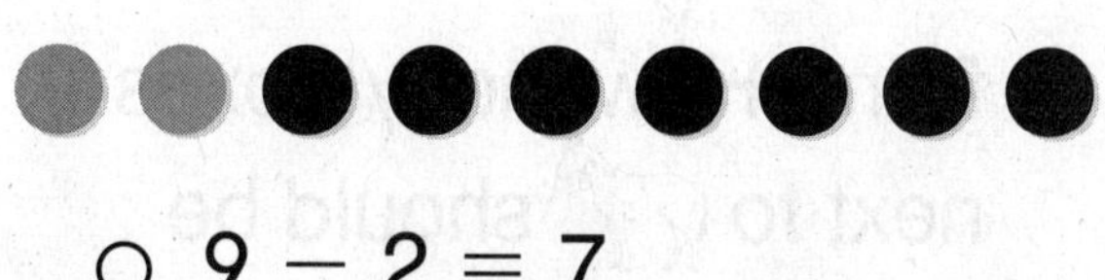

○ $9 - 2 = 7$

○ $7 - 2 = 5$

○ $11 - 2 = 9$

○ $7 - 5 = 2$

28. There were 10 bugs. Some crawled away. Then there were 6 bugs. How many bugs crawled away?

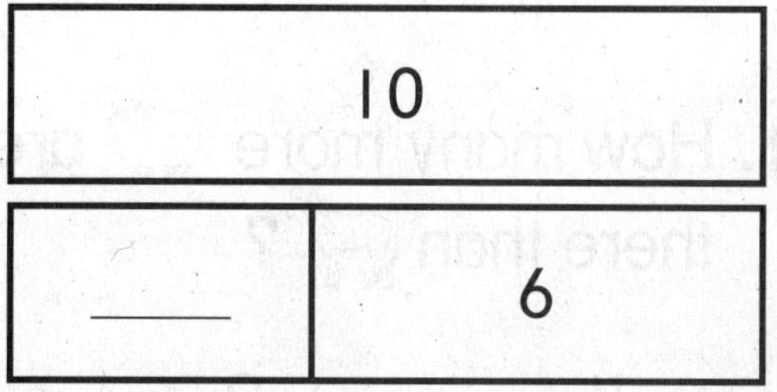

○ 10 ○ 8

○ 6 ○ 4

GO ON

29. How many fewer  are there?

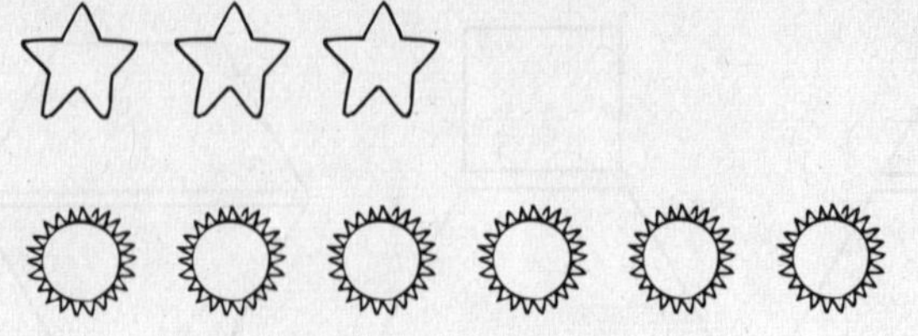

6 − 3 = ______

○ 6 fewer ☆
○ 3 fewer ☆
○ 4 fewer ☆
○ 2 fewer ☆

30. What is the difference?

9 − 0 = ______

○ 0
○ 1
○ 9
○ 10

Use the bar graph for questions 31 and 32.

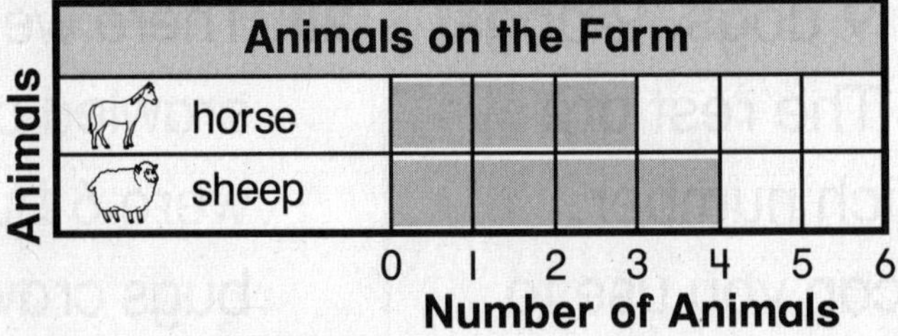

31. How many more 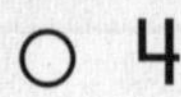 are there than ?

○ 4
○ 2
○ 3
○ 1

32. 2 more come to the farm. How many boxes next to should be shaded now?

○ 6
○ 4
○ 5
○ 2

GO ON

33. How many  are in the band?

Children in the Band		Total
girls	~~IIII~~ II	
boys	IIII	4

- ○ 7
- ○ 4
- ○ 5
- ○ 2

34. Joey crosses out the numbers that are less than 23 and greater than 43. What number is left?

19	32	44	51	53

- ○ 53
- ○ 32
- ○ 44
- ○ 19

35. Which is true?

- ○ $36 > 38$
- ○ $38 < 36$
- ○ $36 < 38$
- ○ $36 = 38$

36. What number is 10 less than 65?

- ○ 55
- ○ 60
- ○ 64
- ○ 75

GO ON

Name ______________________________

37. Count on. What is the sum?

$4 + 1 = \square$

○ 3

○ 4

○ 5

○ 6

38. Which doubles fact helps to solve $5 + 6 = 11$?

○ $7 + 7 = 14$

○ $5 + 5 = 10$

○ $4 + 4 = 8$

○ $3 + 3 = 6$

39. Which shows a way to make a ten to solve $8 + 3$?

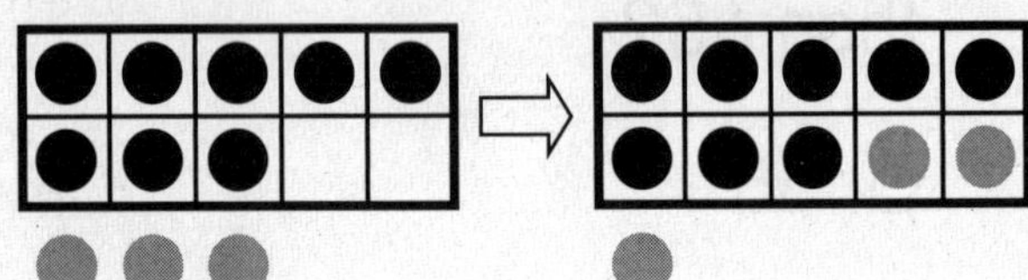

○ $8 + 3 + 1$

○ $8 + 2 + 1$

○ $7 + 3 + 3$

○ $7 + 2 + 1$

40. What is the sum?

$3 + 5 + 2 = \square$

○ 10

○ 8

○ 7

○ 5

STOP

Name ____________________

Choose the correct answer.

1. What is the sum?

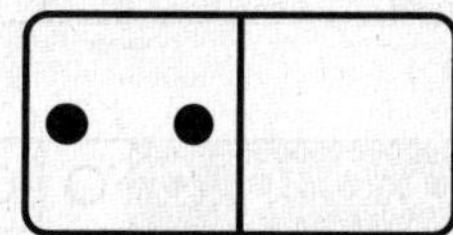

2 + 0 = ____

○ 0 ○ 2

○ 1 ○ 3

2. What is the sum?

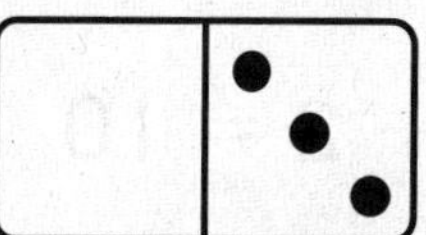

0 + 3 = ____

○ 3 ○ 1

○ 2 ○ 0

3. What is the sum?

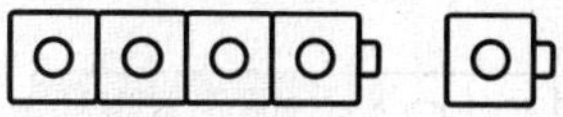

4 + 1 = ____

○ 4 ○ 6

○ 5 ○ 7

4. Which shows 3 + 3 = 6?

○

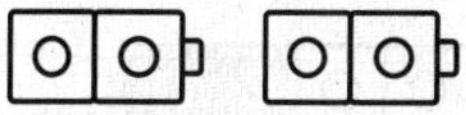

○

○

○

GO ON

5. Which shows the same addends in a different order?

8 + 2 = 10

○ 2 + 6 = 8

○ 2 + 8 = 10

○ 8 + 1 = 9

○ 8 + 2 = 10

6. Which shows a way to make 9?

○

○

○

○

7. Which shows a way to make 6?

○

○

○

○

8. How many fish?

2 fish and 3 more fish _____ fish

5	6	7	8
○	○	○	○

GO ON

Name ___________________________

9. There are 3 red leaves and 4 yellow leaves. How many leaves are there?

$3 + 4 =$ ______

○ 8

○ 7

○ 6

○ 5

10. What is the sum?

$$\begin{array}{r} 6 \\ +\ 1 \\ \hline \end{array}$$

○ 5

○ 6

○ 7

○ 9

11. What is the sum?

$$\begin{array}{r} 8 \\ +\ 2 \\ \hline \end{array}$$

○ 6

○ 8

○ 9

○ 10

12. James has 9 caps. 5 caps are green. The rest are blue. How many caps are blue?

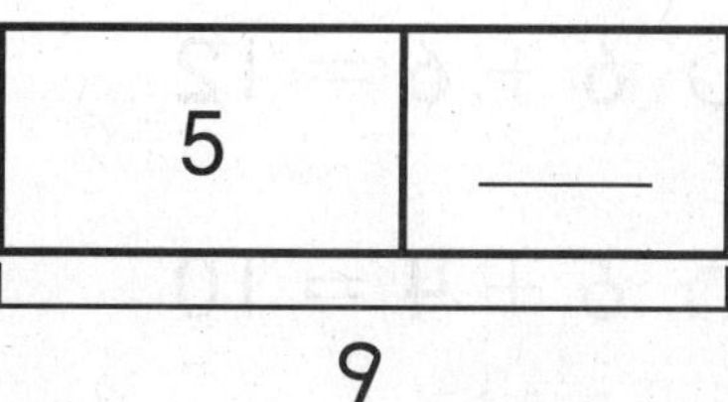

$5 +$ ______ $= 9$

○ 3 ○ 5

○ 4 ○ 6

GO ON

13. What is the sum for 0 + 5?

- ○ 3
- ○ 4
- ○ 5
- ○ 6

14. What is the sum?

3 + 2 = ____

- ○ 5
- ○ 6
- ○ 7
- ○ 8

15. Which shows the same addends in a different order?

6 + 4 = 10

- ○ 6 + 6 = 12
- ○ 6 + 4 = 10
- ○ 4 + 6 = 10
- ○ 4 + 5 = 9

16. Which shows the same addends in a different order?

5 + 3 = 8

- ○ 5 + 3 = 8
- ○ 5 + 8 = 13
- ○ 3 + 8 = 11
- ○ 3 + 5 = 8

GO ON

17. How many worms?

4 worms and 1 more worm _____ worms

8 ○ 7 ○ 6 ○ 5 ○

18. How many cars?

5 cars and 2 more cars _____ cars

6 ○ 7 ○ 8 ○ 9 ○

19. Which shows a way to make 8?

○ 

○ 

○

○

20. There are 2 small flowers and 1 large flower. How many flowers are there?

○ 4 ○ 2

○ 3 ○ 1

GO ON

21. There are 3 big hats and 1 small hat. Which number sentence shows how many hats there are?

○ 3 + 1 = 4

○ 3 + 2 = 5

○ 4 + 1 = 5

○ 3 + 4 = 7

22. What is the sum?

$$\begin{array}{r} 7 \\ +\ 2 \\ \hline \end{array}$$

○ 5

○ 6

○ 8

○ 9

23. There are some frogs on a log. 3 more frogs sit on the log. Then there are 9 frogs on the log. How many frogs were on the log before?

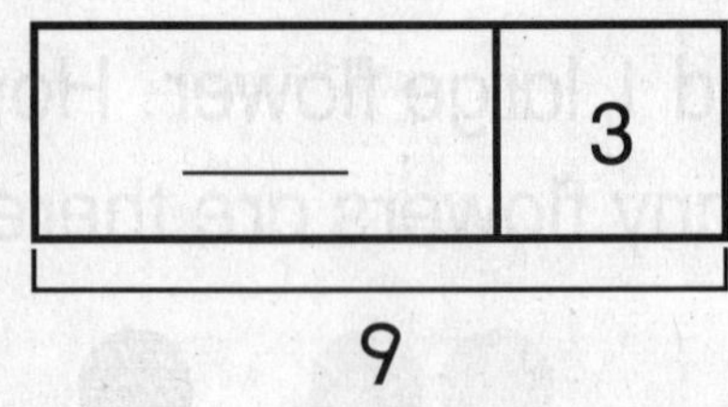

___ + 3 = 9

○ 3 ○ 6

○ 5 ○ 7

24. There are 4 fish swimming. Then 2 more fish join them. How many fish are swimming now?

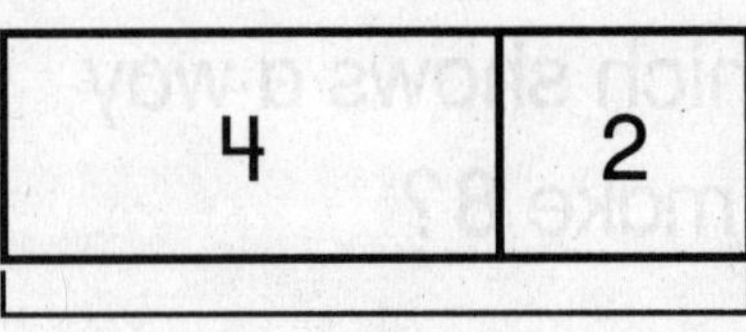

4 + 2 = ___

○ 7 ○ 5

○ 6 ○ 4

STOP

Choose the correct answer.

1. What is the sum?

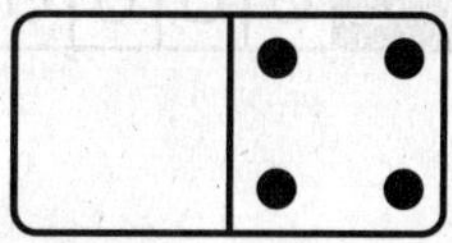

0 + 4 = ____

○ 4 ○ 2

○ 3 ○ 0

2. What is the sum?

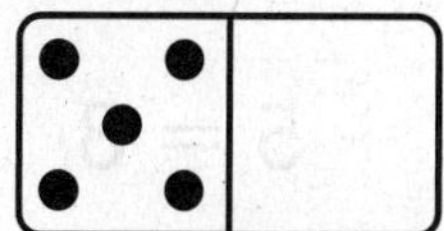

5 + 0 = ____

○ 0 ○ 4

○ 3 ○ 5

3. What is the sum?

4 + 2 = ____

○ 4

○ 5

○ 6

○ 7

4. Which shows 1 + 1 = 2?

○

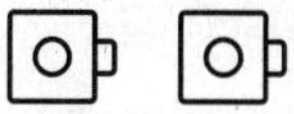

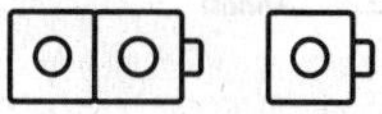

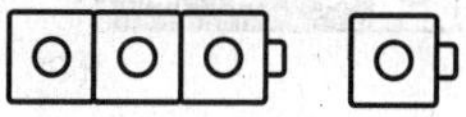

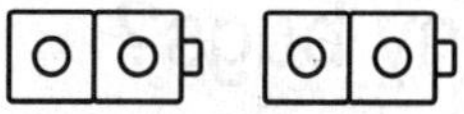

○

○

○

GO ON

5. Which shows the same addends in a different order?

$3 + 5 = 8$

- ○ $3 + 4 = 7$
- ○ $3 + 5 = 8$
- ○ $5 + 4 = 9$
- ○ $5 + 3 = 8$

6. Which shows a way to make 8?

- ○
- ○
- ○
- ○

7. Which shows a way to make 5?

- ○
- ○
- ○ 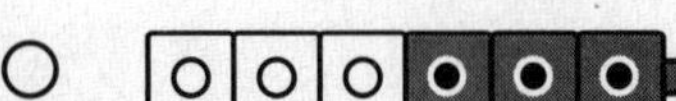
- ○

8. How many bugs?

3 bugs and 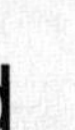 2 more bugs ______ bugs

4	5	6	7
○	○	○	○

GO ON

Name ______________________

9. There are 2 red shirts and 2 green shirts. How many shirts are there?

2 + 2 = ____

- ○ 2
- ○ 3
- ○ 4
- ○ 5

10. What is the sum?

$$\begin{array}{r} 7 \\ +\ 1 \\ \hline \end{array}$$

- ○ 9
- ○ 8
- ○ 7
- ○ 6

11. What is the sum?

$$\begin{array}{r} 6 \\ +\ 3 \\ \hline \end{array}$$

- ○ 3
- ○ 5
- ○ 7
- ○ 9

12. Jesse has 6 hats. 1 hat is blue. The rest are yellow. How many hats are yellow?

1 + ______ = 6

- ○ 3
- ○ 5
- ○ 4
- ○ 6

GO ON

Name ______________________________

Write the correct answer.

13. Write the sum.

$0 + 6 =$ ______

14. Write the sum.

5 cats and 3 more cats

$5 \quad + \quad 3 \quad =$ ______

15. Write the addends in a different order.

$2 + 8 = 10$

______ + ______ = 10

16. Write the addends in a different order.

$0 + 2 = 2$

______ + ______ = 2

GO ON

Name ______________________________

17. How many birds?

5 birds and 1 more bird ______ birds

18. How many boats?

4 boats and 3 more boats ______ boats

19. Color to show a way to make 7.

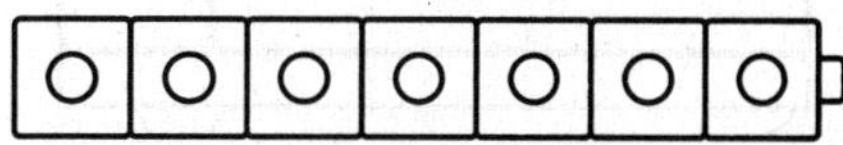

20. There are 4 red birds and 2 blue birds. How many birds are there?

______ birds

GO ON

21. There are 5 red buttons and 4 blue buttons. Write a number sentence to show how many buttons there are.

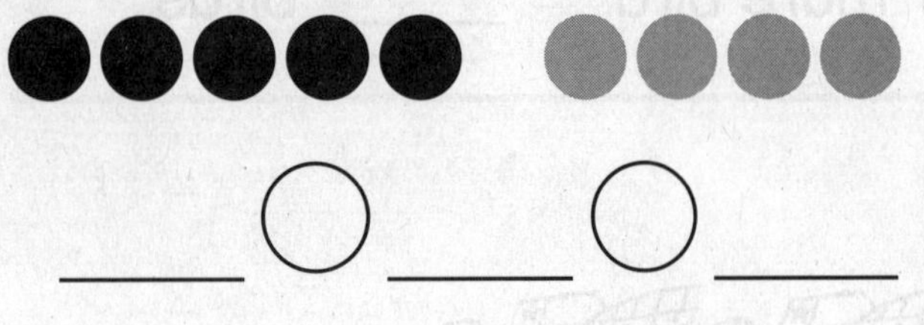

____ ◯ ____ ◯ ____

____ buttons

22. Write the sum.

$$\begin{array}{r} 9 \\ +\ 1 \\ \hline \end{array}$$

23. Some ants are on a log. 2 more ants climb on the log. Then there are 7 ants on the log. How many ants were on the log before?

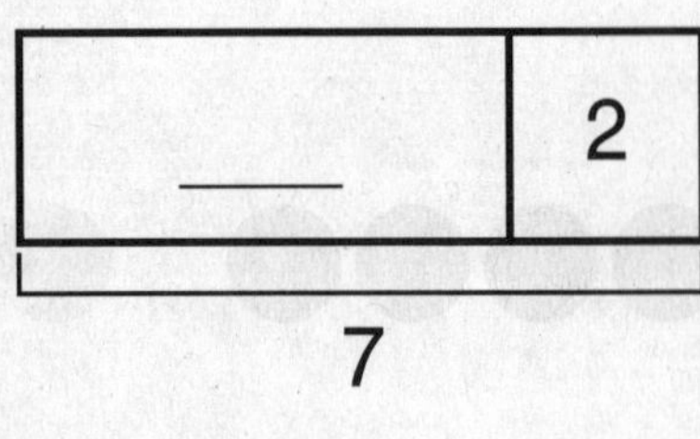

____ + 2 = 7

24. 4 cats are in the yard. Then 1 more cat joins them. How many cats are in the yard now?

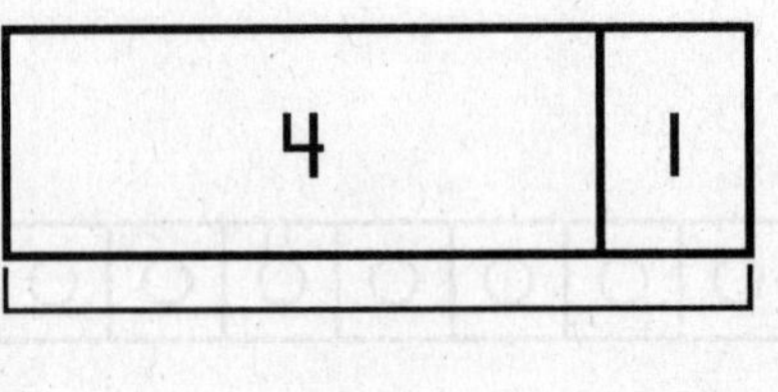

4 + 1 = ____

GO ON

Name ______________________________

Extended Constructed Response

25. Use ▣ ▢ to show all the ways to make 7.
Color to show your cube trains.
Complete the addition sentences to match your drawings.

Cube train	Addition sentence
○○○○○○○	7 = ______ + ______
○○○○○○○	7 = ______ + ______
○○○○○○○	7 = ______ + ______
○○○○○○○	7 = ______ + ______
○○○○○○○	7 = ______ + ______
○○○○○○○	7 = ______ + ______
○○○○○○○	7 = ______ + ______
○○○○○○○	7 = ______ + ______

Circle one addition sentence. Then circle another addition sentence that has the same addends in a different order. Explain how the addition sentences you circled are alike. Explain how they are different.

____

____

Child's Name ______________________________

Extended Constructed Response

The Extended Constructed Response item is scored using the 3-point scoring rubric in the *Assessment Guide*. A child can receive partial credit for answers that are partially correct or partially completed.

Performance Indicators

For Problem 25, a child with a Level 2 paper:

_____ correctly shows all the ways to make 7.

_____ correctly completes the addition sentences to match drawings.

_____ circles two addition sentences that represent the Commutative Property.

_____ gives a reasonable explanation for how the addition sentences are alike and how they are different.

Choose the correct answer.

1. What is the difference?

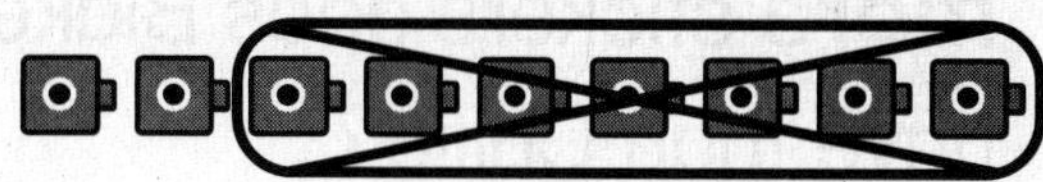

○ 2

○ 3

○ 7

○ 9

2. What is the difference?

$$\begin{array}{r} 7 \\ -\ 1 \\ \hline \end{array}$$

○ 8

○ 7

○ 6

○ 5

3. How many **more** are there?

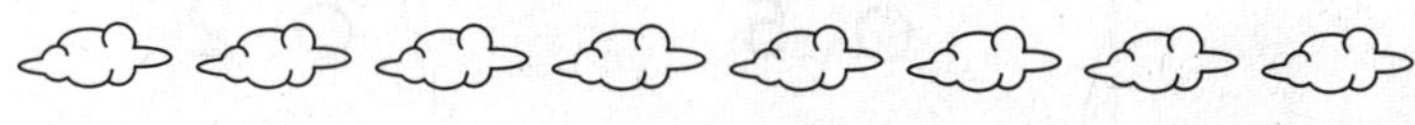

8 − 5 = ____

3 more	2 more	5 more	8 more
○	○	○	○

4. How many **more** are there?

5 − 3 = ____

8 more	5 more	4 more	2 more
○	○	○	○

GO ON

Name ____________________

5. There are 8 bugs. 3 bugs walk away. How many bugs are there now?

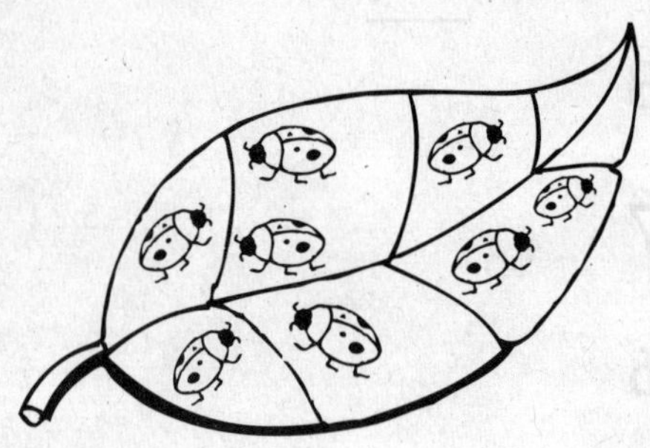

○ 4 ○ 6
○ 5 ○ 8

6. Blake has 5 stickers. Callie has 2 stickers. How many **more** stickers does Blake have than Callie?

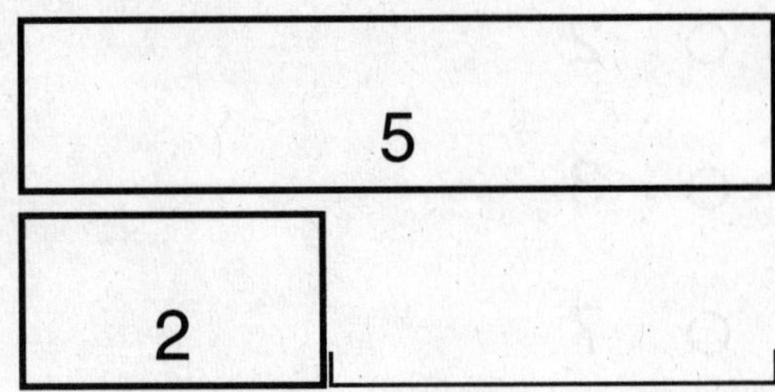

____

○ 4 ○ 3
○ 5 ○ 2

7. There were 7 dogs. Some dogs ran away. Then there were 2 dogs. How many dogs ran away?

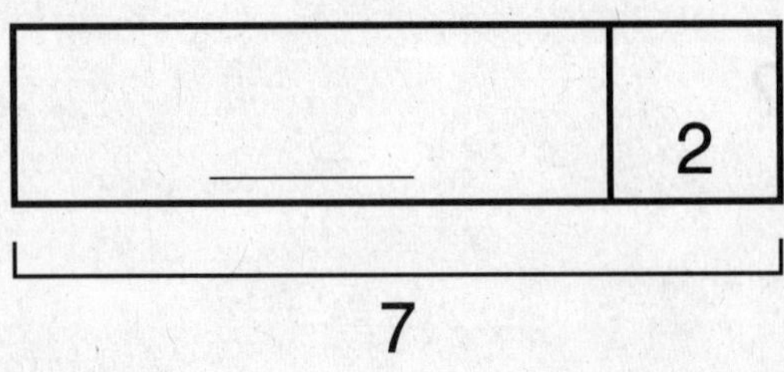

○ 7 ○ 4
○ 5 ○ 2

8. Which shows a way to take apart 4?

○ $4 - 3 = 1$

○ $7 - 4 = 3$

○ $7 - 3 = 4$

○ $4 + 3 = 7$

GO ON

Name ____________________

9. Which shows a way to take apart 8?

- ○ $9 - 1 = 8$
- ○ $9 - 8 = 1$
- ○ $8 + 2 = 10$
- ○ $8 - 2 = 6$

10. What is the difference?

$\_\_\_\_ = 4 - 0$

- ○ 0
- ○ 1
- ○ 4
- ○ 5

11. Which number sentence solves the problem? There are 9 children. 5 are boys. The rest are girls. How many children are girls?

- ○ $9 - 5 = 4$
- ○ $4 + 1 = 5$
- ○ $8 + 1 = 9$
- ○ $9 - 2 = 7$

12. Which number sentence solves the problem? There are 6 apples. 4 apples are red. The rest are green. How many apples are green?

- ○ $2 + 2 = 4$
- ○ $6 - 4 = 2$
- ○ $4 + 5 = 9$
- ○ $6 - 3 = 3$

GO ON

13. What is the difference?

10 − 5 = ______

○ 4

○ 5

○ 10

○ 15

14. What is the difference?

7 − 3 = ______

○ 3

○ 4

○ 7

○ 10

15. What is the difference?

$$\begin{array}{r} 8 \\ -6 \\ \hline \end{array}$$

○ 1

○ 3

○ 2

○ 4

16. How many **fewer** are there?

4 − 3 = ______

○ 1 fewer

○ 4 fewer

○ 3 fewer

○ 7 fewer

GO ON

Name ________________________________

17. There are 5 birds. 1 bird flies away. How many birds are there now?

○ 6

○ 5

○ 4

○ 1

18. Ana has 1 shell. Len has 6 shells. How many **fewer** shells does Ana have than Len?

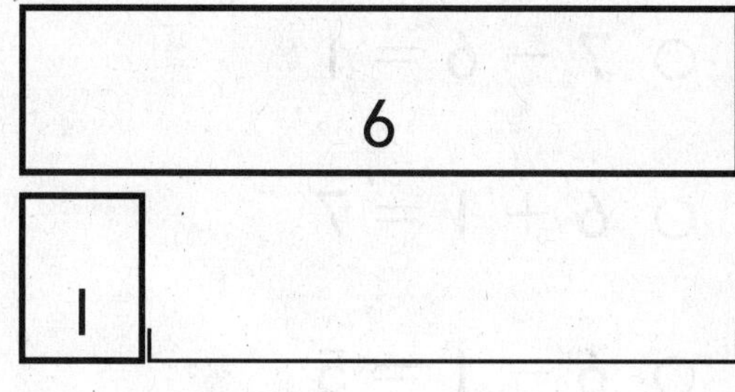

____

○ 1 ○ 5

○ 4 ○ 7

19. There were some fish. 3 fish swam away. Then there were 6 fish. How many fish were there before?

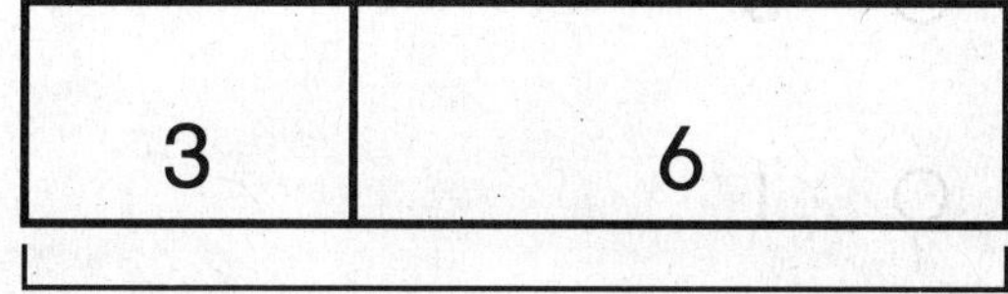

____

○ 12 ○ 6

○ 9 ○ 3

20. There are 8 pencils. 5 pencils are small. The rest are big. How many pencils are big?

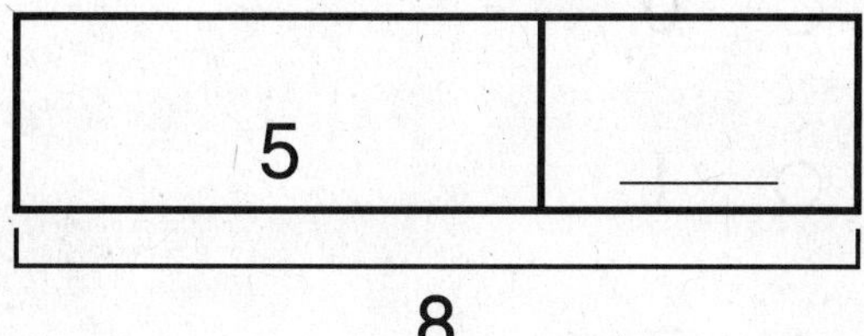

○ 2 ○ 6

○ 3 ○ 13

GO ON

Name ______________________________

21. Which shows a way to take apart 6?

- ○ 7 − 1 = 6
- ○ 7 − 6 = 1
- ○ 6 + 1 = 7
- ○ 6 − 1 = 5

22. Which number sentence solves the problem? There are 5 cars. 2 cars are big. The rest are small. How many cars are small?

- ○ 2 + 5 = 7
- ○ 1 + 2 = 3
- ○ 5 − 2 = 3
- ○ 5 − 5 = 0

23. What is the difference?

8 − 0 = _____

- ○ 0
- ○ 1
- ○ 7
- ○ 8

24. What is the difference?

6 − 6 = _____

- ○ 0
- ○ 1
- ○ 6
- ○ 9

STOP

Choose the correct answer.

1. What is the difference?

○ 7　　○ 3

○ 5　　○ 2

2. What is the difference?

$$\begin{array}{r} 8 \\ -\ 7 \\ \hline \end{array}$$

○ 0　　○ 2

○ 1　　○ 15

3. How many **more**  are there?

10 − 6 = ______

10 more　　8 more 　　6 more　　4 more 

○　　○　　○　　○

4. How many **more** ☆ are there?

9 − 3 = ______

3 more 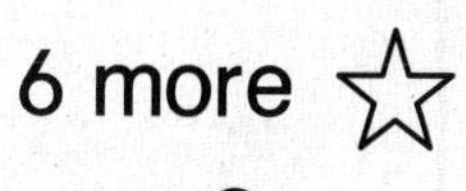　　6 more 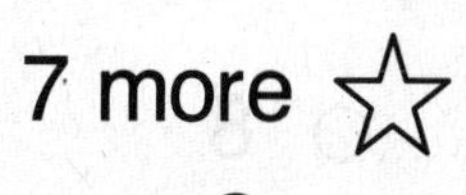　　7 more 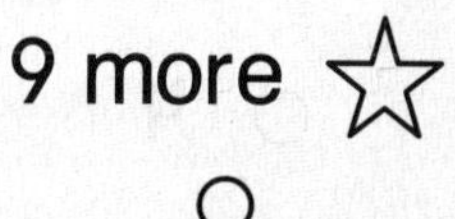　　9 more ☆

○　　○　　○　　○

Name ____________________

5. There are 7 birds. 1 bird flies away. How many birds are there now?

○ 1
○ 6
○ 5
○ 7

6. Frank has 7 books. Jaime has 2 books. How many **more** books does Frank have than Jaime?

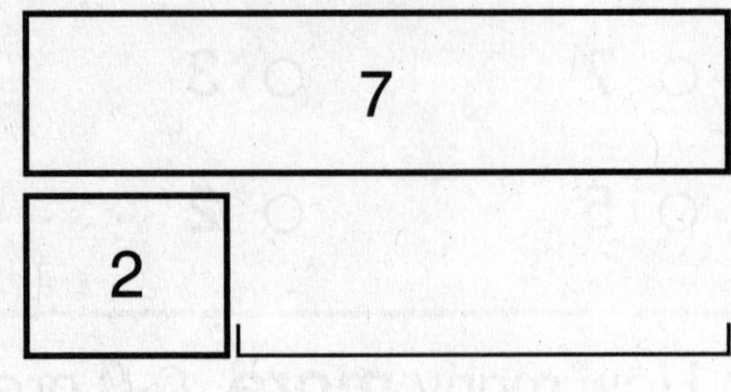

○ 5
○ 7
○ 6
○ 9

7. There were 8 cats. Some cats ran away. Then there were 4 cats. How many cats ran away?

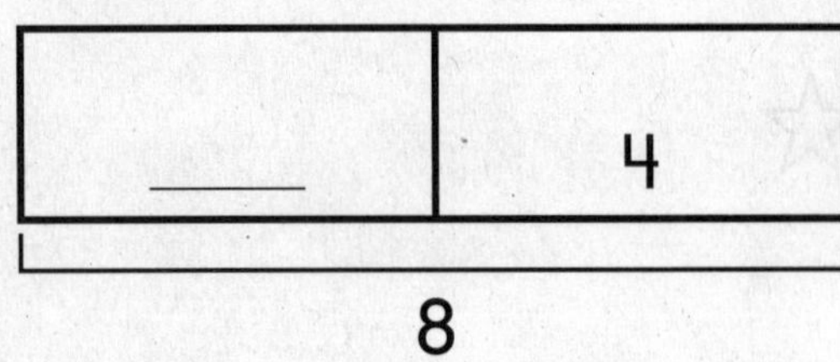

○ 2
○ 6
○ 4
○ 8

8. Which shows a way to take apart 6?

○ $6 + 3 = 9$

○ $8 - 6 = 2$

○ $8 - 2 = 6$

○ $6 - 2 = 4$

GO ON

9. Which shows a way to take apart 9?

- ○ $9 - 8 = 1$
- ○ $10 - 8 = 2$
- ○ $10 - 2 = 8$
- ○ $9 + 1 = 10$

10. What is the difference?

______ $= 2 - 0$

- ○ 0
- ○ 1
- ○ 2
- ○ 3

11. Which number sentence solves the problem?
There are 8 rings in a box. 5 rings are pink. The rest are gold. How many rings are gold?

- ○ $2 + 3 = 5$
- ○ $8 + 2 = 10$
- ○ $8 - 2 = 6$
- ○ $8 - 5 = 3$

12. Which number sentence solves the problem?
There are 7 cows. 3 cows are brown. The rest are black. How many cows are black?

- ○ $7 - 3 = 4$
- ○ $7 + 3 = 10$
- ○ $3 + 3 = 6$
- ○ $10 - 7 = 3$

GO ON

Write the correct answer.

13. What is the difference?

7 − 2 = ______

14. What is the difference?

6 − 3 = ______

15. What is the difference?

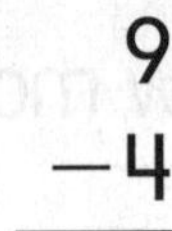

$$\begin{array}{r} 9 \\ -4 \\ \hline \end{array}$$

16. Draw lines to match. Subtract to compare.

8 − 5 = ______

______ fewer (acorn)

GO ON

17. There are 6 bugs. 2 bugs walk away. How many bugs are there now?

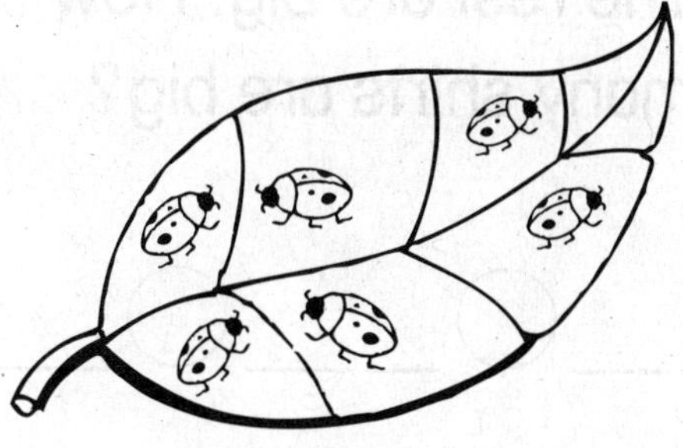

_____ bugs now

18. Jackie has 2 marbles. Ray has 9 marbles. How many **fewer** marbles does Jackie have than Ray?

9	
2	____

_____ fewer marbles

19. There were some dogs. 4 dogs ran away. Then there were 2 dogs. How many dogs were there before?

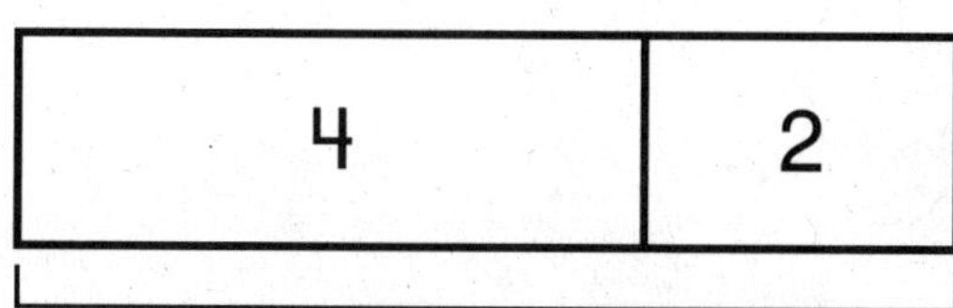

____

_____ − 4 = 2

20. There are 5 flowers. 2 are yellow. The rest are red. How many flowers are red?

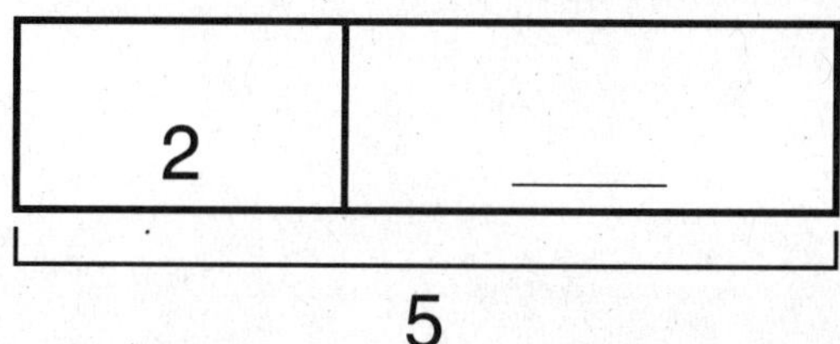

5 − 2 = _____

GO ON

Name ___________________________________

21. Write a number sentence to show a way to take apart 4.

4 − _____ = _____

22. Write the number sentence and how many. There are 5 shirts. 4 shirts are small. The rest are big. How many shirts are big?

_____ ◯ _____ ◯ _____

_____ big shirt

23. What is the difference?

9 − 0 = _____

24. What is the difference?

1 − 1 = _____

GO ON

Name ______________________________

Extended Constructed Response

25. Ali and Nico collect animal cards. Ali has 3 fewer cards than Nico. Nico has 9 cards. How many cards does Ali have?

Use numbers, pictures, or words to show your work.

Write a subtraction sentence.

_____ − _____ = _____

Ali has _____ cards.

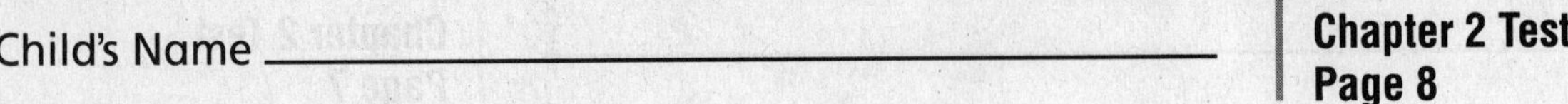
Child's Name ______________________________

Extended Constructed Response

The Constructed Response item is scored using the 3-point scoring rubric in the *Assessment Guide*. A child can receive partial credit for answers that are partially correct or partially completed.

Performance Indicators

For Problem 25, a child with a Level 2 paper:

_____ writes or draws to model comparing and subtracting.

_____ gives reasonable support to show that 6 is 3 fewer than 9.

_____ correctly completes the subtraction sentence.

_____ shows work that is easy to follow and clearly supports the answer given.

Choose the correct answer.

1. Which addition sentence matches the picture?

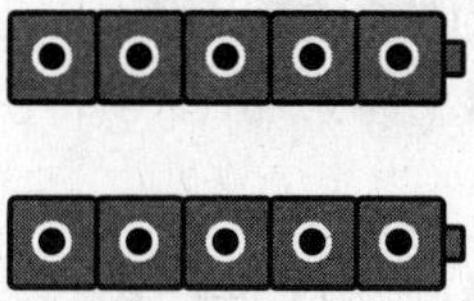

○ 3 + 3 = 6

○ 4 + 4 = 8

○ 5 + 5 = 10

○ 6 + 6 = 12

2. What is the sum of 4 + 1 + 5?

○ 5

○ 6

○ 9

○ 10

3. Which shows the same addends in a different order?

8 + 3 = 11

○ 8 + 2 = 10

○ 3 + 8 = 11

○ 7 + 4 = 11

○ 3 + 9 = 12

4. Which shows a way to make a ten to solve 9 + 5?

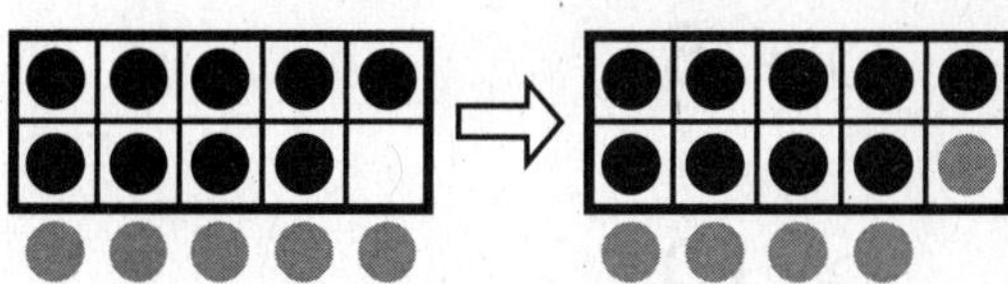

○ 9 + 1 + 4

○ 9 + 1 + 5

○ 5 + 5 + 9

○ 4 + 6 + 5

GO ON

5. Alicia has 4 red markers. She has 3 green markers. She also has 6 blue markers. How many markers does Alicia have?

- ○ 13
- ○ 10
- ○ 9
- ○ 7

6. What number sentence does this model show?

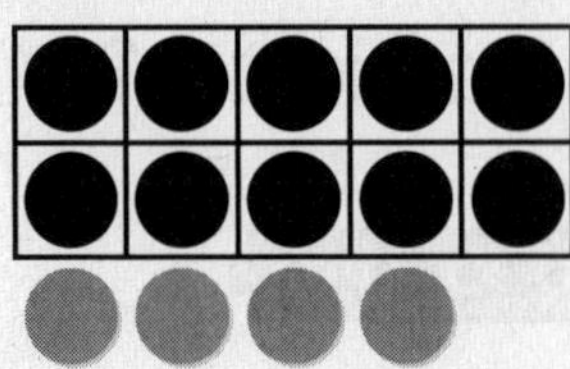

- ○ $10 - 4 = 6$
- ○ $5 + 4 = 9$
- ○ $6 + 4 = 10$
- ○ $10 + 4 = 14$

7. What is the sum of $5 + 7 + 3$?

- ○ 8
- ○ 10
- ○ 15
- ○ 17

8. Count on. What is the sum?

$5 + 2 =$ ______

- ○ 10
- ○ 9
- ○ 8
- ○ 7

GO ON

9. What is the sum?

9 + 8 = ____

○ 16

○ 17

○ 18

○ 19

10. Which shows a way to find the sum of 8 + 9?

○ 9 + 9 + 1

○ 8 + 8 + 1

○ 7 + 7 + 1

○ 6 + 6 + 1

11. Which doubles fact helps you solve 5 + 4 = 9?

○ 3 + 3 = 6

○ 4 + 4 = 8

○ 6 + 6 = 12

○ 7 + 7 = 14

12. What number sentence does this model show?

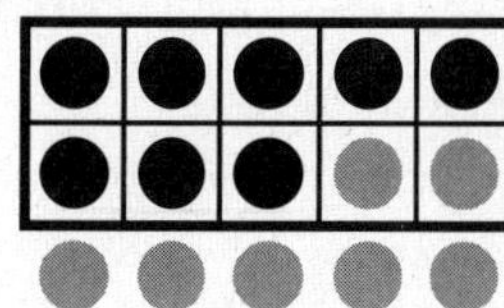

○ 10 + 5 = 15

○ 10 + 2 = 12

○ 8 + 5 = 13

○ 2 + 5 = 7

GO ON

Name ______________________________

13. Which addition sentence matches the picture?

○ 4 + 4 = 8

○ 3 + 3 = 6

○ 2 + 2 = 4

○ 1 + 1 = 2

14. Which shows the same addends in a different order?

9 + 4 = 13

○ 7 + 6 = 13

○ 9 + 3 = 12

○ 4 + 9 = 13

○ 4 + 6 = 10

15. What is the sum?

2 + 6 + 3 = ______

○ 13

○ 11

○ 9

○ 5

16. Which shows a way to make a ten to solve 8 + 4?

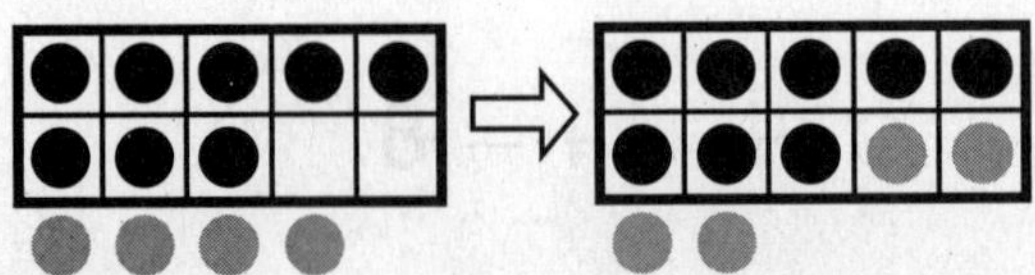

○ 8 + 2 + 4

○ 8 + 2 + 2

○ 4 + 6 + 4

○ 2 + 2 + 4

GO ON

Name ______________________________

17. Bly has 2 cards. Sara has 7 cards. Louis has 2 cards. How many cards do they have altogether?

- ○ 4
- ○ 9
- ○ 10
- ○ 11

18. What number sentence does this model show?

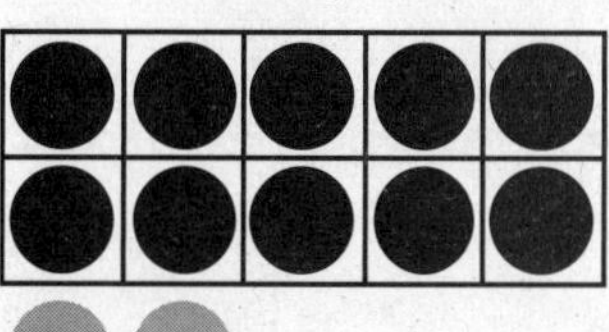

- ○ 5 + 2 = 7
- ○ 12 − 3 = 9
- ○ 10 + 2 = 12
- ○ 10 + 3 = 13

19. What is the sum of 8 + 0 + 8?

- ○ 16
- ○ 14
- ○ 8
- ○ 0

20. Count on. What is the sum?

$$\begin{array}{r} 3 \\ +\ 9 \\ \hline \end{array}$$

- ○ 6
- ○ 12
- ○ 14
- ○ 16

GO ON

21. What is the sum?

$1 + 8 =$ ____

○ 6

○ 7

○ 8

○ 9

22. Stan wants to find the sum of $4 + 5$. Which has the same sum as $4 + 5$?

○ $6 + 6 + 1$

○ $5 + 5 + 1$

○ $4 + 4 + 1$

○ $3 + 3 + 1$

23. Paula wants to find $7 + 8$. Which shows a way Paula can use doubles to find the sum?

○ $8 + 8 + 1$

○ $7 + 7 + 1$

○ $6 + 6 + 1$

○ $5 + 5 + 1$

24. Which shows a way to make a ten to add?

$6 + 5 =$ ___?___

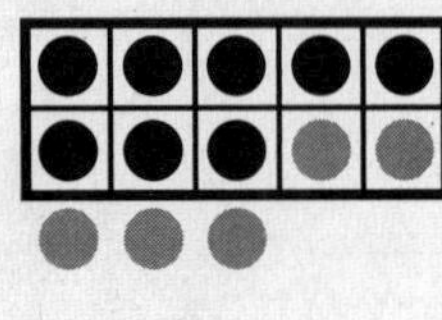

○

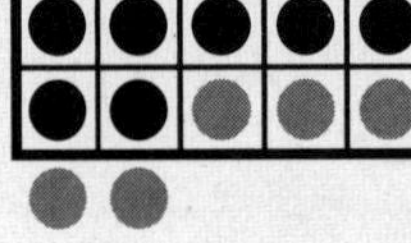

○

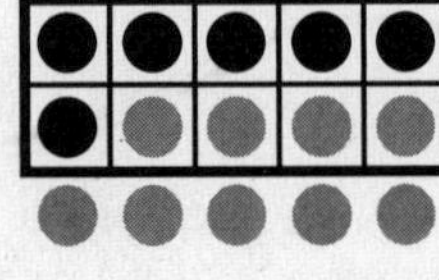

○

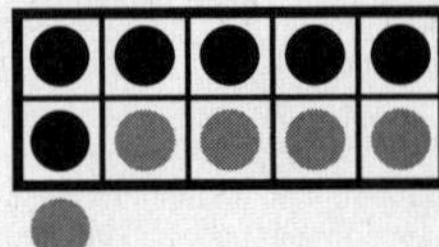

○

STOP

Choose the correct answer.

1. Which addition sentence matches the picture?

- ○ $4 + 4 = 8$
- ○ $5 + 5 = 10$
- ○ $6 + 6 = 12$
- ○ $7 + 7 = 14$

2. What is the sum of $2 + 5 + 4$?

- ○ 6
- ○ 7
- ○ 9
- ○ 11

3. Which shows the same addends in a different order?

$$7 + 4 = 11$$

- ○ $5 + 6 = 11$
- ○ $7 + 3 = 10$
- ○ $4 + 7 = 11$
- ○ $4 + 6 = 10$

4. Which shows a way to make a ten to solve $7 + 4$?

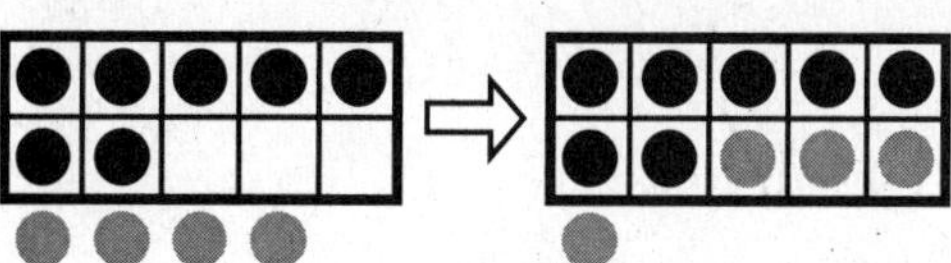

- ○ $7 + 3 + 1$
- ○ $7 + 2 + 1$
- ○ $4 + 6 + 2$
- ○ $1 + 9 + 7$

GO ON

5. Angel has 2 red apples.
He has 8 green apples.
He also has 1 yellow apple.
How many apples does
Angel have?

○ 3

○ 9

○ 10

○ 11

6. What number sentence
does this model show?

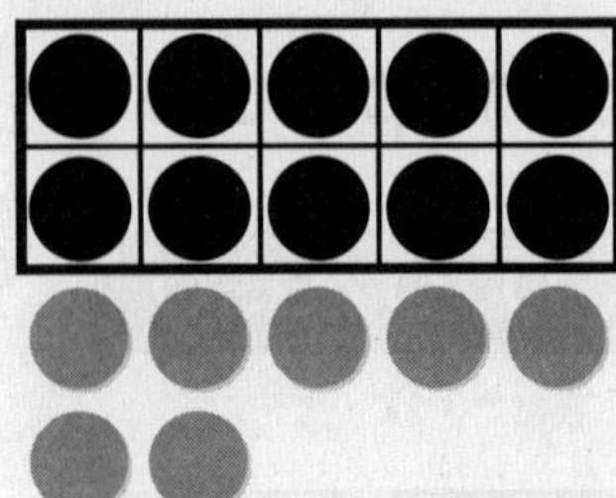

○ $10 + 7 = 17$

○ $9 + 7 = 16$

○ $7 + 3 = 10$

○ $2 + 5 = 7$

7. What is the sum of
$2 + 2 + 7$?

○ 11

○ 9

○ 7

○ 4

8. Count on. What is
the sum?

$8 + 1 =$ ____

○ 10

○ 9

○ 8

○ 7

GO ON

9. What is the sum?

$4 + 5 =$ ____

○ 6

○ 7

○ 8

○ 9

10. Which shows a way to use doubles to find the sum of $5 + 6$?

○ $4 + 4 + 1$

○ $5 + 5 + 1$

○ $6 + 6 + 1$

○ $7 + 7 + 1$

11. Which doubles fact helps you solve $6 + 7 = 13$?

○ $8 + 8 = 16$

○ $7 + 7 = 14$

○ $5 + 5 = 10$

○ $4 + 4 = 8$

12. What number sentence does this model show?

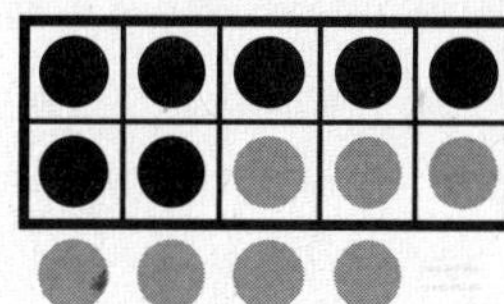

○ $10 + 4 = 14$

○ $10 + 3 = 13$

○ $7 + 4 = 11$

○ $3 + 3 = 6$

GO ON

Write the correct answer.

13. What doubles fact does the picture show?

_____ + _____ = _____

14. Add. Change the order of the addends. Add again.

$$\begin{array}{r} 8 \\ +\ 5 \\ \hline \square \end{array} \qquad \begin{array}{r} \square \\ +\ \square \\ \hline \square \end{array}$$

15. What is the sum?

1 + 9 + 2 = _____

16. Write a way to make a ten to solve 8 + 9.

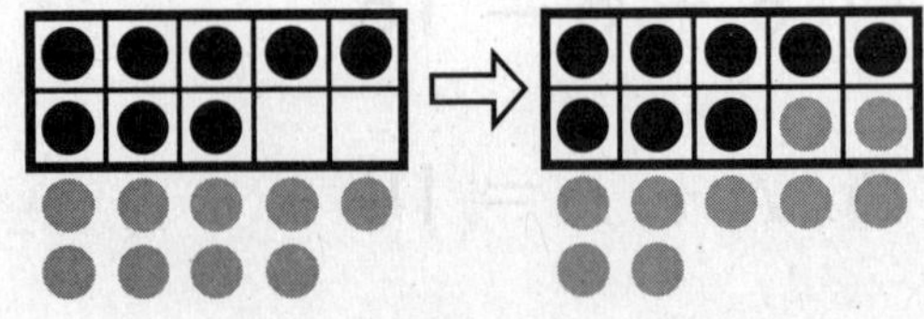

_____ + _____ + _____

GO ON

17. Nikki has 4 pennies. Lucy has 6 pennies. Jamar has 4 pennies. How many pennies do they have altogether?

_______ pennies

18. What number sentence does this model show?

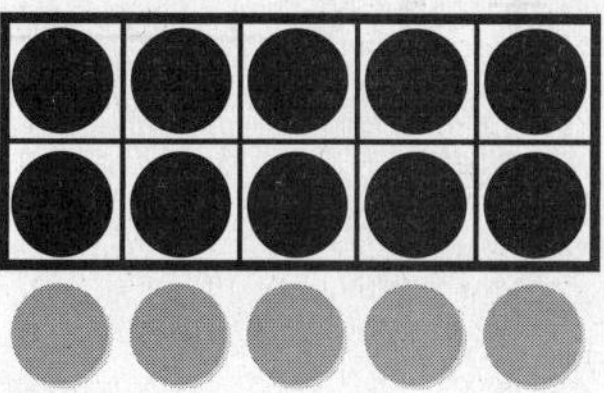

$10 + 5 =$ _______

19. What is the sum?

$$\begin{array}{r} 3 \\ 3 \\ +7 \\ \hline \square \end{array}$$

20. Count on. What is the sum?

$$\begin{array}{r} 3 \\ +\ 6 \\ \hline \square \end{array}$$

GO ON

21. What is the sum?

7 + 3 = ______

22. Tracy wants to find this sum.

8 + 9 = ______

How can Tracy use doubles to find the sum?

______ + ______ + 1 = ______

23. Mark wants to find this sum.

7 + 8 = ______

How can Mark use doubles to find the sum?

______ + ______ + 1 = ______

24. Make a ten to add. Draw to show your work. Write the sum.

8 + 5 = ?

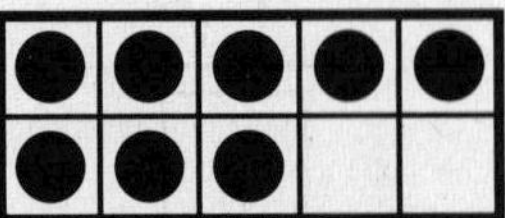

8 + 5 = ______

GO ON

Extended Constructed Response

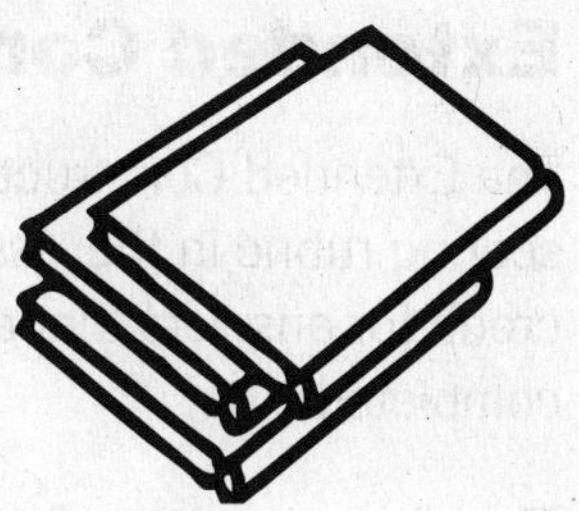

25. Jim has 2 books.
Karla has 8 books.
Manuel has 7 books.
How many books do they have altogether?

Use numbers, pictures, or words to show your work.

__________ books

Name ____________________

Extended Constructed Response

The Extended Constructed Response item is scored using the 3-point scoring rubric in the *Assessment Guide.* A child can receive partial credit for answers that are partially correct or partially completed.

Performance Indicators

For Problem 25, a child with a Level 2 paper:

_____ writes or draws to show a group of 2, 8, and 7.

_____ gives reasonable support to show that the sum of 2 and 8 and 7 is 17.

_____ shows pictures, words, or numbers that are easy to follow and clearly supports the answers given.

Choose the correct answer.

1. Ty had 6 toy cars. He gave 3 toy cars to Po. How many toy cars does Ty have now?

○ 9 ○ 3

○ 4 ○ 2

2. Nina has 9 pictures to color. She colors some of them. Now Nina has 7 pictures left to color. How many pictures did she color?

○ 2 ○ 11

○ 3 ○ 16

3. Which shows how to make a ten to solve 15 − 8?

Step 1

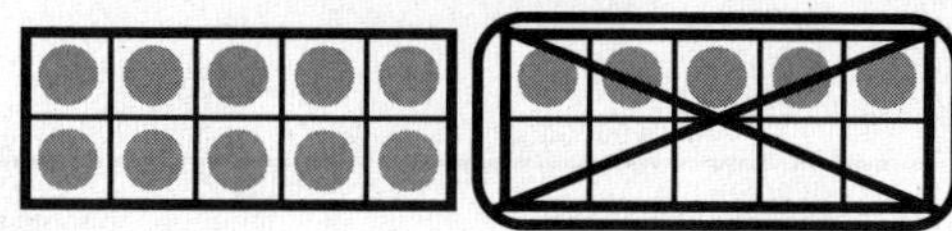

○ 15 − 5

○ 10 − 5

Step 2

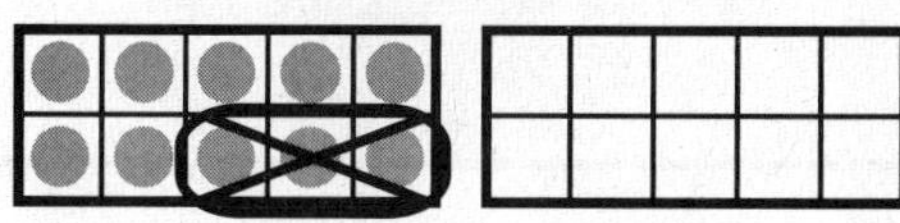

○ 15 − 5 − 3

○ 10 − 5 − 1

4. Which shows how to make a ten to solve 14 − 6?

Step 1

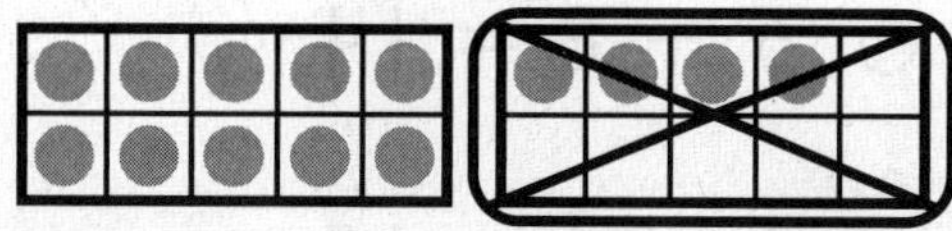

○ 14 − 4 − 2

○ 14 − 4

Step 2

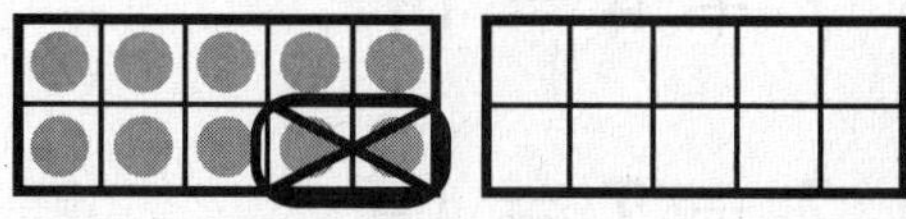

○ 10 − 4 − 2

○ 10 − 4

GO ON

Name ________________________________

5. Ella has 14 flowers. She gives some to her friend. She has 6 left. How many flowers does Ella give her friend?

○ 20

○ 10

○ 8

○ 7

6. Brian had some baseball cards. He gave 5 cards to his sister. Now Brian has 7 cards. How many cards did Brian start with?

○ 13

○ 12

○ 5

○ 2

7. Which addition fact helps you solve 11 − 4?

○ 4 + 4 = 8

○ 8 + 3 = 11

○ 7 + 4 = 11

○ 7 + 7 = 14

8. Which addition fact helps you solve 15 − 6?

○ 9 + 6 = 15

○ 8 + 7 = 15

○ 6 + 8 = 14

○ 6 + 6 = 12

9. What is 9 − 4?

Think:

4 + ___?___ = 9

○ 13 ○ 4

○ 5 ○ 1

10. What is 17 − 8?

Think:

8 + ___?___ = 17

○ 5 ○ 8

○ 7 ○ 9

11. Which shows a way to make a ten to subtract?

12 − 8 = ___?___

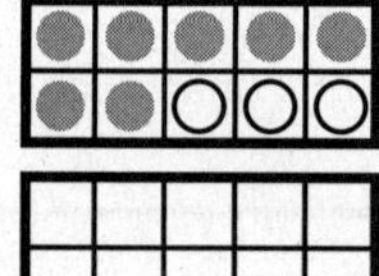 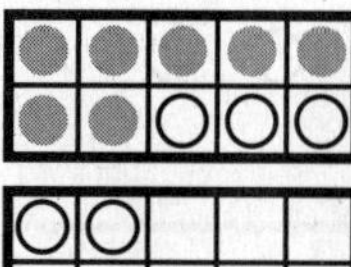 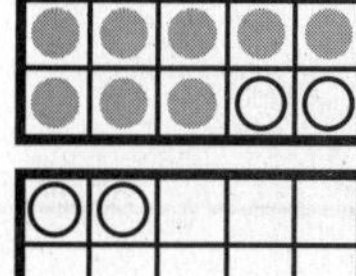 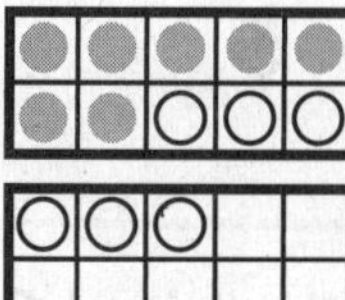

○ ○ ○ ○

12. Which shows a way to make a ten to subtract?

14 − 9 = ___?___

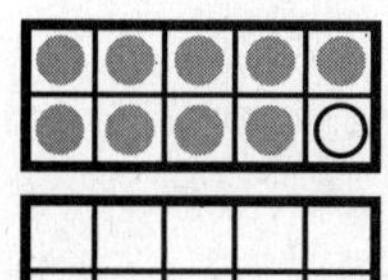 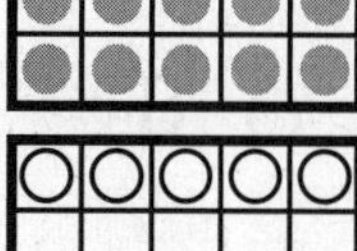 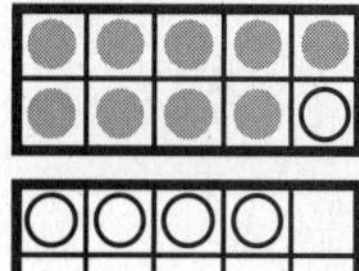 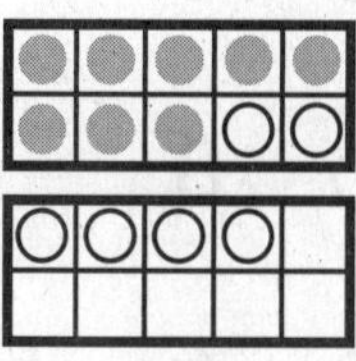

○ ○ ○ ○

GO ON

Name ______________________________

13. Shawn has 7 cherries. He eats 1 of them. How many cherries does he have now?

- ○ 8
- ○ 7
- ○ 6
- ○ 5

14. Cho has 8 books. She gives 3 books to her sister. How many books does Cho have now?

- ○ 8
- ○ 5
- ○ 4
- ○ 3

15. What is 10 − 8?

Think:

$8 + \underline{\quad ? \quad} = 10$

- ○ 10
- ○ 8
- ○ 6
- ○ 2

16. What is 16 − 7?

Think:

$7 + \underline{\quad ? \quad} = 16$

- ○ 9
- ○ 8
- ○ 7
- ○ 6

GO ON

Name ______________________

17. Angel has 16 grapes. He eats some of them. He has 7 grapes left. How many grapes does Angel eat?

- ○ 9
- ○ 8
- ○ 7
- ○ 6

18. Max has 13 pens. He gives some to his sister. He has 8 pens left. How many pens does Max give his sister?

- ○ 4
- ○ 5
- ○ 6
- ○ 21

19. Which addition sentence helps you solve 12 − 5?

- ○ 7 + 5 = 12
- ○ 5 + 5 = 10
- ○ 5 + 8 = 13
- ○ 6 + 5 = 11

20. Which addition sentence helps you solve 13 − 4?

- ○ 8 + 6 = 14
- ○ 8 + 5 = 13
- ○ 9 + 3 = 12
- ○ 9 + 4 = 13

GO ON

21. Jaime had 12 toy bears on a shelf. He takes 2 off the shelf. How many bears are on the shelf now?

○ 14 ○ 10

○ 12 ○ 8

22. There are 13 bugs on a rock. Some crawl away. Now there are 4 bugs on the rock. How many bugs crawl away?

○ 4 ○ 9

○ 7 ○ 10

23. Which shows how to make a ten to solve $14 - 7$?

Step 1

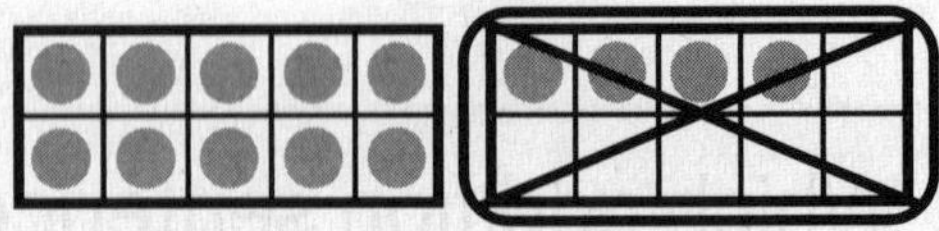

Step 2

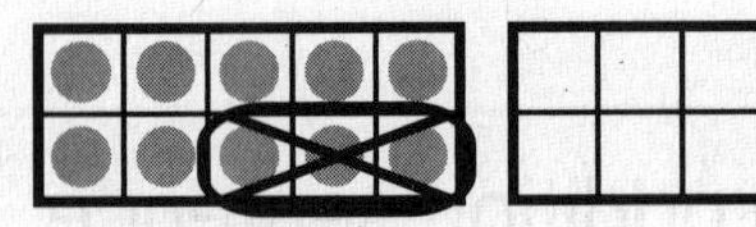

○ $14 - 4 - 3$

○ $10 - 4 - 3$

○ $14 - 4 - 1$

○ $10 - 4 - 1$

24. Which shows a way to make a ten to subtract?

$16 - 8 = \underline{\ ?\ }$

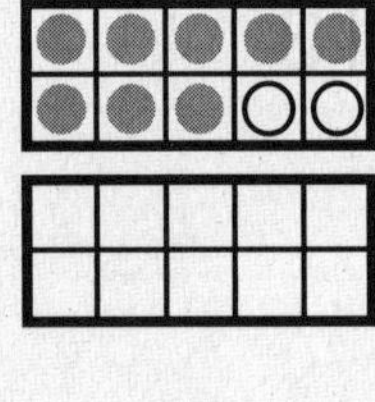

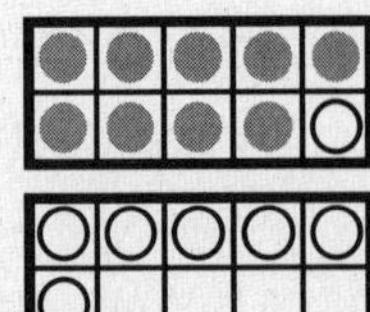

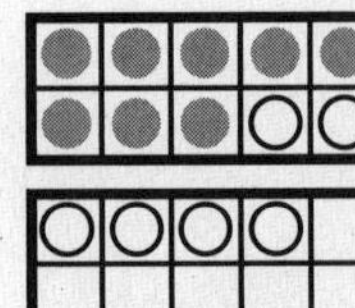

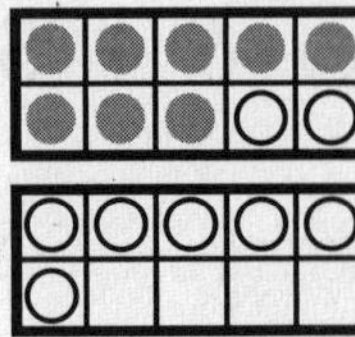

○ ○ ○ ○

STOP

Name ____________________

Choose the correct answer.

1. Moe had 10 stickers. He gave 3 stickers to Jen. How many stickers does Moe have now?

○ 8 ○ 6
○ 7 ○ 3

2. Hannah has 8 pages to read. She reads some of them. Now Hannah has 6 pages left to read. How many pages did she read?

○ 2 ○ 6
○ 4 ○ 8

3. Which shows how to make a ten to solve 12 − 5?

Step 1

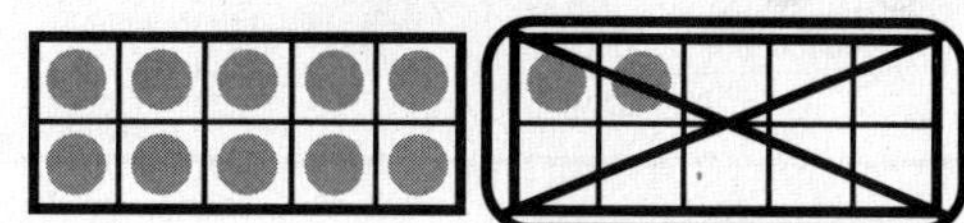

○ 12 − 2
○ 10 − 2

Step 2

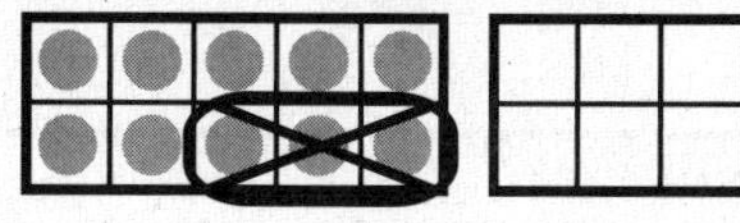

○ 12 − 2 − 3
○ 10 − 2 − 2

4. Which shows how to make a ten to solve 14 − 8?

Step 1

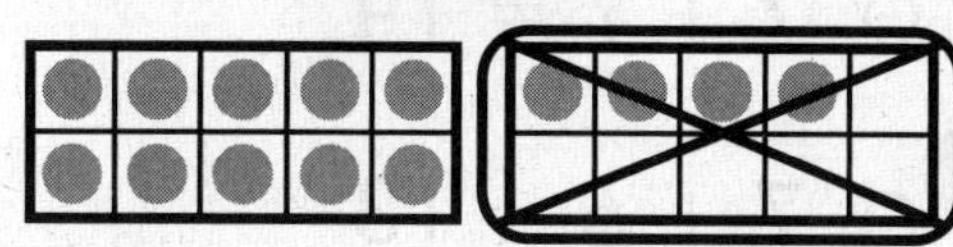

○ 14 − 4 − 6
○ 14 − 4 − 4

Step 2

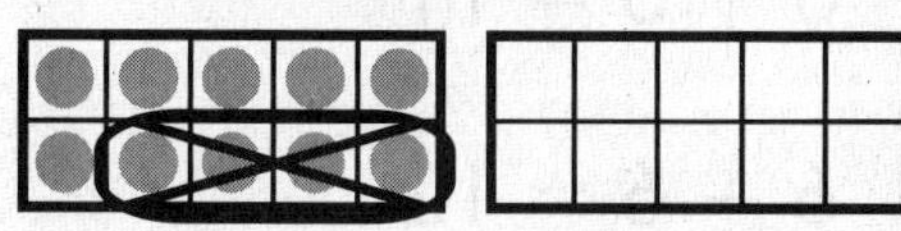

○ 10 − 4 − 4
○ 10 − 4

GO ON

5. Maria has 18 pears. She gives some away. She has 9 pears left. How many pears does Maria give away?

- ○ 18
- ○ 10
- ○ 9
- ○ 8

6. Kris has 11 pencils. She gives 8 pencils to her brother. How many pencils does Kris have now?

- ○ 2
- ○ 3
- ○ 4
- ○ 5

7. Which addition fact helps you solve $11 - 5$?

- ○ $5 + 5 = 10$
- ○ $7 + 4 = 11$
- ○ $6 + 5 = 11$
- ○ $6 + 6 = 12$

8. Which addition fact helps you solve $15 - 8$?

- ○ $7 + 8 = 15$
- ○ $8 + 6 = 14$
- ○ $7 + 7 = 14$
- ○ $7 + 6 = 13$

9. What is 13 − 6?

Think:

6 + __?__ = 13

○ 19

○ 8

○ 7

○ 5

10. What is 14 − 5?

Think:

5 + __?__ = 14

○ 5

○ 9

○ 11

○ 20

11. Which shows a way to make a ten to subtract?

13 − 8 = __?__

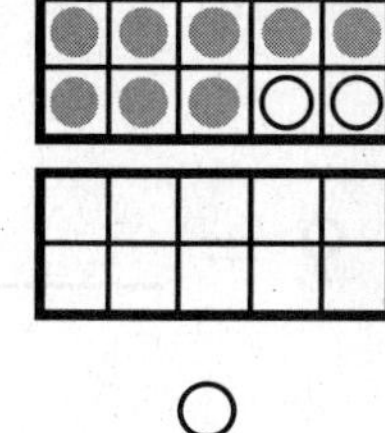
○

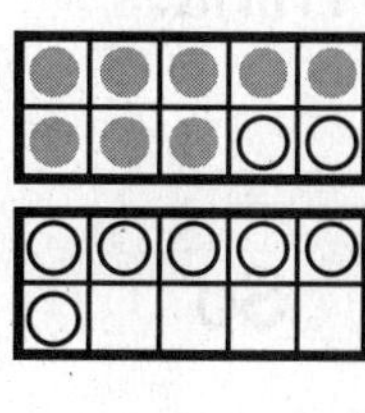
○

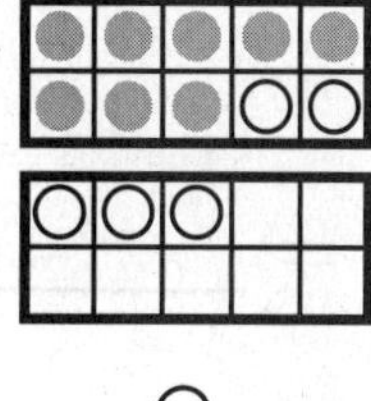
○

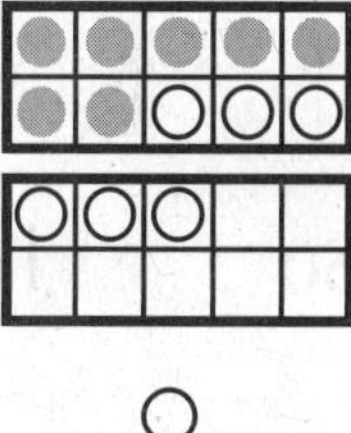
○

12. Which shows a way to make a ten to subtract?

15 − 9 = __?__

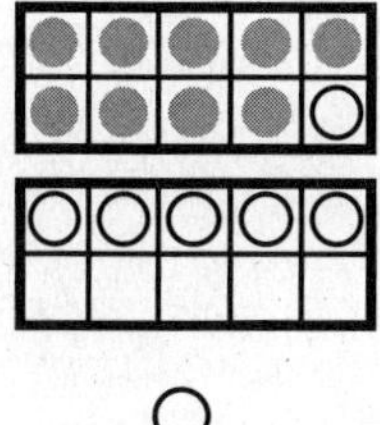
○

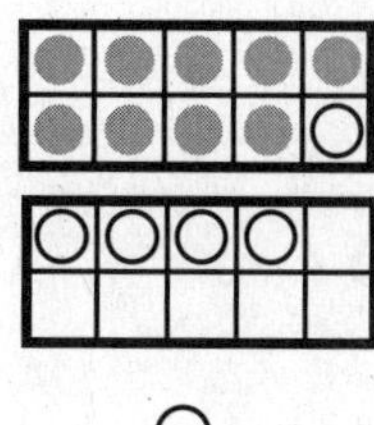
○

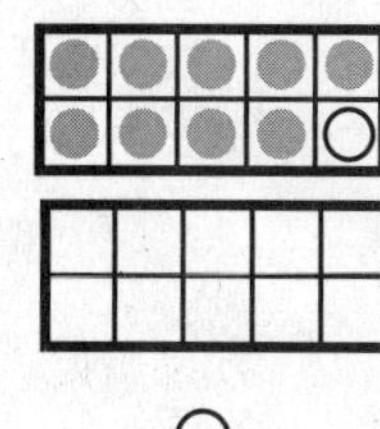
○

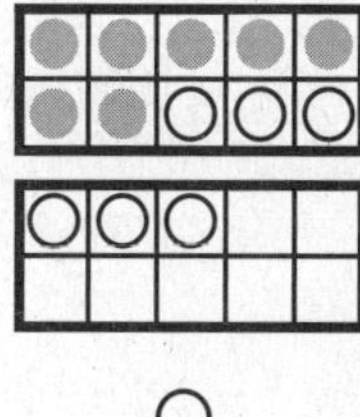
○

GO ON

Name ______________________________

Write the correct answer.

13. April has 9 stamps. She uses 1 of them. How many stamps does April have now?

____ stamps

14. Pat has 7 crackers. He eats 3 crackers. How many crackers does Pat have now?

____ crackers

15. What is 11 − 6?

Think: 6 + __?__ = 11

So 11 − 6 = ______

16. What is 17 − 9?

Think: 9 + __?__ = 17

So 17 − 9 = ______

GO ON

Name ______________________

17. Meg has 11 berries. She eats some of them. She has 7 berries left. How many berries does Meg eat?

Meg eats _____ berries.

18. Al makes 14 cards. He gives away some cards. He has 9 cards left. How many cards does Al give away?

Al gives away _____ cards.

19. Write an addition sentence that can help you solve 12 − 8.

_____ + _____ = 12

20. Write an addition sentence that can help you solve 14 − 6.

_____ + _____ = 14

GO ON

21. Mark has 16 pencils. 9 pencils are green. The rest are red. How many pencils are red?

______ red pencils

22. There are 13 birds in a tree. Some of the birds fly away. Now there are 5 birds in the tree. How many birds fly away?

______ birds

23. Write how to make a ten to solve 15 − 6.

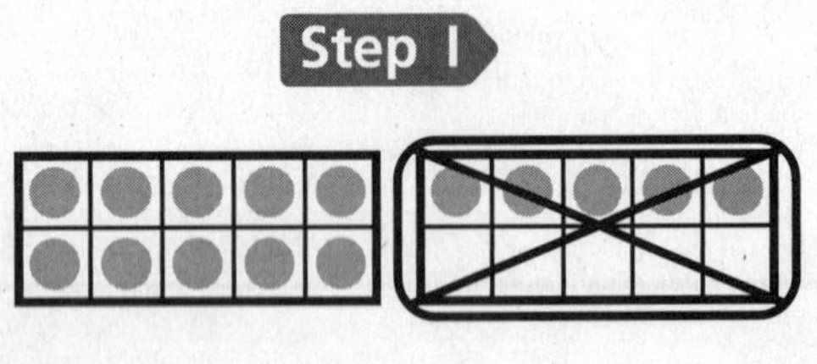

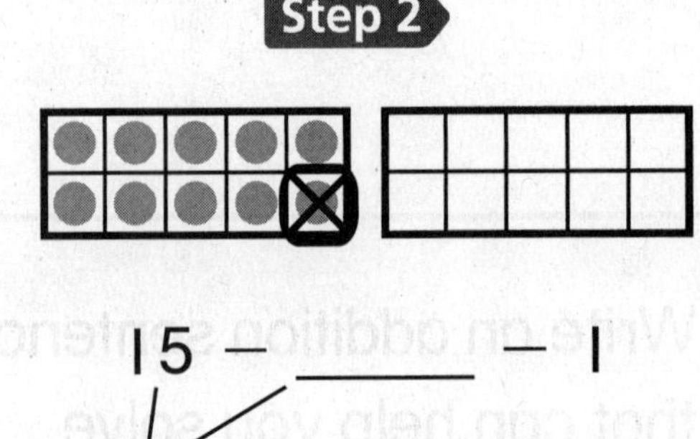

15 − ______ − 1

10 − ______ = ______

So, 15 − 6 = ______.

24. Draw a circle around the picture that shows a way to make a ten to subtract.

12 − 9 = ?

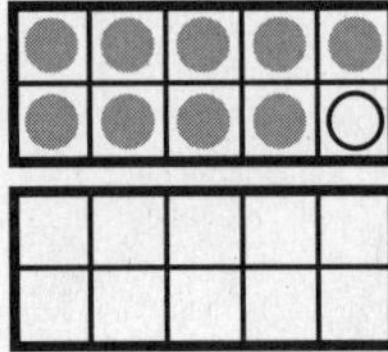

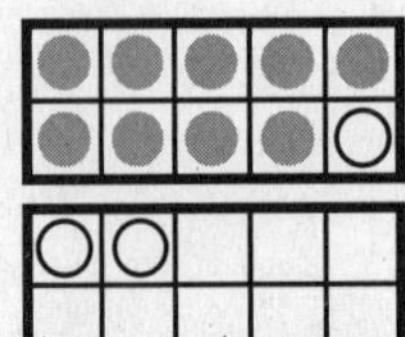

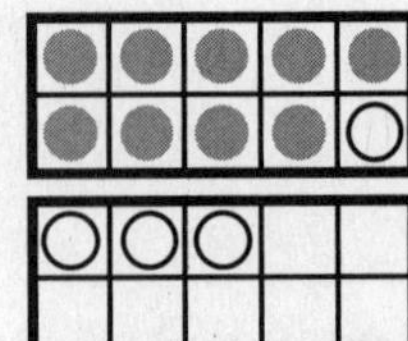

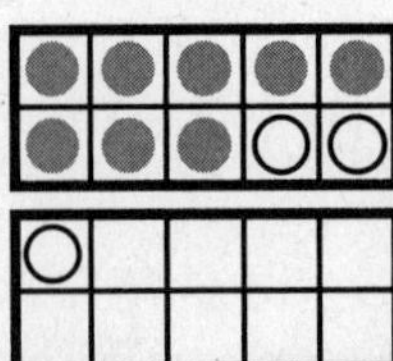

GO ON

Name ______________________________

Extended Constructed Response

25. Ron has 2 crayons on a table.
He has some more crayons in a box.
He has 11 crayons in all.
How many crayons are in the box?

____ crayons

Use words, numbers or pictures.
Show how you solved the problem.

How many more crayons are there in the box than on the table?

Write the subtraction sentence you can use to solve this problem.

____ – ____ = ____

____ more crayons

Child's Name ______________________________

Extended Constructed Response

The Extended Constructed Response item is scored using the 3-point scoring rubric in the *Assessment Guide.* A child can receive partial credit for answers that are partially correct or partially completed.

Performance Indicators

For Problem 25, a child with a Level 2 paper:

_____ correctly finds the differences.

_____ gives a reasonable explanation for a strategy used to solve the problem.

_____ correctly writes the number sentence for the comparing situation.

_____ shows work that is easy to follow and clearly supports the answers given.

Name ______________________________

Choose the correct answer.

1. Lisa bakes 6 muffins. Max bakes 8 more muffins than Lisa bakes. Which number sentence shows how to find the number of muffins Max bakes?

   ○ $8 - 6 = 2$

   ○ $8 - 2 = 6$

   ○ $6 + 8 = 14$

   ○ $14 - 7 = 7$

2. Jason and Lucy eat 13 raisins. Jason eats 8 raisins. Which number sentence shows how to find the number of raisins Lucy eats?

   ○ $13 + 8 = 21$

   ○ $9 + 4 = 13$

   ○ $5 + 5 = 10$

   ○ $13 - 8 = 5$

3. Look at the pairs of facts. Which shows related facts?

   ○ $6 + 5 = 11$, $5 + 1 = 6$

   ○ $6 - 1 = 5$, $5 + 1 = 6$

   ○ $6 + 5 = 11$, $5 + 5 = 10$

   ○ $16 - 8 = 8$, $5 + 9 = 14$

4. Look at the pairs of facts. Which shows related facts?

   ○ $7 + 7 = 14$, $8 + 8 = 16$

   ○ $7 + 8 = 15$, $8 + 9 = 17$

   ○ $1 + 7 = 8$, $17 - 8 = 9$

   ○ $7 + 7 = 14$, $14 - 7 = 7$

GO ON

5. Jack uses these 3 numbers to write related facts.

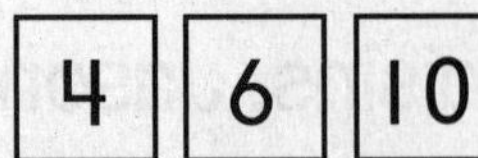

Which could be one of Jack's related facts?

○ $4 + 6 = 10$

○ $6 - 4 = 2$

○ $9 + 4 = 13$

○ $9 + 6 = 15$

6. Lara uses these numbers to write related facts.

5	8	13

Which is **not** one of Lara's related facts?

○ $13 - 5 = 8$

○ $8 + 5 = 13$

○ $5 + 8 = 13$

○ $12 - 8 = 4$

7. Which is a related fact?

$5 + 3 = 8$
$3 + 5 = 8$
$8 - 5 = 3$

○ $8 - 3 = 5$

○ $8 + 5 = 13$

○ $8 + 3 = 11$

○ $6 - 5 = 1$

8. Which number is missing from these related facts?

$\square + 3 = 11$ $\quad 11 - 3 = \square$

$3 + \square = 11$ $\quad 11 - \square = 3$

○ 1 ○ 8

○ 3 ○ 9

GO ON

9. Mr. Stuart buys 11 erasers. He gives 7 erasers away. How many erasers does he have left?

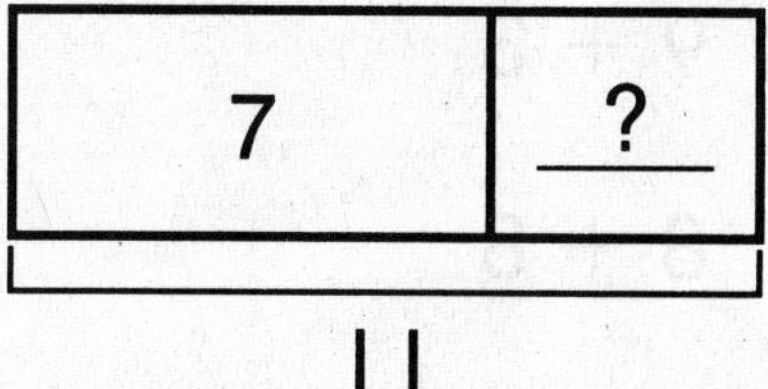

○ 3
○ 4
○ 7
○ 18

10. Mitchell finds 6 shells on the beach. Now he has 13 shells. How many shells did Mitchell start with?

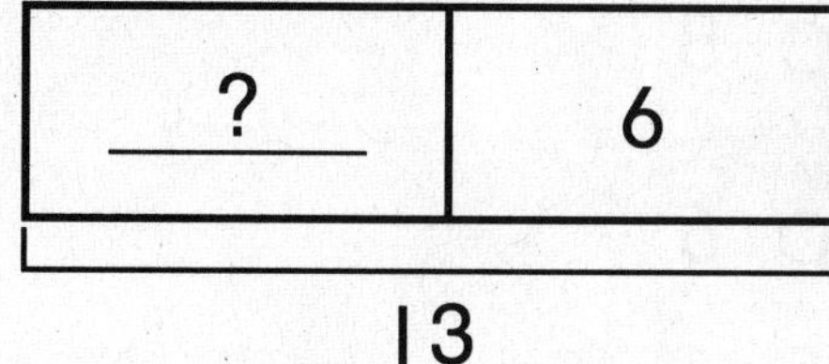

○ 6
○ 7
○ 13
○ 19

11. What is the missing number?

$13 - 5 = \square$

$5 + \square = 13$

○ 4
○ 5
○ 8
○ 9

12. What is the missing number?

$8 + \square = 16$

○ 1
○ 6
○ 8
○ 10

GO ON

Name ____________________

13. Which number makes the sentence **true**?

$3 + 4 = 9 - \square$

○ 8

○ 6

○ 5

○ 2

14. Which makes the sentence **false**?

$8 + 4 =$ ____

○ $9 + 3$

○ $8 + 8$

○ $7 + 5$

○ $6 + 6$

15. Which makes the sentence **true**?

$5 + 8 = 14 - \square$

○ 13

○ 7

○ 5

○ 1

16. Which addition fact helps you solve $14 - 6$?

○ $6 + 6 = 12$

○ $6 + 8 = 14$

○ $7 + 8 = 15$

○ $8 + 8 = 16$

GO ON

17. Which addition fact helps you solve $13 - 9$?

○ $4 + 5 = 9$

○ $3 + 9 = 12$

○ $9 + 4 = 13$

○ $9 + 5 = 14$

18. The table shows ways to make 14. Which shows a different way to make 14?

14
$7 + 7$
$3 + 6 + 5$

○ $8 + 6$ ○ $15 - 0$

○ $9 + 6$ ○ $12 - 7$

19. Which way makes 19?

○ $1 + 9$

○ $10 - 9$

○ $4 + 5 + 9$

○ $5 + 5 + 9$

20. Alba solves this subtraction sentence.

$15 - 7 = \square$

Which addition sentence can Alba use to check her subtraction?

○ $6 + 9 = 15$

○ $7 + 1 = 8$

○ $8 + 7 = 15$

○ $7 + 7 = 14$

Name ____________________

21. Which addition sentence can you use to check the subtraction?

9 − 3 = ☐

○ 9 + 6 = 15

○ 6 + 3 = 9

○ 4 + 2 = 6

○ 9 + 4 = 13

22. Flora has 8 pencils. Pat has 4 pencils. How many pencils do Flora and Pat have?

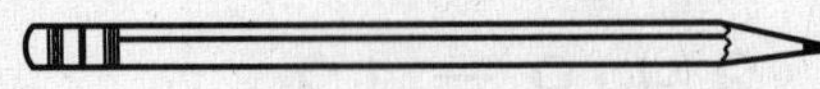

○ 2

○ 4

○ 11

○ 12

23. What is 8 + 7?

○ 1

○ 7

○ 15

○ 16

24. What is 9 − 0?

○ 0

○ 1

○ 6

○ 9

STOP

Name ______________________

Choose the correct answer.

1. Mali plants 5 roses. Justin plants 7 more roses than Mali. Which number sentence shows how to find the number of roses Justin plants?

○ $5 + 2 = 7$

○ $7 - 5 = 2$

○ $5 + 7 = 12$

○ $12 - 5 = 7$

2. Alice and Gavin eat 11 apples. Alice eats 6 apples. Which number sentence shows how to find the number of apples Gavin eats?

○ $7 + 4 = 11$

○ $9 + 6 = 15$

○ $3 + 3 = 6$

○ $11 - 6 = 5$

3. Look at the pairs of facts. Which shows related facts?

$5 + 8 = 13$ $8 + 5 = 13$ ○	$8 - 5 = 3$ $8 + 5 = 13$ ○
$5 + 8 = 13$ $8 + 8 = 16$ ○	$5 + 8 = 13$ $5 + 3 = 8$ ○

4. Look at the pairs of facts. Which shows related facts?

$8 + 9 = 17$ $8 + 8 = 16$ ○	$9 + 9 = 18$ $9 - 8 = 1$ ○
$7 + 6 = 13$ $7 + 1 = 8$ ○	$8 - 2 = 6$ $8 - 6 = 2$ ○

GO ON

Name ____________________

5. Tom uses these numbers to write related facts.

8	9	17

Which could be one of Tom's related facts?

- ○ $8 + 9 = 17$
- ○ $9 - 1 = 8$
- ○ $9 - 8 = 1$
- ○ $16 - 8 = 8$

6. Dawn uses these numbers to write related facts.

4	7	11

Which is **not** one of Dawn's related facts?

- ○ $11 - 7 = 4$
- ○ $4 + 7 = 11$
- ○ $7 + 4 = 11$
- ○ $10 - 7 = 3$

7. Which is a related fact?

$6 + 7 = 13$
$7 + 6 = 13$
$13 - 7 = 6$

- ○ $7 + 7 = 14$
- ○ $13 - 6 = 7$
- ○ $6 + 6 = 12$
- ○ $7 - 6 = 1$

8. Which number is missing from these related facts?

$\square + 9 = 13$ $13 - 9 = \square$

$9 + \square = 13$ $13 - \square = 9$

- ○ 9
- ○ 8
- ○ 4
- ○ 3

GO ON

Name ____________________

9. Julia buys 12 books. She gives 9 books away. How many books does she have left?

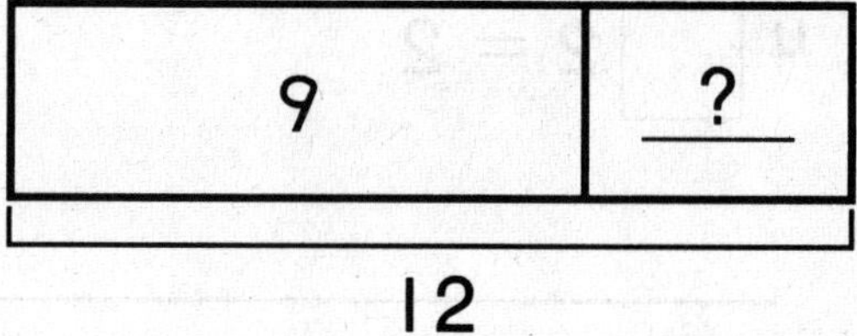

○ 21 ○ 9

○ 12 ○ 3

10. Carrie finds 4 pencils on the floor. Now she has 12 pencils. How many pencils did Carrie start with?

?	4

12

○ 16 ○ 8

○ 12 ○ 4

11. What is the missing number?

$5 + \square = 12$

$12 - \square = 5$

○ 17 ○ 7

○ 12 ○ 5

12. What is the missing number?

$9 + \square = 17$

○ 16

○ 9

○ 8

○ 6

GO ON

Write the correct answer.

13. Write the number that makes the sentence **true**.

$9 - 2 = 3 + \square$

____

14. Make the sentence **true**. Use + or −.

$4 \square 2 = 2$

____

15. Write the number that makes the sentence **true**.

$7 - 2 = 1 + \square$

____

16. Write the number that completes the related fact.

$7 + 4 = 11$

$11 - \_\_\_\_ = 4$

____

GO ON

17. Write an addition fact that helps you solve $12 - 7$.

____

18. The table shows ways to make 12. Write a different way to make 12.

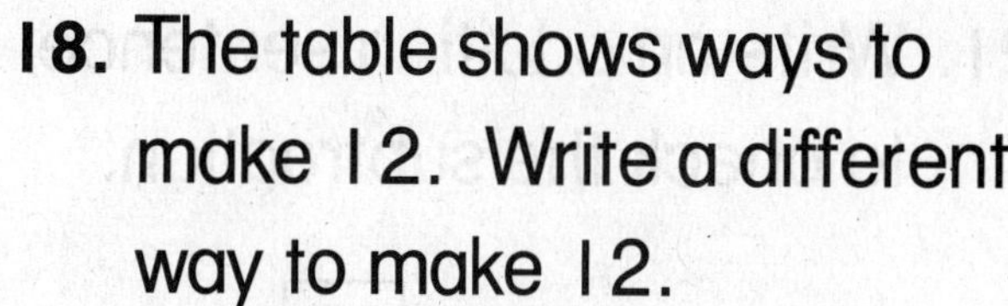

12
$6 + 6$
$3 + 5 + 4$

____

19. Write the number that makes the sentence **true**.

$5 + 7 + \square = 17$

____

20. Brian solves this subtraction sentence.

$17 - 8 = \square$

Write an addition sentence Brian can use to check his subtraction.

____

GO ON

Name ______________________________

21. Write an addition sentence to check the subtraction.

$11 - 3 = \square$

____

22. Mike has 7 jump ropes. Kristi has 5 jump ropes. How many jump ropes do Mike and Kristi have?

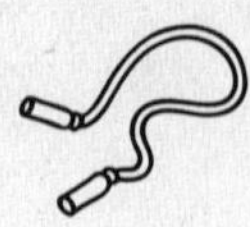

________ jump ropes

23. What is $4 + 6$?

____

24. What is $7 - 0$?

____

GO ON

Name ______________________________

Extended Constructed Response

25. Bobby is at the lake.
He sees 13 ducks.
_____ ducks are swimming.
_____ ducks are sleeping.

- Choose and write numbers to complete the story problem.
- Draw a picture to explain.
- Then write the related facts for your story problem.

Show how to solve your problem.
Use numbers, pictures, or words.

Show your work.

_____ ducks are swimming.

_____ ducks are sleeping.

_____ + _____ = _____   _____ − _____ = _____

_____ + _____ = _____   _____ − _____ = _____

STOP

Child's Name ____________________

Extended Constructed Response

The Extended Constructed Response item is scored using the 3-point scoring rubric in the *Assessment Guide.* A child can receive partial credit for answers that are partially correct or partially completed.

Performance Indicators

For Problem 25, a child with a Level 2 paper:

_____ correctly identifies two numbers with a sum of 13.

_____ draws a picture to represent the problem about ducks.

_____ write four related facts for the problem about ducks.

Name ____________________

Choose the correct answer.

1. What number does the model show?

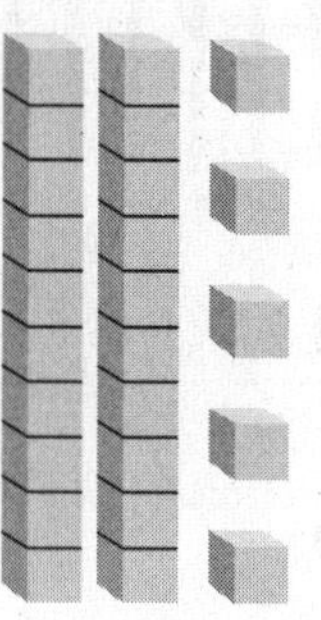

○ 15 ○ 30

○ 25 ○ 52

2. Count forward. What number is missing?

104, 105, 106, ____, 108

○ 103

○ 107

○ 109

○ 110

3. What number does the model show?

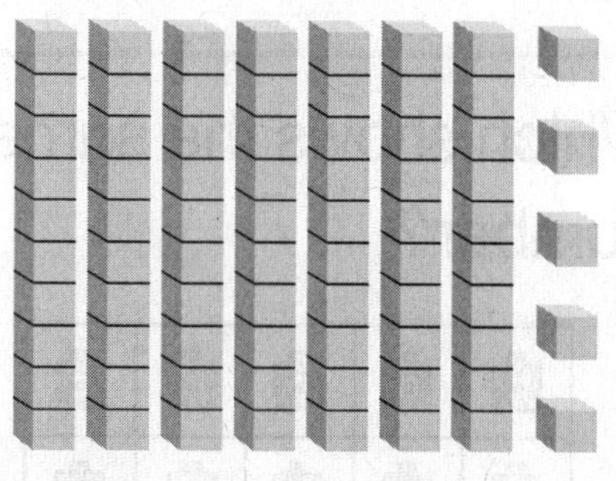

○ 75 ○ 57

○ 65 ○ 12

4. Count by tens. What number is missing?

27, 37, 47, ____, 67

○ 48

○ 50

○ 57

○ 77

GO ON

5. Which is a different way to show the same number?

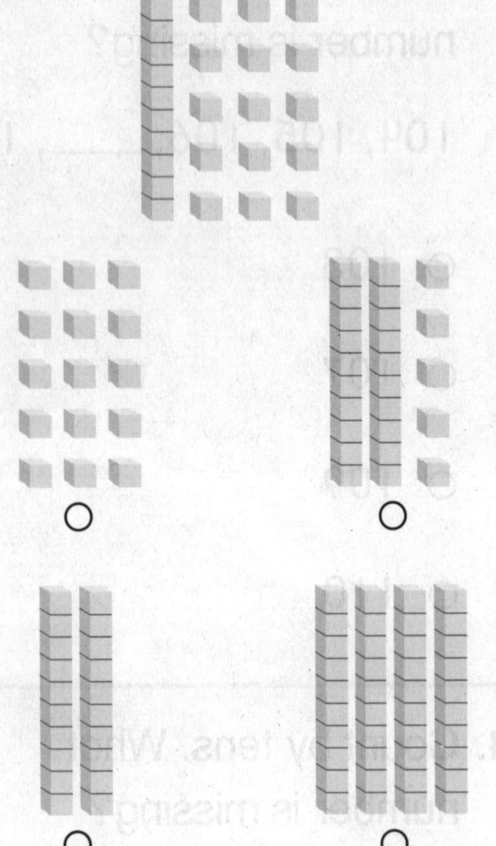

6. What number does the model show?

○ 110

○ 109

○ 108

○ 100

7. Which shows the same number?

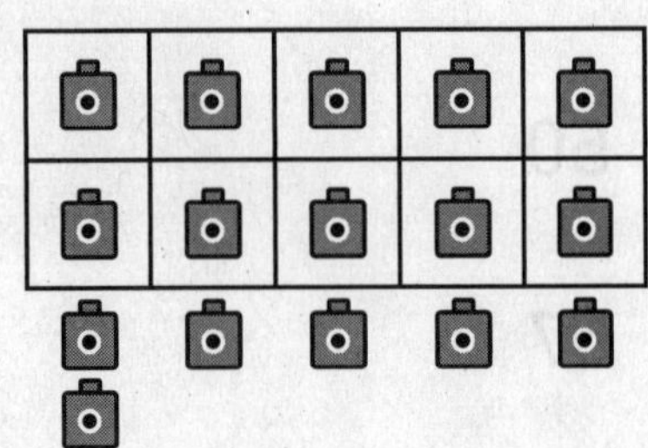

○ 10 + 6 ○ 10 + 7

○ 10 − 6 ○ 10 − 7

8. Which shows the same number?

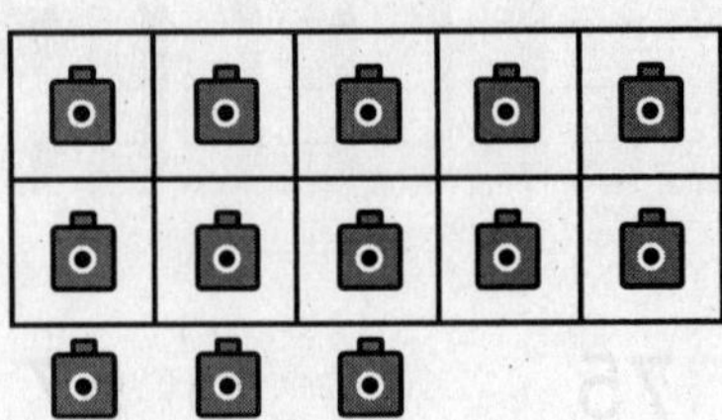

○ 10 + 4 ○ 10 + 3

○ 10 − 4 ○ 10 − 3

GO ON

Name ____________________

9. What number does the model show?

○ 140 ○ 113

○ 114 ○ 103

10. How many tens and ones make this number?

19
nineteen

○ 1 ten 8 ones

○ 1 ten 9 ones

○ 8 tens 1 one

○ 9 tens 1 one

11. What number does the model show?

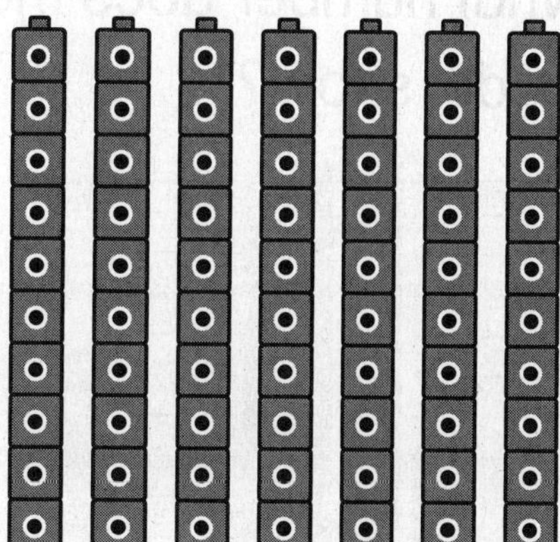

○ 7 ○ 60

○ 35 ○ 70

12. What number does the model show?

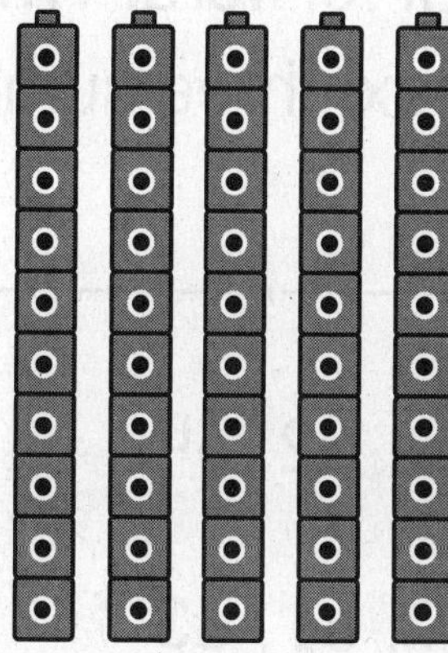

○ 70 ○ 40

○ 50 ○ 25

GO ON

Name ________________________________

13. What number does the model show?

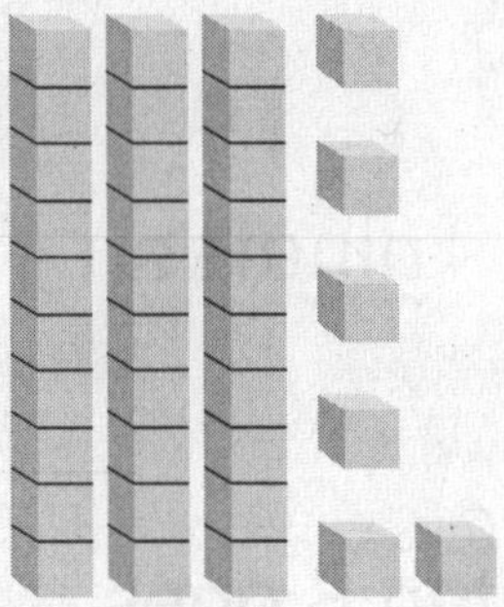

○ 35

○ 36

○ 38

○ 41

14. How many tens and ones are shown?

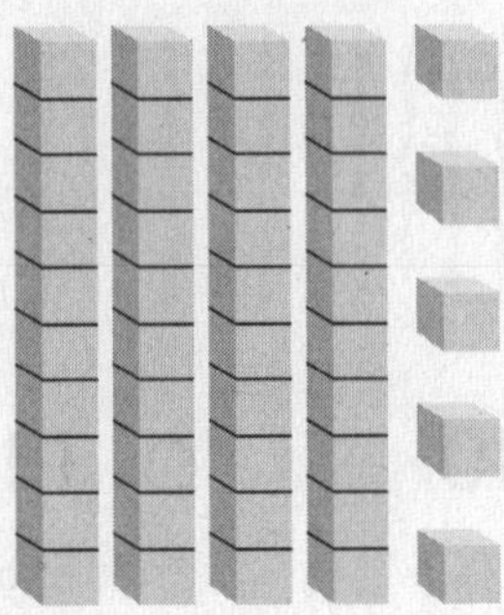

○ 3 tens 5 ones

○ 4 tens 5 ones

○ 5 tens 4 ones

○ 6 tens 4 ones

15. Count forward. What are the next three numbers?

58, _____, _____, _____

○ 60, 62, 64

○ 59, 61, 63

○ 59, 60, 61

○ 57, 56, 55

16. What number does the model show?

○ 78 ○ 14

○ 73 ○ 68

Name ______________________________

17. Count by tens. What number is missing?

30, 40, 50, ______

○ 55

○ 60

○ 65

○ 70

18. Which is a different way to show the same number?

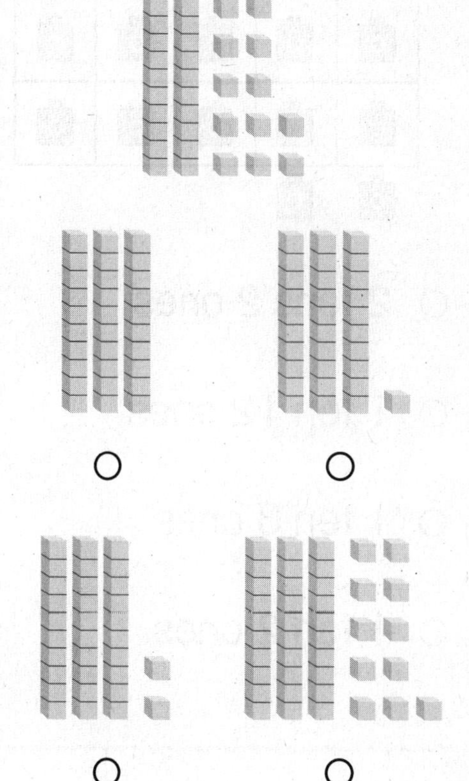

19. What number does the model show?

○ 105 ○ 115

○ 110 ○ 150

20. What number does the model show?

○ 120 ○ 110

○ 112 ○ 105

GO ON

21. Which shows the same number?

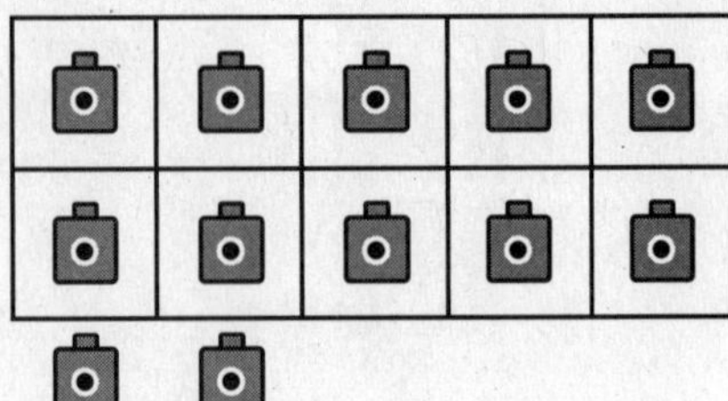

○ 2 tens 2 ones

○ 1 ten 12 ones

○ 1 ten 3 ones

○ 1 ten 2 ones

22. What number does the model show?

○ 116

○ 115

○ 107

○ 106

23. How many tens and ones make this number?

18
eighteen

○ 1 ten 1 one

○ 1 ten 8 ones

○ 8 tens 1 one

○ 8 tens 8 ones

24. What number does the model show?

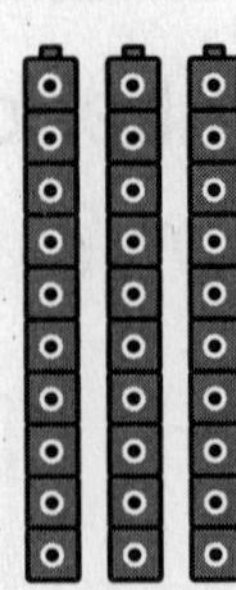

○ 3 ○ 30

○ 15 ○ 40

Choose the correct answer.

1. How many tens and ones are shown?

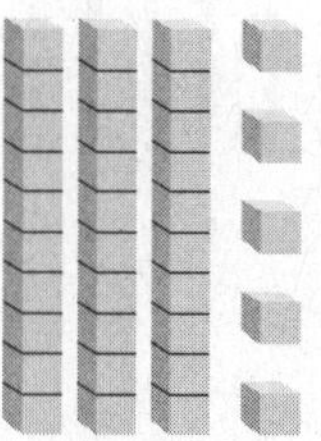

- ○ 2 tens 5 ones
- ○ 3 tens 5 ones
- ○ 4 tens 5 ones
- ○ 5 tens 3 ones

2. Count forward. What number is missing?

103, 104, 105, ____, 107

- ○ 109
- ○ 108
- ○ 106
- ○ 102

3. What number does the model show?

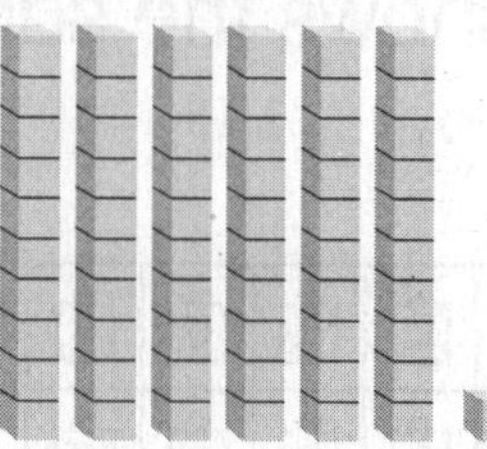

- ○ 7
- ○ 61
- ○ 31
- ○ 70

4. Count by tens. What number is missing?

25, 35, 45, ____, 65

- ○ 46
- ○ 55
- ○ 50
- ○ 66

GO ON

Name ________________

5. Which is a different way to show the same number?

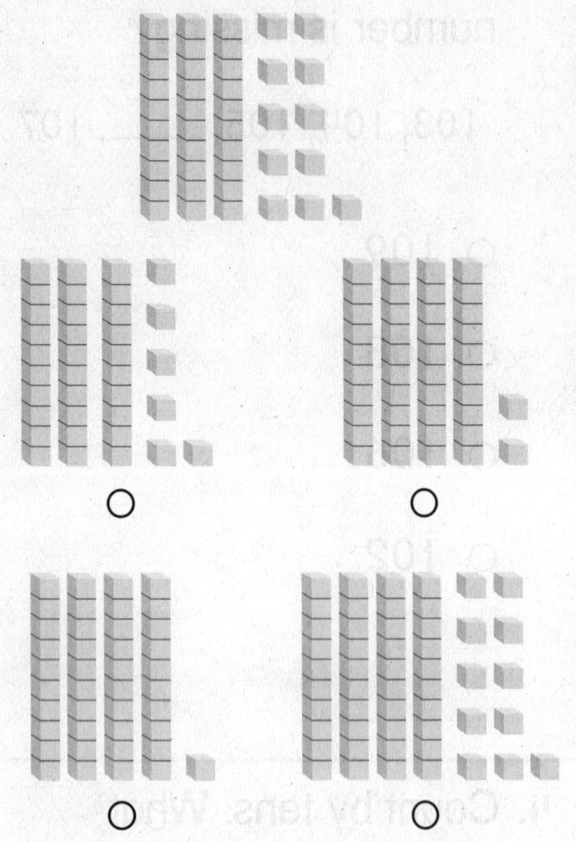

6. What number does the model show?

○ 100

○ 107

○ 108

○ 170

7. Which shows the same number?

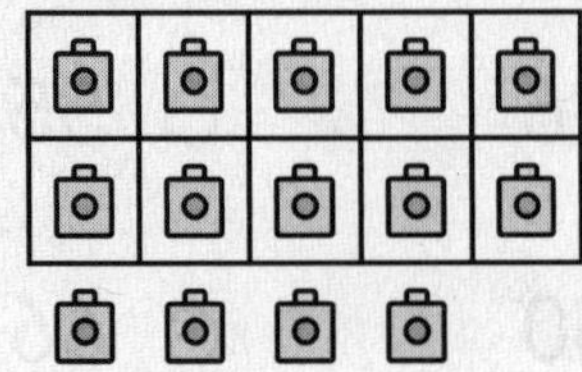

○ 10 + 4 ○ 10 − 3

○ 10 − 4 ○ 10 + 3

8. Which shows the same number?

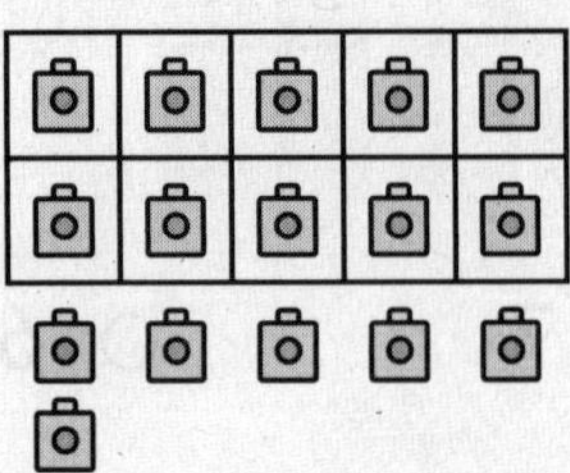

○ 10 − 6 ○ 10 − 7

○ 10 + 6 ○ 10 + 7

GO ON

Name ________________________________

9. What number does the model show?

○ 109 ○ 114

○ 110 ○ 119

10. How many tens and ones make this number?

13
thirteen

○ 1 ten 1 one

○ 1 ten 3 ones

○ 3 tens 1 one

○ 3 tens 3 ones

11. What number does the model show?

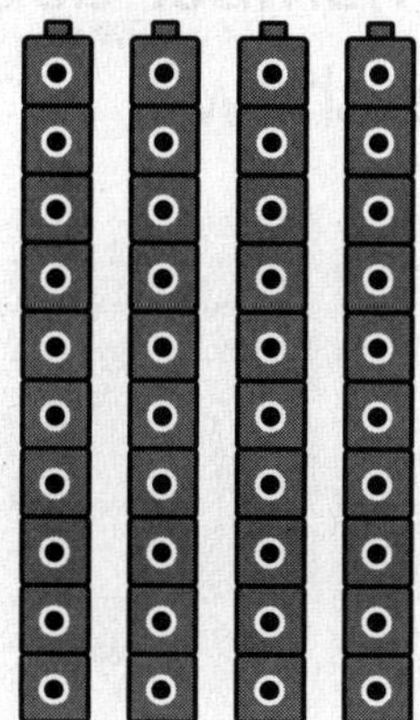

○ 50 ○ 10

○ 40 ○ 4

12. What number does the model show?

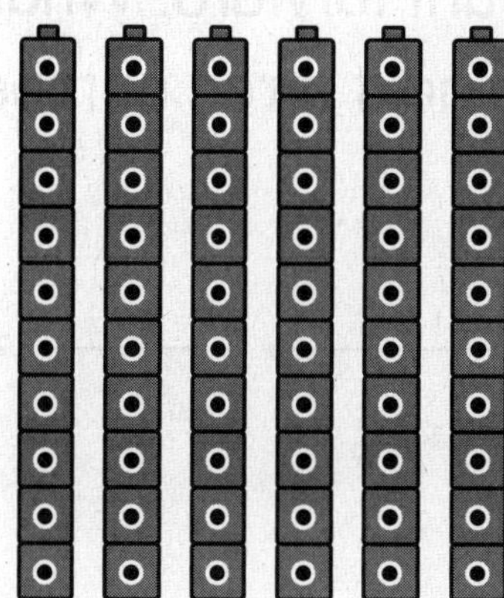

○ 70 ○ 30

○ 60 ○ 6

GO ON

Write the correct answer.

13. What number does the model show?

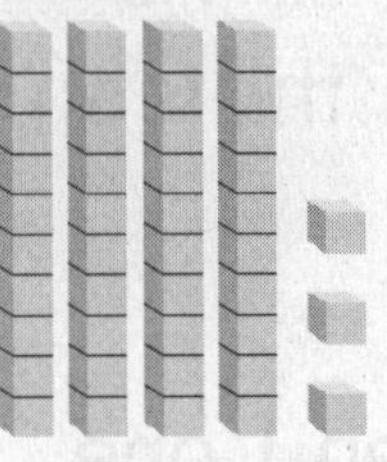

______

14. How many tens and ones are shown?

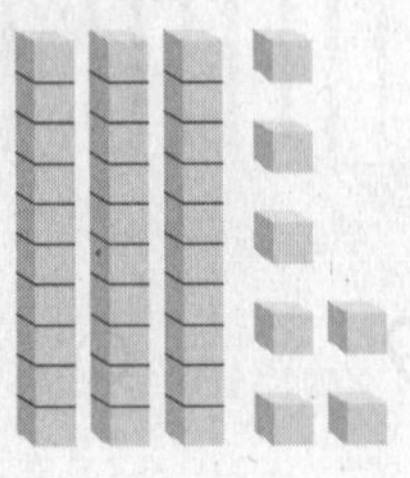

______ tens ______ ones

15. Count forward. What are the next three numbers?

35, ______, ______, ______

16. What number does the model show?

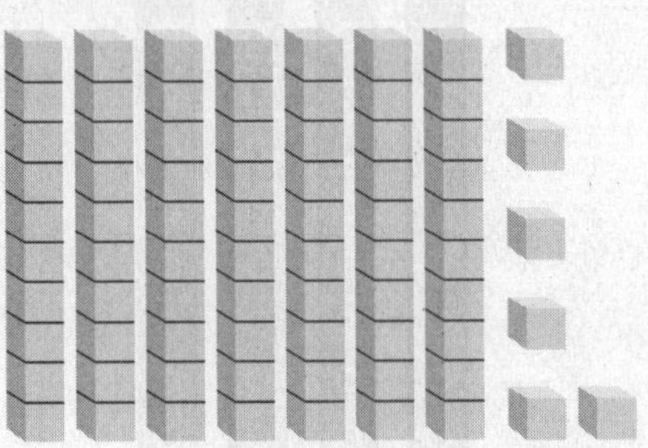

______

GO ON

17. Count by tens.
What are the next two numbers?

48, 58, 68, ______, ______

18. Draw a quick picture to show a different way to make the same number.

19. What number does the model show?

______

20. What number does the model show?

______

GO ON

Name ____________________

21. Write the number in two different ways.

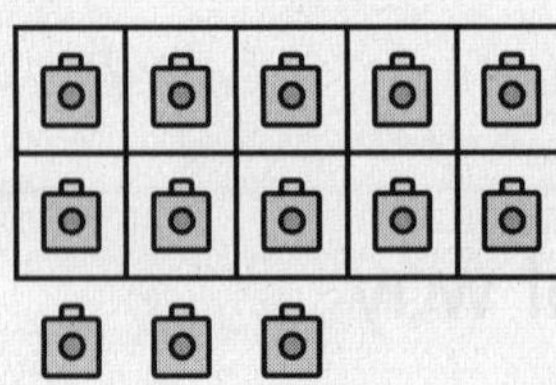

_____ ten _____ ones

_____ + _____

22. What number does the model show?

_____

23. Write how many tens and ones.

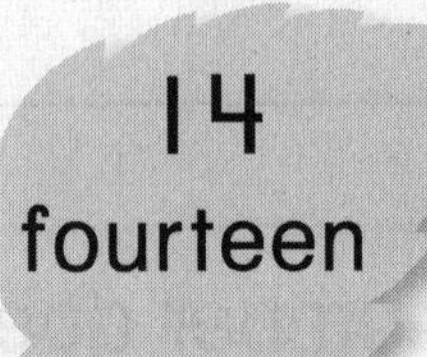

_____ ten _____ ones

24. Use the model. Write the tens and ones.

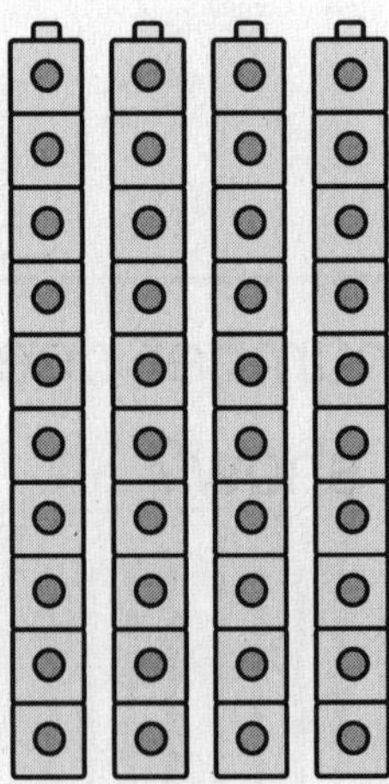

_____ tens _____ ones

GO ON

Name ____________________

Extended Constructed Response

25. Carlos and Jacy each want 36 stickers. There are 4 sheets of 10 stickers and 40 single stickers.

How could Carlos and Jacy each take 36 stickers?

- Use [tens block] [ones cube] to show the number two different ways.
- Draw a quick picture of each way.
- Write how many tens and ones are in each picture. Write the number each picture shows.

Carlos	Jacy
____ tens ____ ones	____ tens ____ ones

____ = ____

Extended Constructed Response

The Extended Constructed Response item is scored using the 3-point scoring rubric in the *Assessment Guide*. A child can receive partial credit for answers that are partially correct or partially completed.

Performance Indicators

For Problem 25, a child with a Level 2 paper:

_____ draws quick pictures of two different ways to make 36.

_____ correctly writes how many tens and ones are in each drawing.

_____ correctly writes the number shown by each drawing.

_____ shows work that is easy to follow and clearly supports the answers given.

Choose the correct answer.

1. Which number is **greater than** 74?

- ○ 17
- ○ 47
- ○ 68
- ○ 78

2. Which number is **greater than** 45?

- ○ 18
- ○ 20
- ○ 34
- ○ 51

3. Which is **true**?

- ○ 35 is greater than 38.
- ○ 47 is greater than 74.
- ○ 62 is greater than 60.
- ○ 71 is greater than 89.

4. The number of pens that Jill has is **greater than** 38. What could be a number of pens Jill has?

- ○ 19
- ○ 29
- ○ 37
- ○ 43

5. Which symbol is missing?

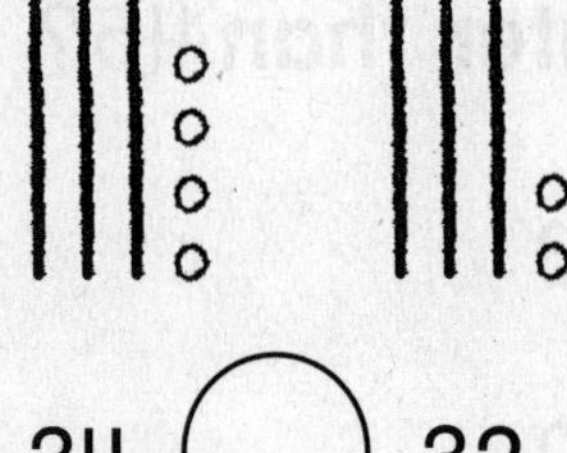

34 ◯ 32

○ $<$

○ $>$

○ $+$

○ $=$

6. Which symbol is missing?

37 ◯ 52

○ $<$

○ $>$

○ $+$

○ $=$

7. Which number is **less than** 44?

○ 54

○ 45

○ 44

○ 34

8. Which number is **less than** 17?

○ 7

○ 18

○ 27

○ 71

GO ON

Name ______________________________

9. The number of dimes that Matt has is **less than** 30. Which could be a number of dimes Matt has?

- ○ 40
- ○ 32
- ○ 30
- ○ 22

10. Which is **true**?

- ○ $62 > 69$
- ○ $62 < 69$
- ○ $69 < 62$
- ○ $69 = 62$

11. The number of books Chad has is **less than** 25. Which could be a number of books Chad has?

- ○ 12
- ○ 34
- ○ 45
- ○ 52

12. Which is **true**?

- ○ 53 is less than 35.
- ○ 64 is less than 60.
- ○ 79 is less than 69.
- ○ 81 is less than 85.

GO ON

13. Ted has 18 marbles. Jamie has **10 more** marbles than Ted. How many marbles does Jamie have?

- ○ 38
- ○ 37
- ○ 28
- ○ 8

14. Theo writes a number that is **10 less** than 41. What number does Theo write?

- ○ 14
- ○ 31
- ○ 40
- ○ 51

15. Stan collects coins. He has **10 more** than 17 coins. How many coins does Stan have?

- ○ 37
- ○ 27
- ○ 18
- ○ 7

16. Which symbol is missing?

- ○ =
- ○ >
- ○ <
- ○ +

GO ON

Name ____________________

17. Which number is **10 less** than 54?

○ 34

○ 44

○ 54

○ 64

18. Which symbol is missing?

76 ◯ 76

○ =

○ >

○ <

○ +

19. Which symbol is missing?

25 ◯ 18

○ >

○ <

○ =

○ +

20. Which number is **10 more** than 49?

○ 39

○ 48

○ 50

○ 59

GO ON

Name ______________________________

21. Juan crosses out the numbers that are **less than** 66 and **greater than** 81. What number is left?

36	49	58	74	90

○ 90 ○ 74

○ 58 ○ 49

22. Traci crosses out the numbers that are **less than** 42 and **greater than** 45. What number is left?

41	43	46	48	49

○ 41 ○ 43

○ 46 ○ 49

23. Kim has these number cards. She gives away cards that are **less than** 29 and **greater than** 39. What numbers are on the cards Kim keeps?

20	25	31	37	46

○ 20 and 25

○ 25 and 31

○ 31 and 37

○ 37 and 46

24. Stella has these number cards. She gives away cards that are **less than** 56 and **greater than** 62. What numbers are on the cards Stella keeps?

55	57	60	64	65

○ 55 and 57

○ 57 and 60

○ 60 and 64

○ 64 and 65

Name ____________________

Choose the correct answer.

1. Which number is **greater than** 32?

   ○ 12

   ○ 23

   ○ 30

   ○ 43

2. Which number is **greater than** 64?

   ○ 72

   ○ 62

   ○ 58

   ○ 46

3. Which is **true**?

   ○ 27 is greater than 31.

   ○ 46 is greater than 64.

   ○ 71 is greater than 77.

   ○ 82 is greater than 70.

4. The number of erasers that Debby has is **greater than** 29. What could be a number of erasers Debby has?

   ○ 19

   ○ 21

   ○ 27

   ○ 32

GO ON

5. Which symbol is missing?

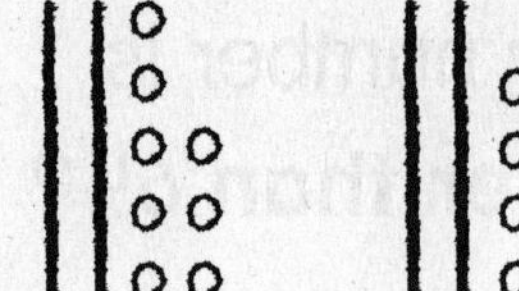

28 ◯ 24

- ○ <
- ○ >
- ○ +
- ○ =

6. Which symbol is missing?

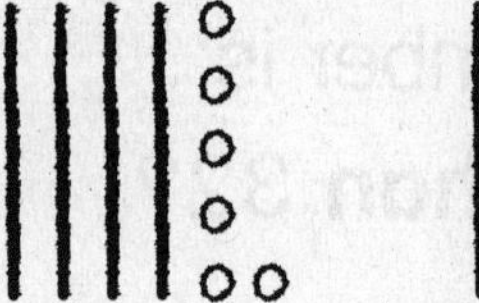

46 ◯ 58

- ○ <
- ○ >
- ○ +
- ○ =

7. Which number is **less than** 83?

- ○ 96
- ○ 91
- ○ 85
- ○ 82

8. Which number is **less than** 47?

- ○ 74
- ○ 56
- ○ 48
- ○ 39

GO ON

Name ______________________________

9. The number of balloons that Rick has is **less than** 38. Which could be a number of balloons Rick has?

○ 29

○ 38

○ 39

○ 83

10. Which is **true**?

○ 52 > 57

○ 52 < 57

○ 57 < 52

○ 57 = 52

11. The number of acorns Chris has is **less than** 28. Which could be a number of acorns Chris has?

○ 19

○ 29

○ 36

○ 82

12. Which is **true**?

○ 18 is less than 16.

○ 25 is less than 24.

○ 37 is less than 43.

○ 59 is less than 32.

GO ON

Write the correct answer.

13. Stuart has 15 pennies. Lauren has **10 more** pennies than Stuart. How many pennies does Lauren have?

_______ pennies

14. Ryan writes a number that is **10 less** than 72. What number does Ryan write?

____

15. Holly collects stamps. She has **10 more** than 12 stamps. How many stamps does Holly have?

_______ stamps

16. Write <, >, or =.

42 ◯ 63

Name ______________________

17. Write the number that is **10 less** than 47.

______

18. 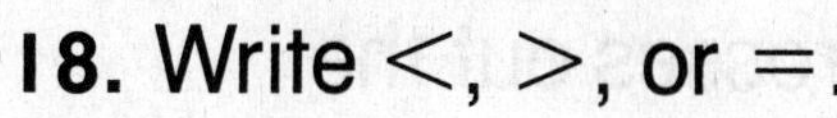
Write <, >, or =.

39 ◯ 39

19. Write <, >, or =.

23 ◯ 17

20. Write the number that is **10 more** than 85.

______

GO ON

21. Lee crosses out the numbers that are **less than** 61 and **greater than** 67. What number is left?

59	60	64	68	69

____

22. Colleen crosses out the numbers that are **less than** 38 and **greater than** 41. What number is left?

37	39	43	45	46

____

23. Jose has these number cards. He gives away cards that are **less than** 22 and **greater than** 27. What numbers are on the cards Jose keeps?

20	25	26	28	30

__________ and __________

24. Fred has these number cards. He gives away cards that are **less than** 78 and **greater than** 86. What numbers are on the cards Fred keeps?

72	75	79	82	87

__________ and __________

Name ______________________________

Extended Constructed Response

25. Emma draws pictures of shapes.
She draws fewer circles than squares.
She draws 10 more triangles than squares.
How many of each shape could Emma have drawn?

Use numbers, pictures, or words to show your work.

STOP

Extended Constructed Response

The Extended Constructed Response item is scored using the 3-point scoring rubric in the *Assessment Guide.* A child can receive partial credit for answers that are partially correct or partially completed.

Performance Indicators

For Problem 25, a child with a Level 2 paper:

_____ correctly shows three groups of shapes.

_____ gives reasonable support to show that the shape with the least number is a circle, the shape with the next greater number is a square, and the shape with the number that is 10 more than the number of squares is a triangle.

_____ shows numbers, pictures, or words that are easy to follow and clearly support the answers given.

Name ______________________

Choose the correct answer.

1. How many tens are in the sum?

20 + 70 = ?

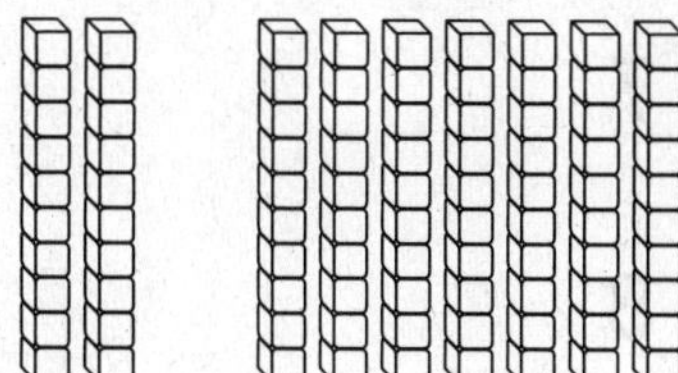

○ 2 tens

○ 5 tens

○ 7 tens

○ 9 tens

2. What is the sum?

50 + 10 = ______

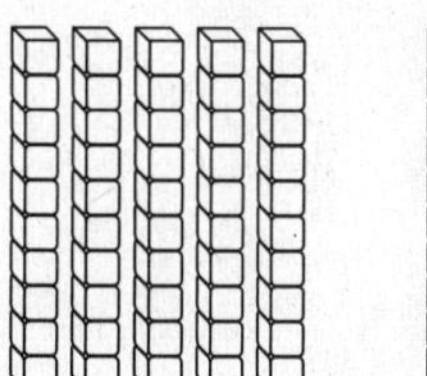

○ 6

○ 40

○ 60

○ 70

3. What is the sum?

60 + 30 = ______

○ 9

○ 30

○ 63

○ 90

4. What is the sum?

9 + 4 = ______

○ 15

○ 13

○ 11

○ 5

GO ON

5. What is the difference?

15 − 8 = _____

○ 7

○ 9

○ 13

○ 23

6. What is the sum?

$$\begin{array}{r} 12 \\ +\ 7 \\ \hline \end{array}$$

○ 5

○ 17

○ 18

○ 19

7. How many tens are in the difference?

90 − 40 = ?

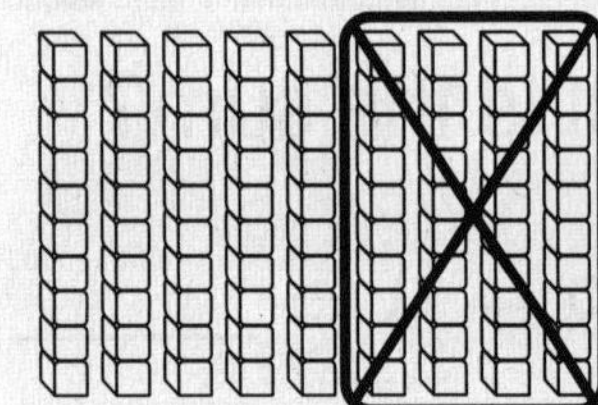

○ 3 tens

○ 4 tens

○ 5 tens

○ 6 tens

8. What is the difference?

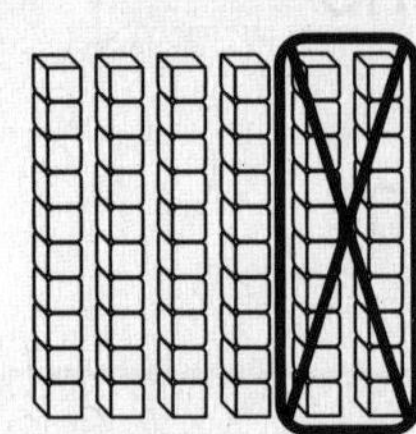

60 − 20 = _____

○ 80

○ 60

○ 40

○ 20

GO ON

9. What is the difference?

70 − 30 = ______

○ 4

○ 10

○ 40

○ 73

10. What is the sum?

17 + 20 = ______

○ 37

○ 30

○ 27

○ 19

11. Count on by ones.
What is the sum?

22 + 3 = ______

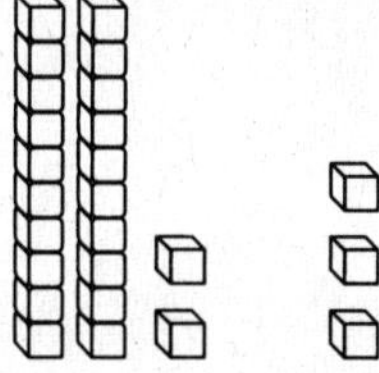

○ 19

○ 25

○ 27

○ 52

12. Count on by tens.
What is the sum?

31 + 60 = ______

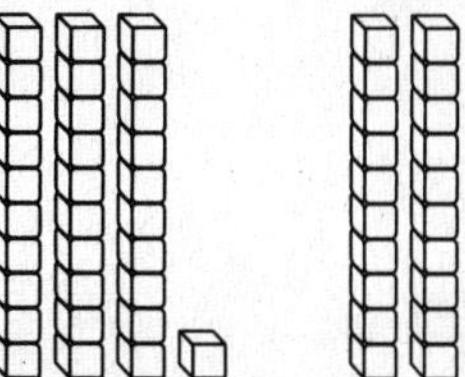

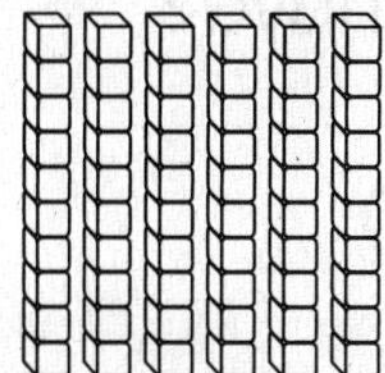

○ 97

○ 91

○ 61

○ 37

GO ON

13. How many tens and ones are in the sum?

$$\begin{array}{r} 56 \\ +\ 33 \\ \hline \end{array}$$

- ○ 2 tens and 3 ones
- ○ 2 tens and 9 ones
- ○ 8 tens and 9 ones
- ○ 8 tens and 3 ones

14. How many tens and ones are in the sum?

$$\begin{array}{r} 47 \\ +\ 32 \\ \hline \end{array}$$

- ○ 1 ten and 5 ones
- ○ 1 ten and 9 ones
- ○ 7 tens and 9 ones
- ○ 7 tens and 5 ones

15. Jack has 15 shells. He collects 25 more shells. How many shells does Jack have?

- ○ 10
- ○ 30
- ○ 35
- ○ 40

16. Mai has 38 pennies. Jared has 21 pennies. How many pennies do Mai and Jared have?

- ○ 59
- ○ 58
- ○ 39
- ○ 17

Name ____________________

Use the hundred chart for questions 17 and 18.

1	2	3	4	5	6	7	8	9	10
11	12	13	14	15	16	17	18	19	20
21	22	23	24	25	26	27	28	29	30
31	32	33	34	35	36	37	38	39	40
41	42	43	44	45	46	47	48	49	50
51	52	53	54	55	56	57	58	59	60
61	62	63	64	65	66	67	68	69	70
71	72	73	74	75	76	77	78	79	80
81	82	83	84	85	86	87	88	89	90
91	92	93	94	95	96	97	98	99	100

17. Count on by ones. What is the sum?

$45 + 4 =$ ______

○ 48 ○ 59

○ 49 ○ 85

18. Count on by tens. What is the sum?

$17 + 30 =$ ______

○ 14 ○ 20

○ 40 ○ 47

19. Use [tens and ones blocks]. Make a ten. What is the sum?

$14 + 9 =$ ______

○ 5 ○ 23

○ 20 ○ 24

20. Use [tens and ones blocks]. Make a ten. What is the sum?

$57 + 23 =$ ______

○ 80 ○ 77

○ 70 ○ 34

GO ON

21. What is the sum?

58 + 4 = ____

○ 98

○ 90

○ 62

○ 54

22. What is the sum?

$$\begin{array}{r} 40 \\ +\ 35 \\ \hline \end{array}$$

○ 15

○ 39

○ 70

○ 75

23. What is the difference?

$$\begin{array}{r} 16 \\ -\ 9 \\ \hline \end{array}$$

○ 13

○ 10

○ 7

○ 5

24. What is the sum?

42 + 15 = ____

○ 27

○ 37

○ 47

○ 57

Choose the correct answer.

1. How many tens are in the sum?

30 + 50 = ?

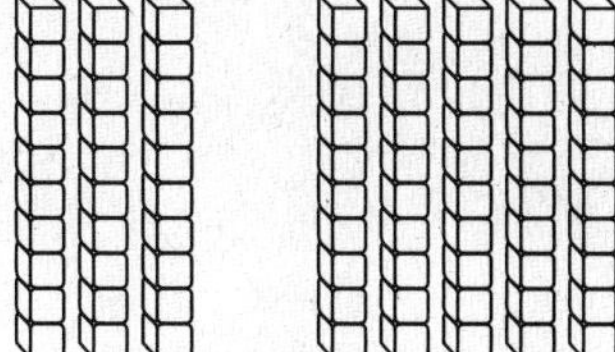

- ○ 10 tens
- ○ 8 tens
- ○ 5 tens
- ○ 2 tens

2. What is the sum?

40 + 20 = ______

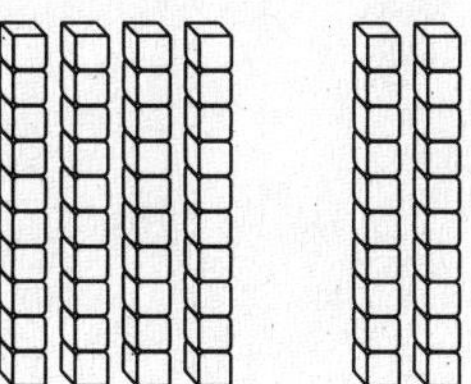

- ○ 6
- ○ 20
- ○ 60
- ○ 70

3. What is the sum?

30 + 40 = ______

- ○ 7
- ○ 34
- ○ 40
- ○ 70

4. What is the sum?

7 + 8 = ______

- ○ 17
- ○ 16
- ○ 15
- ○ 14

GO ON

5. What is the difference?

17 − 8 = ______

○ 11

○ 9

○ 8

○ 7

6. What is the sum?

$$\begin{array}{r} 10 \\ +\ 6 \\ \hline \end{array}$$

○ 16

○ 15

○ 5

○ 4

7. How many tens are in the difference?

70 − 30 = ?

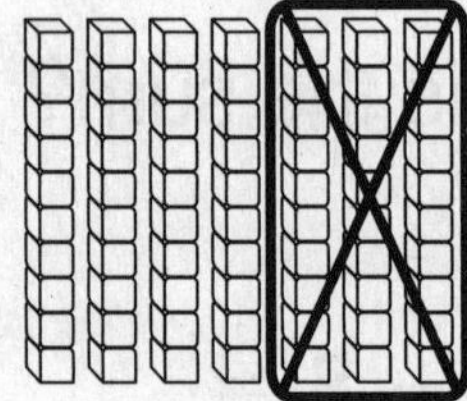

○ 10 tens

○ 7 tens

○ 4 tens

○ 3 tens

8. What is the difference?

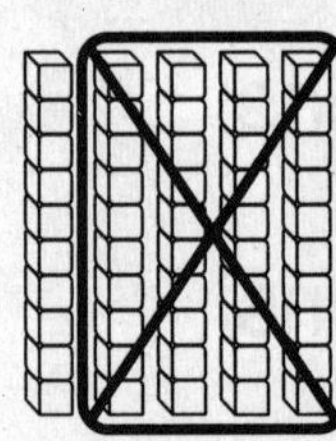

50 − 40 = ______

○ 90

○ 50

○ 40

○ 10

GO ON

9. What is the difference?

80 − 10 = ____

○ 90

○ 80

○ 70

○ 7

10. What is the sum?

19 + 20 = ____

○ 21

○ 29

○ 30

○ 39

11. Count on by ones.
What is the sum?

16 + 3 = ____

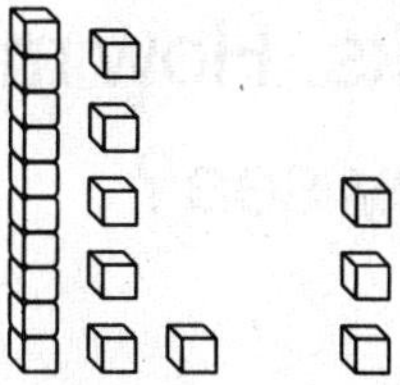

○ 20

○ 19

○ 13

○ 9

12. Count on by tens.
What is the sum?

32 + 20 = ____

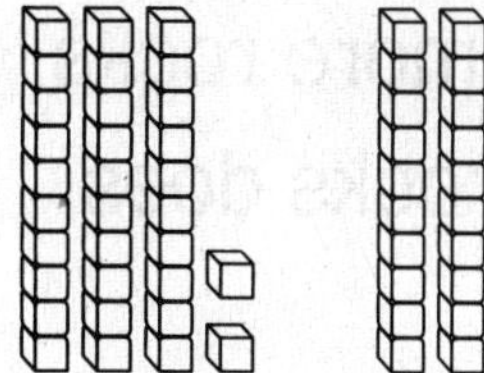

○ 70

○ 52

○ 34

○ 12

GO ON

Name ____________________

Write the correct answer.

13. How many tens and ones are in the sum?

41 + 27 = _____ tens and _____ ones.

14. How many tens and ones are in the sum?

63 + 14 = _____ tens and _____ ones.

15. Pat has 11 rocks. He collects 17 more rocks. How many rocks does Pat have?

_____ rocks

16. Jake sees 12 ducks. Cam sees 20 ducks. How many ducks do they see?

_____ ducks

GO ON

Use the hundred chart for questions 17 and 18.

1	2	3	4	5	6	7	8	9	10
11	12	13	14	15	16	17	18	19	20
21	22	23	24	25	26	27	28	29	30
31	32	33	34	35	36	37	38	39	40
41	42	43	44	45	46	47	48	49	50
51	52	53	54	55	56	57	58	59	60
61	62	63	64	65	66	67	68	69	70
71	72	73	74	75	76	77	78	79	80
81	82	83	84	85	86	87	88	89	90
91	92	93	94	95	96	97	98	99	100

17. Count on by ones. What is the sum?

$34 + 2 =$ ______

18. Count on by tens. What is the sum?

$15 + 40 =$ ______

19. Use tens and ones blocks. Make a ten. What is the sum?

$17 + 4 =$ ______

20. Use tens and ones blocks. Make a ten. What is the sum?

$65 + 7 =$ ______

21. What is the sum?

58 + 5 = ______

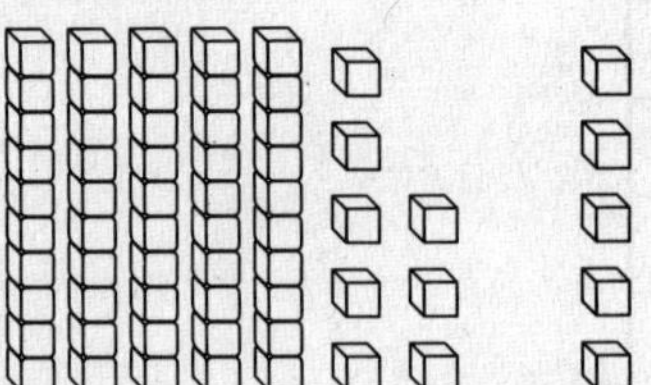

22. What is the sum?

$$\begin{array}{r} 62 \\ +\ 24 \\ \hline \end{array}$$

______

23. What is the difference?

$$\begin{array}{r} 44 \\ -\ 2 \\ \hline \end{array}$$

______

24. What is the sum?

50 + 10 = ______

GO ON

Name ______________________________

Extended Constructed Response

25. Stan is at the park. He sees 32 people walking. Then he sees 19 people riding bikes. How many people does Stan see?

Use numbers, pictures, or words to show your work.

Extended Constructed Response

The Extended Constructed Response item is scored using the 3-point scoring rubric in the *Assessment Guide.* A child can receive partial credit for answers that are partially correct or partially completed.

Performance Indicators

For Problem 25, a child with a Level 2 paper:

_____ writes or draws to show a group of 32 and a group of 19.

_____ gives reasonable support to show that the sum of 32 and 19 is 51.

_____ shows pictures, words, or numbers that are easy to follow and clearly support the answers given.

Name ______________________

Choose the correct answer.

1. Look at the hour hand. What is the time?

○ 1:00 ○ 11:00

○ 12:00 ○ 10:00

2. Look at the hour hand. What is the time?

○ 8:00 ○ 6 o'clock

○ 7:00 ○ 5 o'clock

3. What time is it?

○ 6:00

○ 6:30

○ 9:00

○ 9:30

4. Look at the hour hand. What is the time?

○ 3:00

○ half past 3:00

○ 4:00

○ half past 4:00

GO ON

5. A black ribbon is longer than a white ribbon.
The white ribbon is longer than a gray ribbon.
Which is correct?

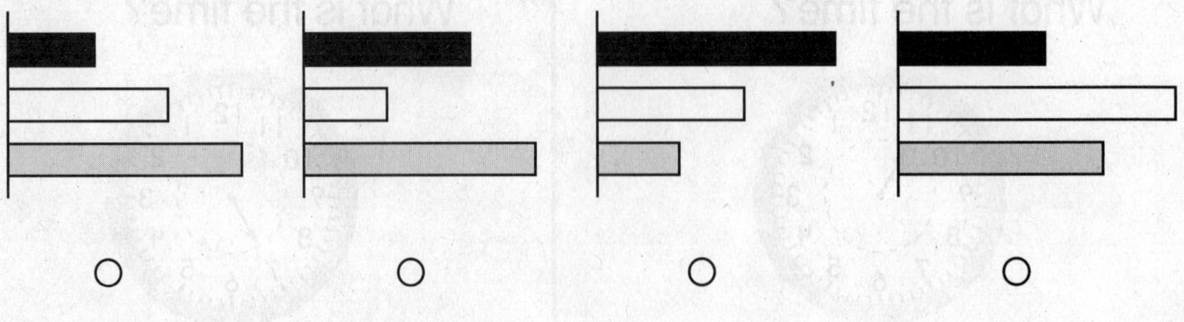

○ ○ ○ ○

6. A white crayon is shorter than a gray crayon.
The gray crayon is shorter than a black crayon.
Which is correct?

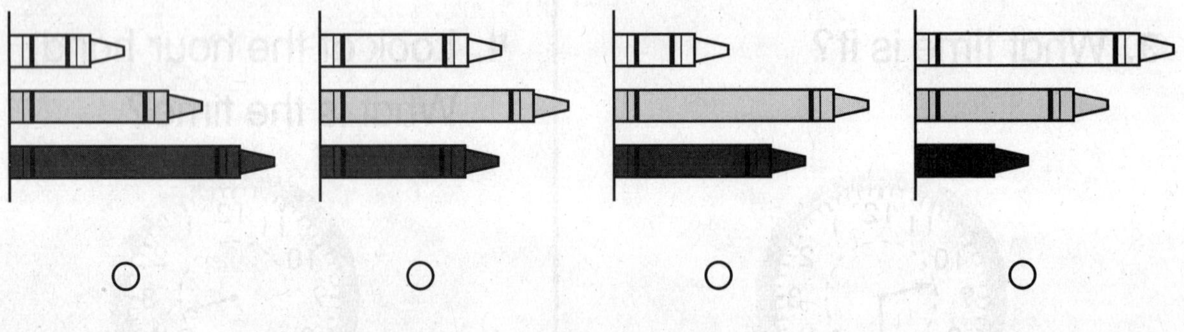

○ ○ ○ ○

7. Which shows the ropes in order from shortest to longest?

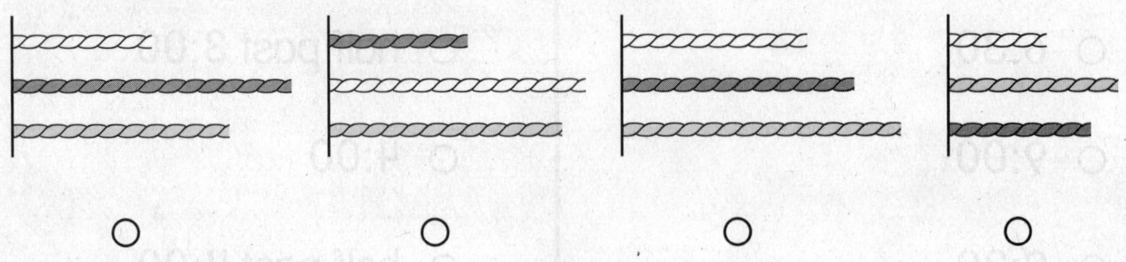

○ ○ ○ ○

Name ____________________

8. Use ■. Ty measures a paper clip with ■. About how long is the paper clip?

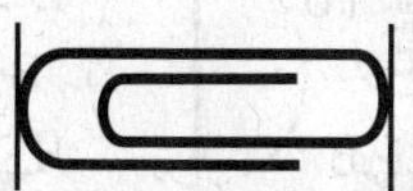

- ○ about 1 ■ long
- ○ about 2 ■ long
- ○ about 3 ■ long
- ○ about 4 ■ long

9. Use ■. Carla measures the eraser with ■. About how long is the eraser?

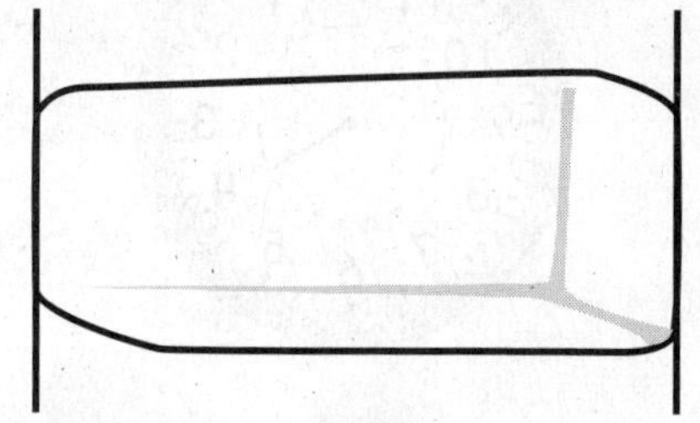

- ○ about 1 ■
- ○ about 2 ■
- ○ about 4 ■
- ○ about 6 ■

10. Which clock shows 2:30?

○

○

○

○

11. Which clock shows 1:00?

○

○

○

○

GO ON

Name ____________________

12. Look at the hour hand. What is the time?

- ○ 6:00
- ○ 5:00
- ○ 4 o'clock
- ○ 3 o'clock

13. What time is it?

- ○ 12:00
- ○ 12:30
- ○ 6:00
- ○ 6:30

14. What time is it?

- ○ 7:30
- ○ 8:00
- ○ 9:00
- ○ 9:30

15. Look at the hour hand. What is the time?

- ○ 9:00
- ○ half past 9:00
- ○ 10:00
- ○ half past 10:00

GO ON

Name ______________________

16. Look at the hour hand.
What is the time?

○ 6:00 ○ 7:00

○ half past 6:00 ○ half past 7:00

17. A white arrow is shorter than a gray arrow.
The gray arrow is shorter than a black arrow.
Which is correct?

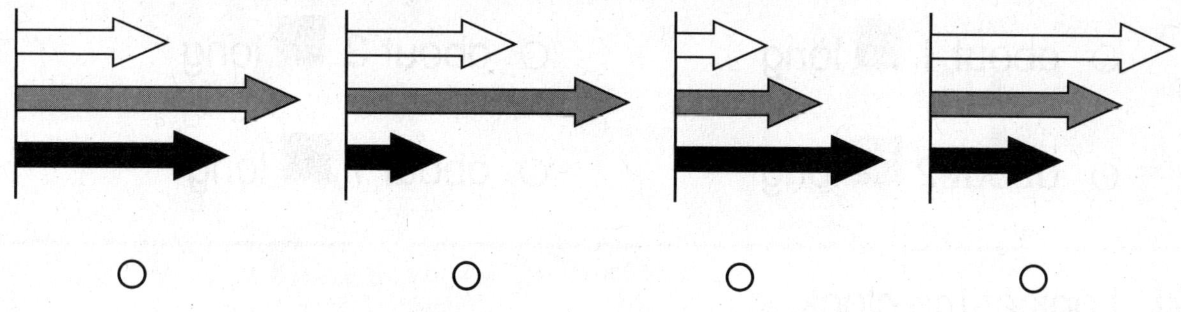

○ ○ ○ ○

18. Which shows the pencils in order
from longest to shortest?

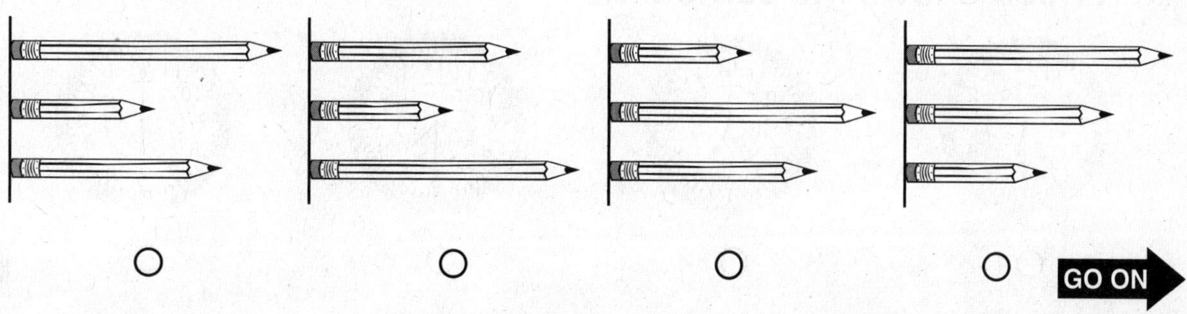

○ ○ ○ ○

GO ON

19. Use ■. Calvin measures the marker with ■.
About how long is a marker?

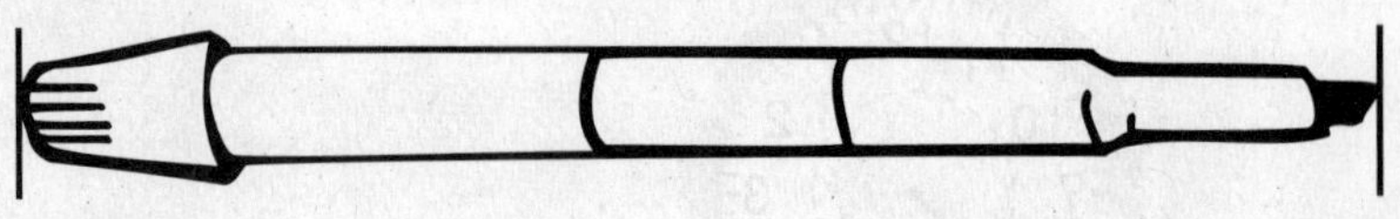

○ about 2 ■ long
○ about 4 ■ long
○ about 6 ■ long
○ about 8 ■ long

---

20. Use ■. Ella measures her ribbon with ■.
About how long is Ella's ribbon?

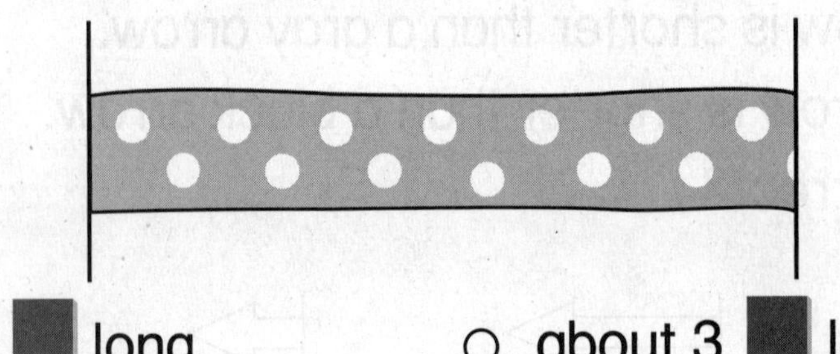

○ about 1 ■ long
○ about 2 ■ long
○ about 3 ■ long
○ about 7 ■ long

---

21. Look at the clock.

Which shows the same time?

○

○

○

Choose the correct answer.

1. Look at the hour hand.
What is the time?

○ 2:00 ○ 4 o'clock

○ 3:00 ○ 5 o'clock

2. Look at the hour hand.
What is the time?

○ 4:00 ○ 6 o'clock

○ 5:00 ○ 12 o'clock

3. What time is it?

○ 12:00

○ 12:30

○ 1:00

○ 2:00

4. Look at the hour hand.
What is the time?

○ 4:00

○ half past 4:00

○ 5:00

○ half past 5:00

GO ON

Name ______________________

5. A gray ribbon is longer than the black ribbon.
The black ribbon is longer than a white ribbon.
Which is correct?

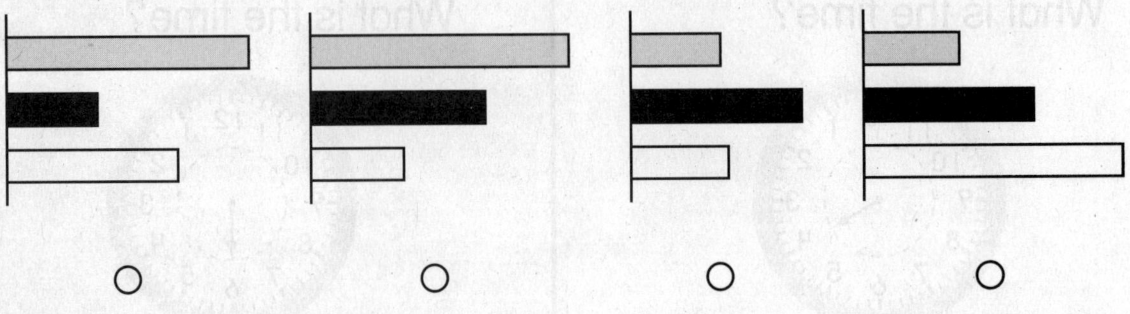

○ ○ ○ ○

6. A black crayon is shorter than the white crayon.
The white crayon is longer than a gray crayon.
Which is correct?

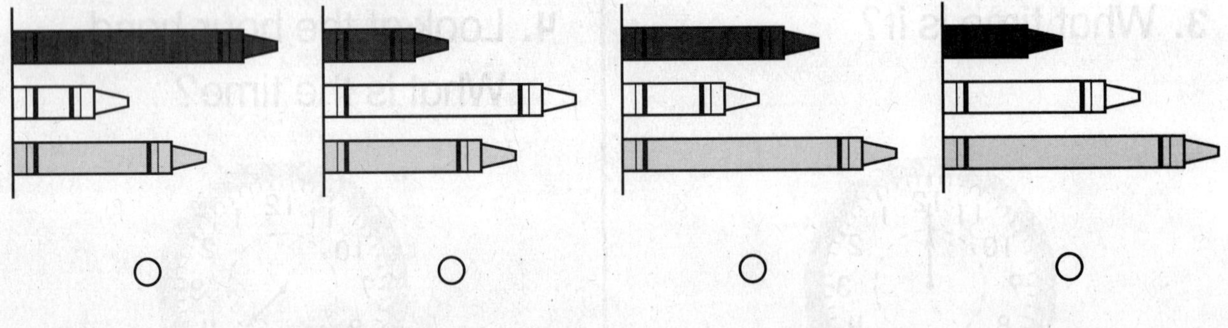

○ ○ ○ ○

7. Which shows the ropes in order from shortest to longest?

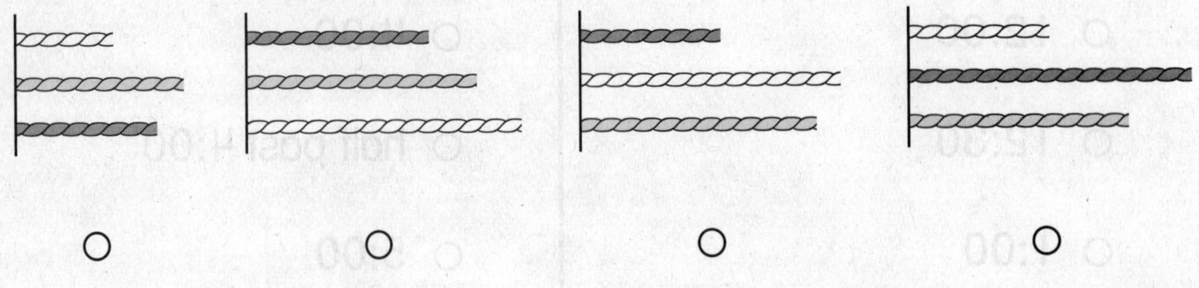

○ ○ ○ ○

GO ON

Name ____________________

8. Use ■. Alexis measures the pencil with ■. About how long is the pencil?

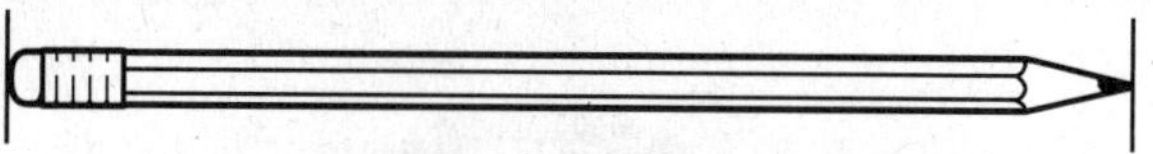

○ about 1 ■ long

○ about 3 ■ long

○ about 5 ■ long

○ about 7 ■ long

9. Kris measures the ribbon with ■. About how long is the ribbon?

○ about 2 ■

○ about 3 ■

○ about 4 ■

○ about 5 ■

10. Which clock shows 9:30?

 ○

 ○

 ○

 ○

11. Which clock shows 11:00?

 ○

 ○

 ○

 ○

GO ON

Name ______________________________

Write the correct answer.

12. Look at the hour hand.
What time is it?

____

13. What time is it?

14. What time is it?

15. Look at the hour hand.
What is the time?

____

GO ON

Name ______________________________

16. What is the time? Circle your answer.

half past 7:00

half past 8:00

17. Use the clues. Circle **shorter** or **longer** to complete the sentence. Then draw to prove your answer.

Clue 1: A blue line is shorter than a red line.
Clue 2: The red line is shorter than a green line.

So, the blue line is shorter / longer than the green line.

blue	
red	
green	

18. Draw three pieces of string in order from **longest** to **shortest**.

longest	
shortest	

19. Use ■. Anna measures a paintbrush with ■.
About how long is the paintbrush?

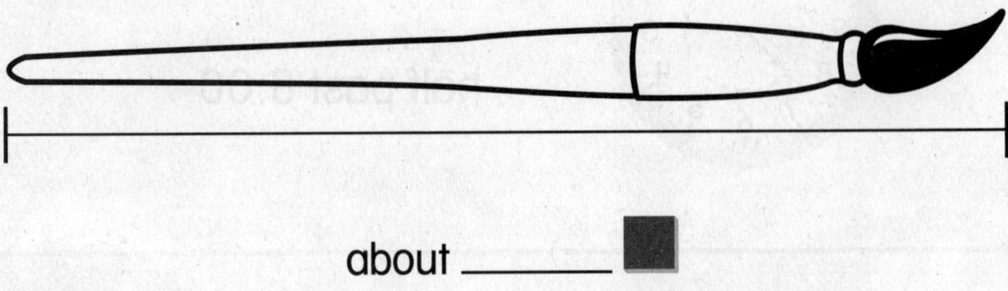

about ________ ■

20. Use ■. Ava measures the ribbon with ■.
About how long is the ribbon?

about ________ ■

21. Use the hour hand to write the time.
Draw the minute hand.

Name ______________________________

Extended Constructed Response

22. Choose three objects to measure.

- Measure the length of each object with .
- Order the objects from longest to shortest.

Write each measurement.
Use pictures, words, or numbers to show how you ordered the lengths of the objects.

Show your work.

Child's Name ______

Extended Constructed Response

The Constructed Response item is scored using the 3-point scoring rubric in the *Assessment Guide*. A child can receive partial credit for answers that are partially correct or partially completed.

Performance Indicators

For Problem 22, a child with a Level 2 paper:

_____ correctly measures the lengths of three objects using paper clips.

_____ orders the objects from longest to shortest.

_____ writes the measurement of each object.

_____ shows work that is easy to follow and clearly supports the answers given.

Choose the correct answer.

Use the tally chart for questions 1–4.

Our Favorite Sport		Total
hockey	||	2
football	|||	
soccer		1

1. How many children chose football?

   ○ 4 ○ 2

   ○ 3 ○ 1

2. How many fewer children chose soccer than football?

   ○ 1 ○ 4

   ○ 2 ○ 5

3. How many children chose soccer?

   | ○ 
   || ○

   ||| ○ |||| ○

4. How many children chose hockey?

   | ○ ||| ○

   || ○ |||| ○

GO ON

Name ____________________

Use the bar graph for questions 5–8.

Children Playing at the Park

Boy or Girl

boys

girls

0 1 2 3 4 5 6

Number of Children

5. How many more are playing at the park than ?

○ 2 ○ 5

○ 4 ○ 8

6. How many are playing at the park?

○ 1 ○ 5

○ 3 ○ 8

7. 1 more joins the children. How many are there now?

○ 7 ○ 5

○ 6 ○ 4

8. 2 more come to the park. How many are there now?

○ 8 ○ 5

○ 6 ○ 3

Name ________________________________

Use the picture graph for questions 9–12.

Pets We Have							
dog	옷	옷	옷	옷	옷	옷	
cat	옷	옷	옷	옷	옷		
hamster	옷	옷					

Each 옷 stands for 1 child.

9. How many children in all have cat and hamster?

○ 3 ○ 7

○ 4 ○ 11

10. How many more children have dog than cat?

○ 1 ○ 6

○ 2 ○ 10

11. 1 more child gets dog. How many 옷 will be in the dog row now?

2 ○ 6 ○

5 ○ 7 ○

12. 2 more children get hamster. How many 옷 will be in the hamster row now?

4 ○ 2 ○

3 ○ 1 ○

GO ON

Name ______________________________

Use the tally chart for questions 13–16.

Our Favorite Lunch		Total
pizza		8
salad	𝍸	
spaghetti	|||	

13. How many more children chose salad than spaghetti?

○ 5 ○ 2

○ 3 ○ 1

14. How many fewer children chose spaghetti than pizza?

3 ○ 8 ○

5 ○ 11 ○

15. Which shows 8 tally marks?

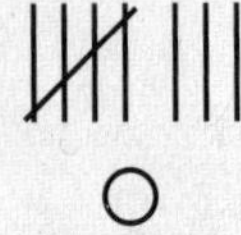
○

○

○

○

16. How many children chose salad?

5 ○ 8 ○

6 ○ 12 ○

GO ON

Use the bar graph for questions 17–20.

Toys at the Store

Kind of Toys						
yo yo	■	■	■	■	■	
doll	■	■	■			
jump rope	■	■	■	■	■	■

0 1 2 3 4 5 6

Number of Toys

17. How many more does the store have than ?

○ 8 ○ 2

○ 3 ○ 1

18. How many and does the store have in all?

○ 14 ○ 8

○ 9 ○ 2

19. The store got 1 more

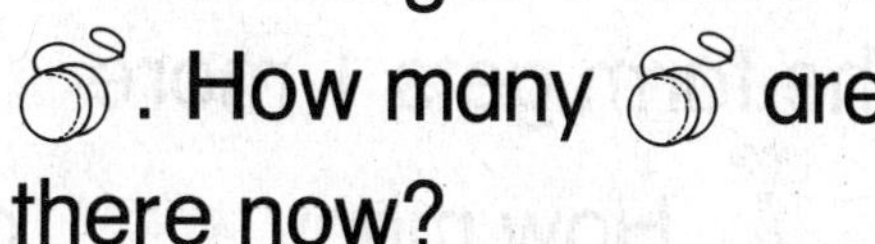

. How many are there now?

○ 2 ○ 4

○ 3 ○ 6

20. The store got 2 more . How many are there now?

○ 5 ○ 3

○ 4 ○ 1

Name ________________________________

Use the picture graph for questions 21–24.

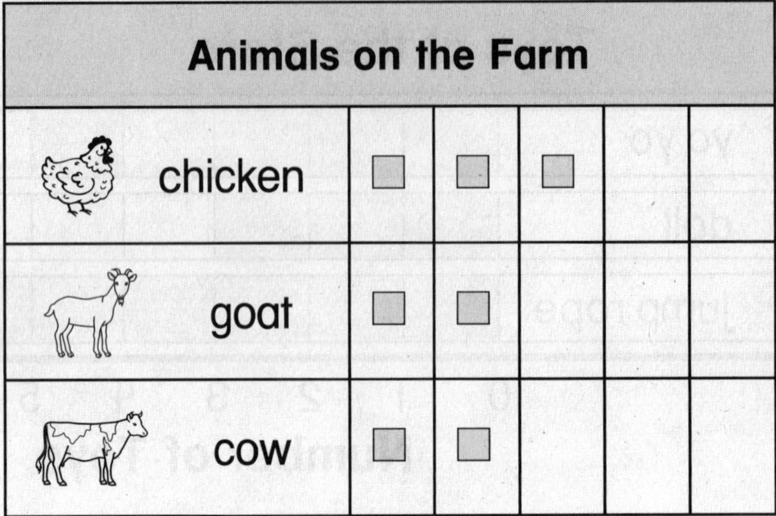

Animals on the Farm					
chicken	■	■	■		
goat	■	■			
cow	■	■			

Each ■ stands for 1 animal.

21. How many and are on the farm in all?

○ 2 ○ 4

○ 3 ○ 7

22. How many are on the farm?

○ 1 ○ 3

○ 2 ○ 4

23. The farm gets 2 more

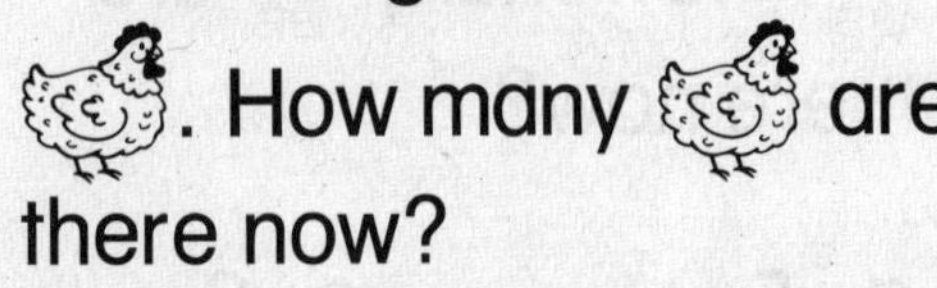

. How many are there now?

○ 1 ○ 4

○ 2 ○ 5

24. The farm gets 1 more

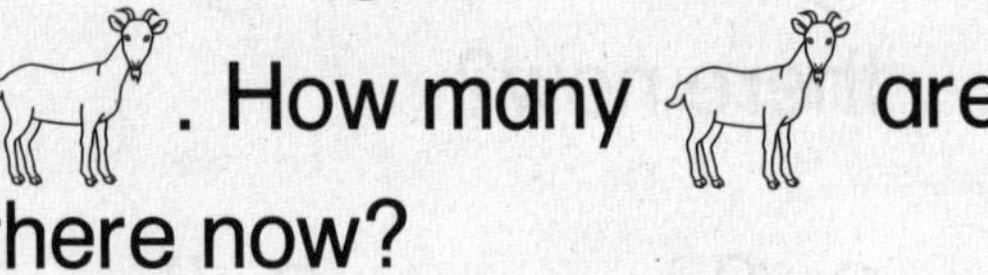

. How many are there now?

○ 4 ○ 2

○ 3 ○ 1

Name ________________________________

Choose the correct answer.

Use the tally chart for questions 1–4.

Animals on the Farm		Total
chicken	|||	3
goat		2
cow	||	

1. How many cows are on the farm?

○ 5 ○ 2

○ 3 ○ 1

2. How many more chickens than cows are on the farm?

○ 4 ○ 2

○ 3 ○ 1

3. How many goats are on the farm?

|||| ○ || ○

||| ○ | ○

4. How many chickens are on the farm?

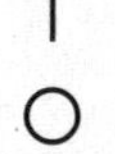
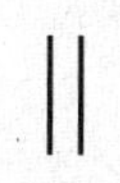

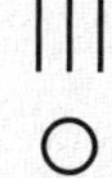

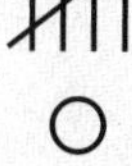

| ○ ||| ○

|| ○ 𝍸 ○

GO ON

Use the bar graph for questions 5–8.

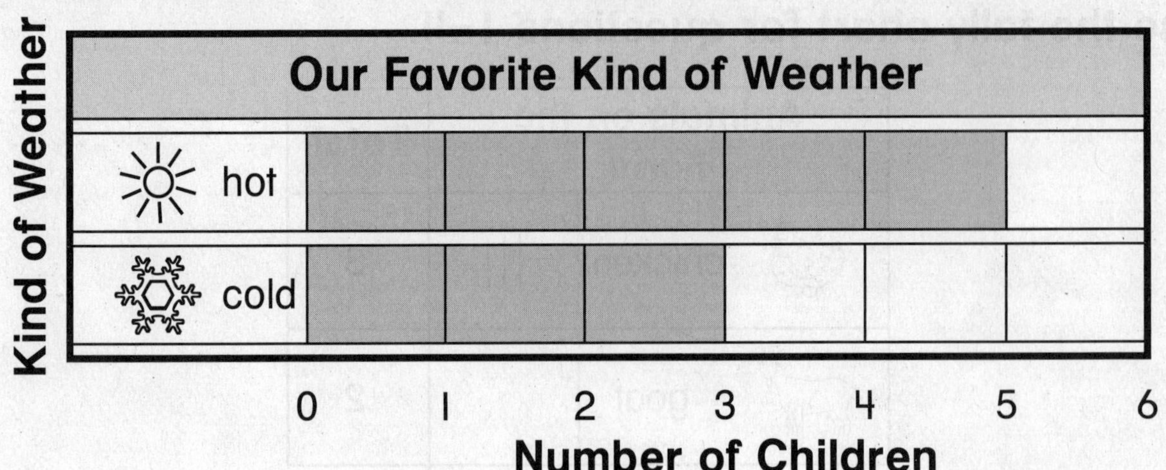

5. How many more children chose than ?

○ 5 ○ 2

○ 3 ○ 1

6. How many children chose ?

○ 1 ○ 3

○ 2 ○ 5

7. 2 more children choose . How many are there now?

○ 5 ○ 3

○ 4 ○ 1

8. 1 more child chooses . How many are there now?

○ 2 ○ 5

○ 3 ○ 6

Name ______________________________

Use the picture graph for questions 9–12.

Our Favorite Place							
home	🧍	🧍	🧍	🧍			
school	🧍	🧍	🧍	🧍	🧍		
park	🧍	🧍	🧍	🧍	🧍	🧍	

Each 🧍 stands for 1 child.

9. How many children in all chose and ?

○ 9 ○ 4

○ 5 ○ 1

10. How many more children chose than ?

○ 1 ○ 6

○ 2 ○ 10

11. 2 more children chose

. How many children chose  now?

○ 7 ○ 5

○ 6 ○ 4

12. 2 more children chose . How many children chose

 now?

○ 4 ○ 6

○ 5 ○ 7

Write the correct answer.

Use the tally chart for questions 13–16.

Our Favorite Yogurt Flavor		Total
peach		5
cherry	卌 ||	
banana		2

13. How many more children chose cherry than banana?

______ more children

14. How many fewer children chose peach than cherry?

______ fewer children

15. 5 children chose peach. Draw tally marks to show the number 5.

______

16. 2 children chose banana. Draw tally marks to show the number 2.

______

Use the bar graph for questions 17–20.

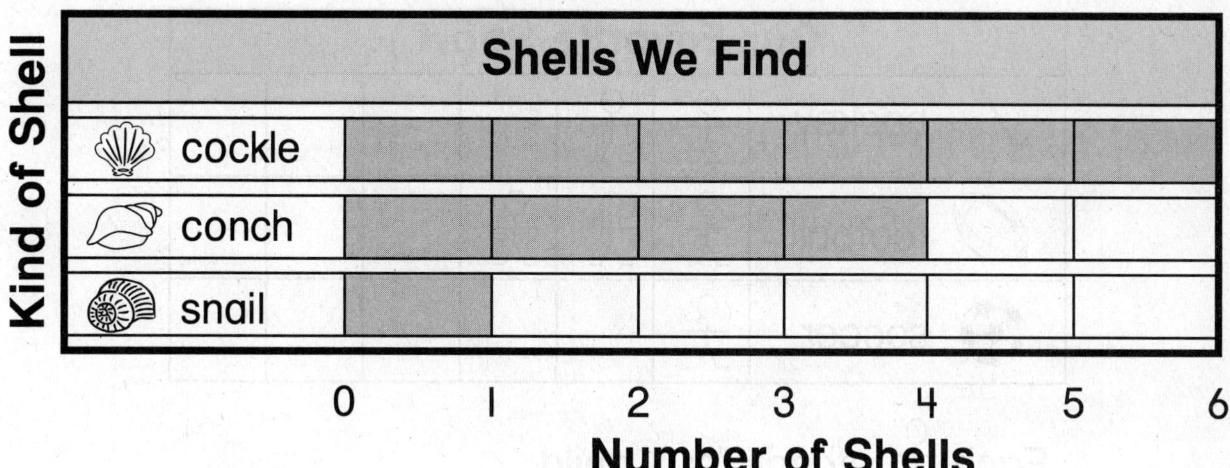

17. How many more do the children find than ?

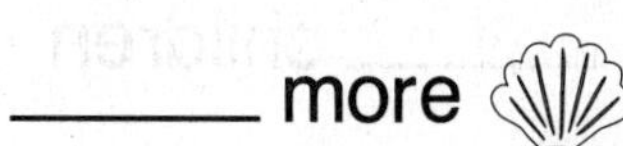

18. How many and do the children find in all?

______ in all

19. Children found 2 more . How many are there now?

20. Children found 1 more . How many are there now?

GO ON

Use the picture graph for questions 21–24.

Our Favorite Sport						
hockey	웃	웃				
football	웃	웃	웃			
soccer	웃					

Each 웃 stands for 1 child.

21. How many more children chose football than soccer?

______ more children

22. How many children chose hockey?

______ children

23. 3 more children chose soccer. How many children in all chose soccer?

______ children

24. 1 more child chooses hockey. How many children in all chose hockey?

______ children

Name ______________________

Extended Constructed Response

25. Rita has 2 toy bears.
Lamar has 2 more toy bears than Rita.
Theo has 1 more toy bear than Lamar.
How many toy bears does Theo have?

Make a bar graph to solve.

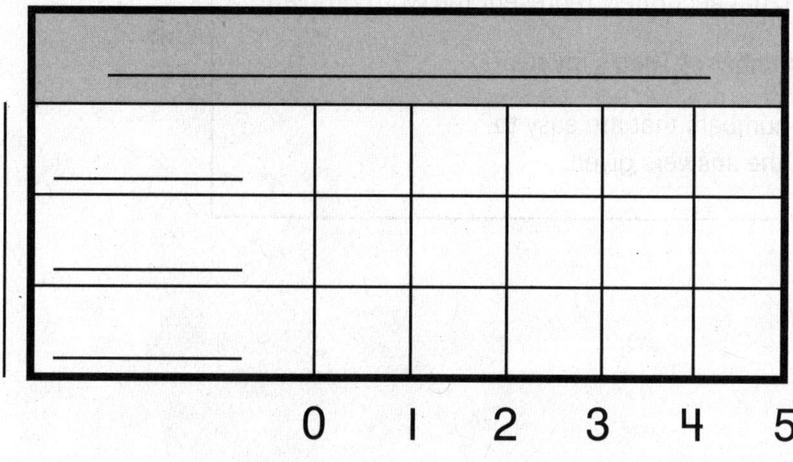

Theo has ________ toy bears.

Use words, numbers, or pictures to tell how many toy bears in all.

______ toy bears

Child's Name ____________________________

Extended Constructed Response

The Extended Constructed Response item is scored using the 3-point scoring rubric in the *Assessment Guide*. A child can receive partial credit for answers that are partially correct or partially completed.

Performance Indicators

For Problem 25, a child with a Level 2 paper:

_____ correctly labels the graph.

_____ displays bars on the graph that accurately represent the word problem.

_____ correctly determines the number of Theo's toy bears.

_____ shows pictures, words, or numbers that are easy to follow and clearly support the answers given.

Choose the correct answer.

1. What is the name of the shape?

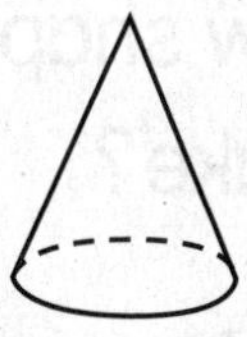

- ○ sphere
- ○ cylinder
- ○ cube
- ○ cone

2. What is the name of the shape?

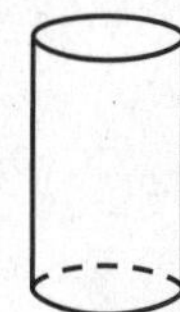

- ○ cone
- ○ cube
- ○ cylinder
- ○ sphere

3. Mira traces around the flat surfaces of a cube.

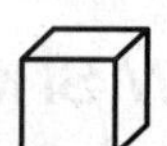

What shape can Mira draw?

○

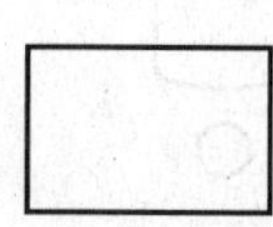
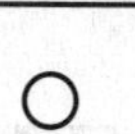

○

○

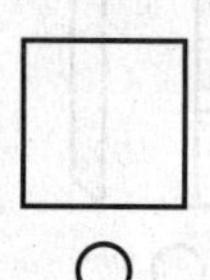

○

4. Tom traces around the flat surface of a cone.

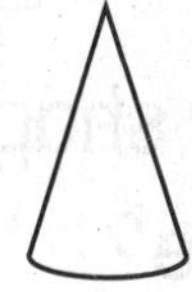

What shape can Tom draw?

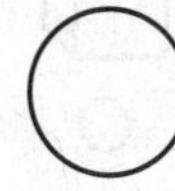

○

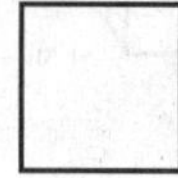

○

○

○

GO ON

5. Which flat surface does a cylinder have?

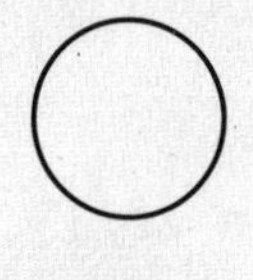
○
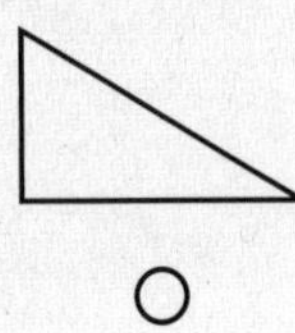
○
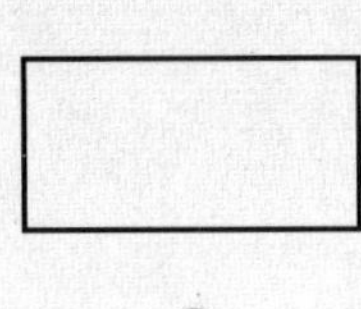
○
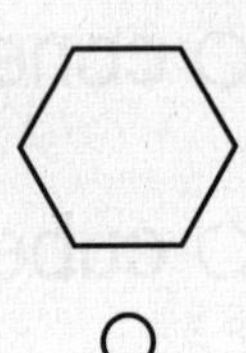
○

6. Cheri combines these shapes.

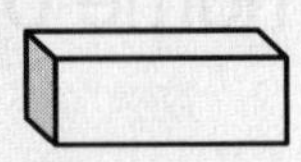

What new shape can Cheri make?

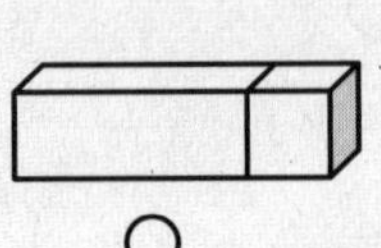
○
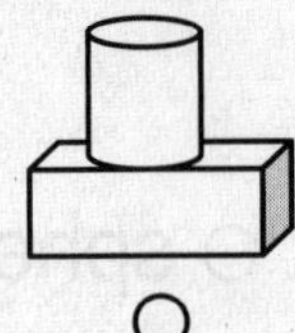
○
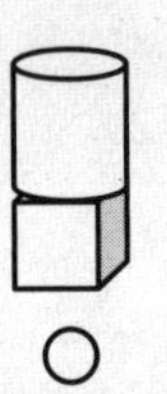
○
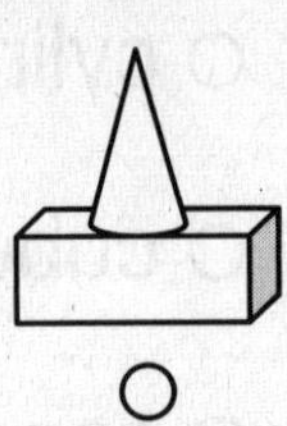
○

7. Joey combines these shapes.

What new shape can Joey make?

○
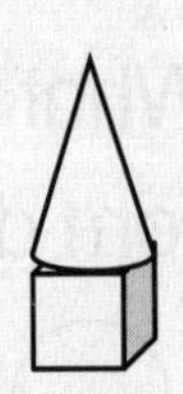
○

○

○

8. Rita combines these shapes.

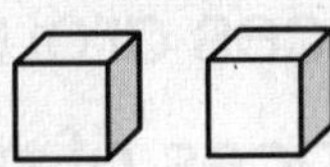

Which new shape can Rita make?

○
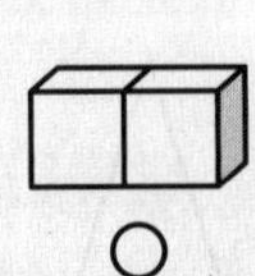
○
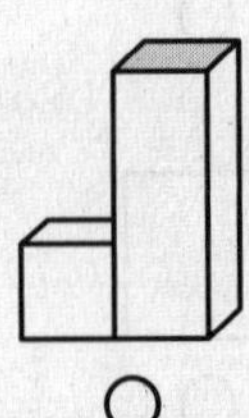
○
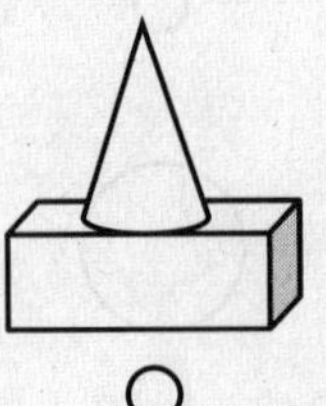
○

Name ____________________

9. Hannah makes another tower just like this tower. Then she combines her towers.

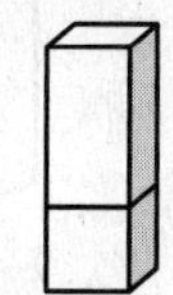

Which new shape could Hanna make?

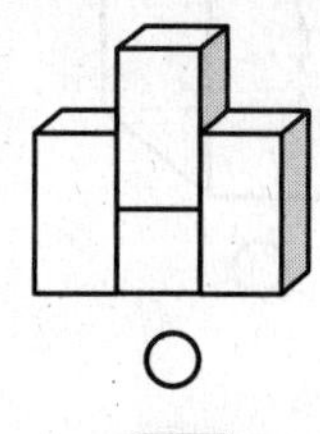
○

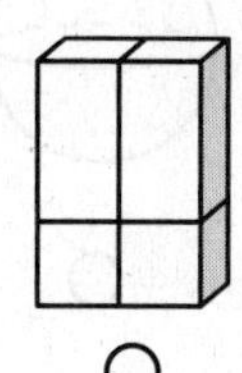
○

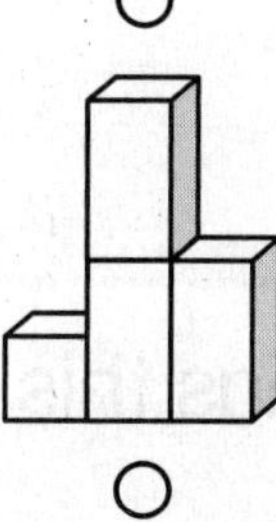
○

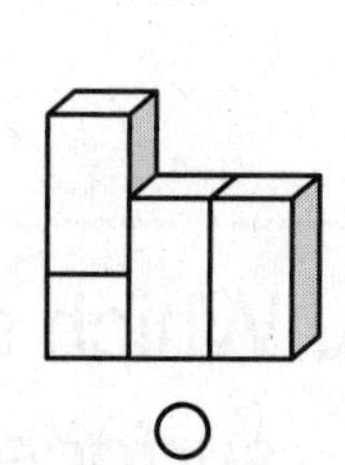
○

10. Look at the shape.

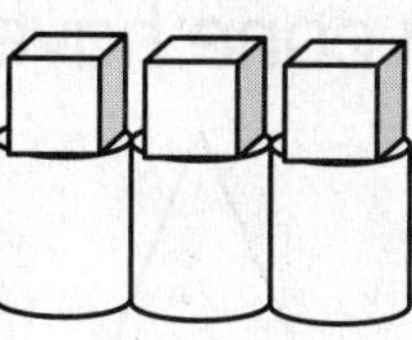

How many [shape] are used to make the shape?

○ 1 ○ 3

○ 2 ○ 4

11. Which shapes did Rosa use to build this tower?

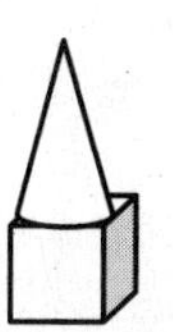

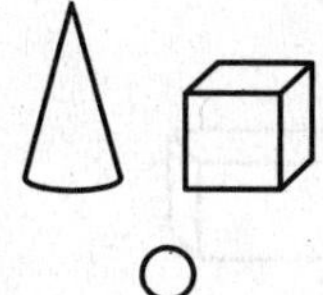
○

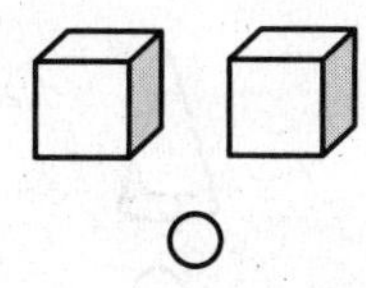
○

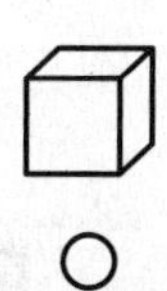
○

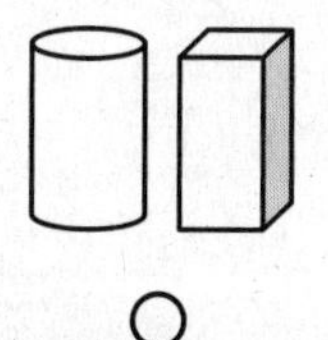
○

12. Dara uses shapes to build this gate. What shapes does Dara use?

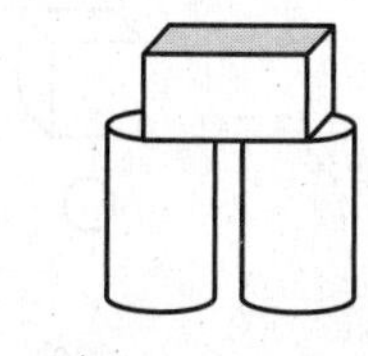

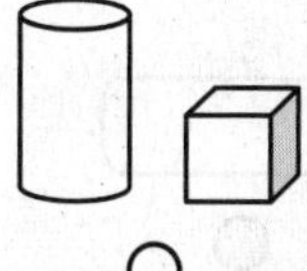
○

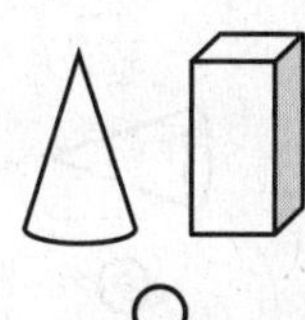
○

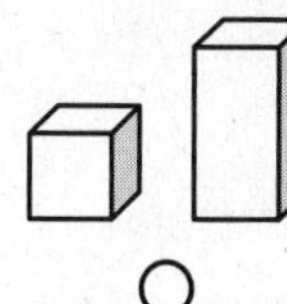
○

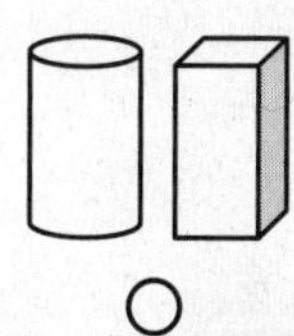
○

GO ON

13. How many flat surfaces does a cone have?

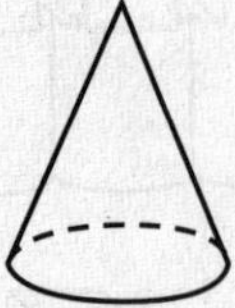

- ○ 1
- ○ 2
- ○ 4
- ○ 6

14. Which shape has **only** a curved surface?

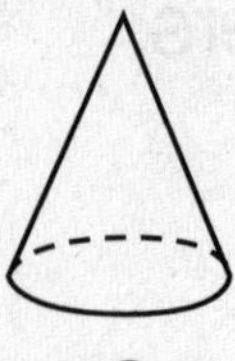
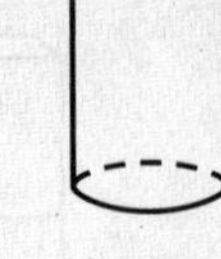

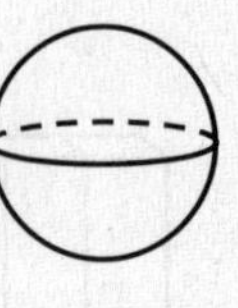
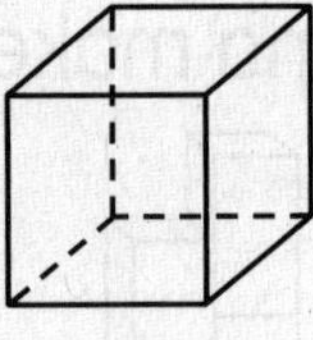

15. Which shape has this flat surface?

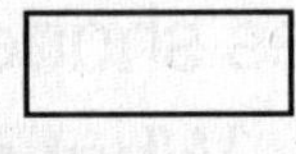

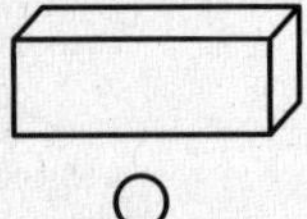
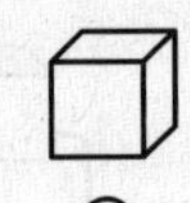

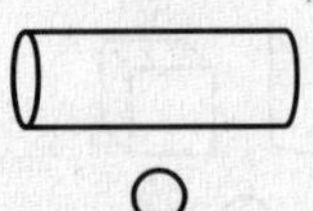

16. Which shape has this flat surface?

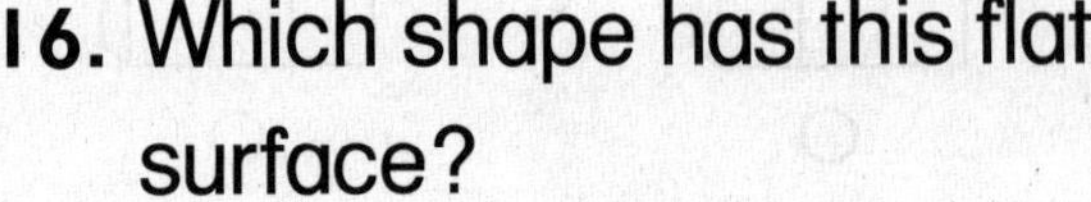

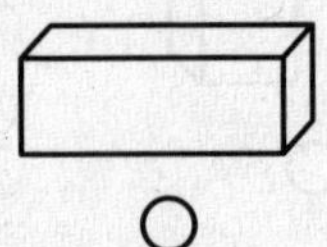

GO ON

17. Suki traces this block.

What shape can Suki draw?

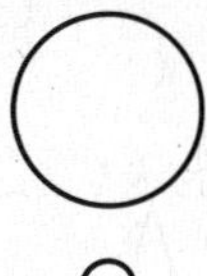

○

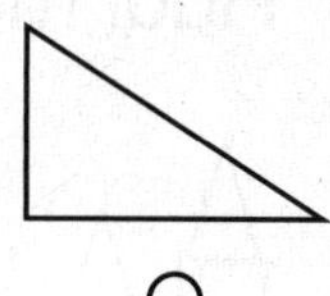

○

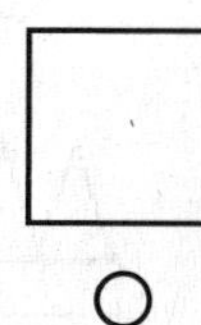

○

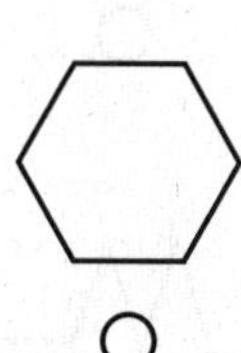

○

18. Paco made this shape.

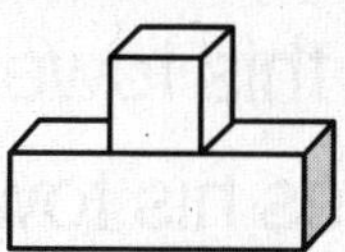

Which is another way to show the same shape?

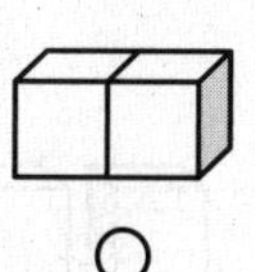

○

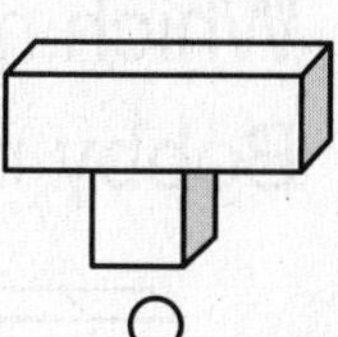

○

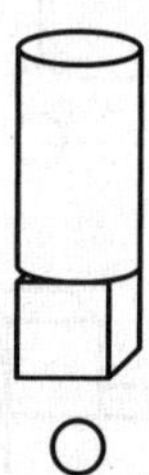

○

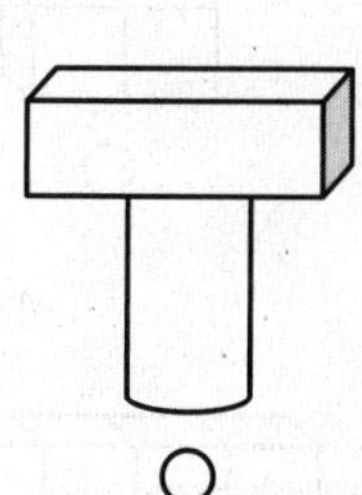

○

19. Jan combines these shapes.

What new shape can Jan make?

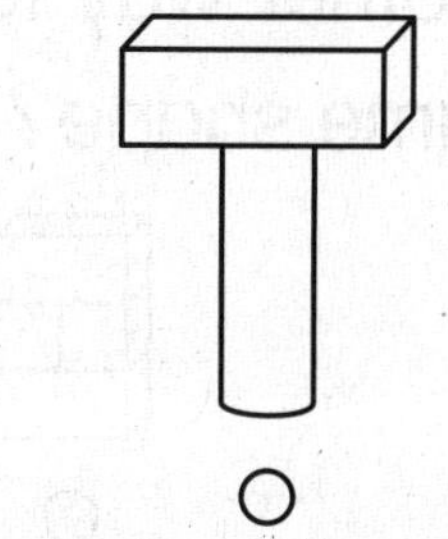

○

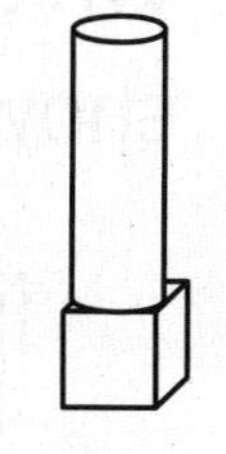

○

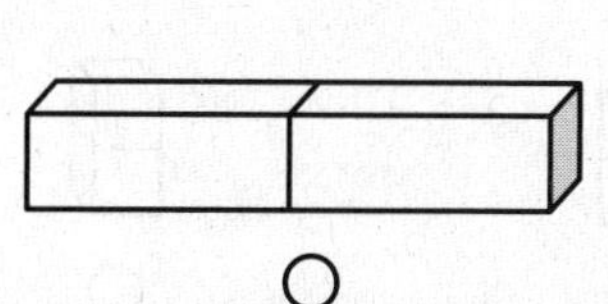

○

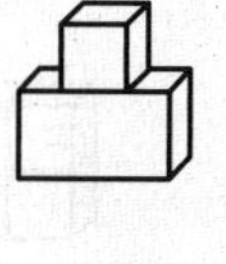

○

20. Ben combines these shapes.

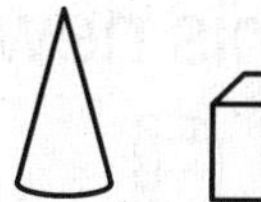

What new shape can Ben make?

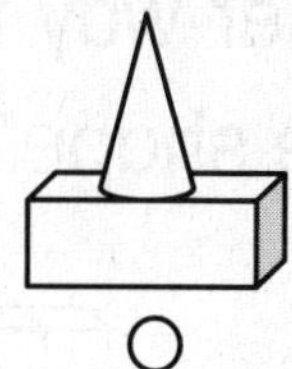

○

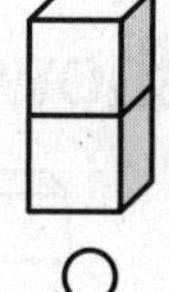

○

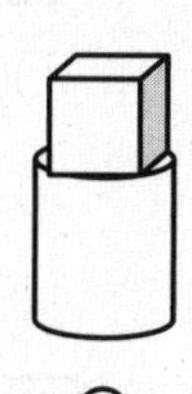

○

○

GO ON

Name ________________________________

21. Bobby makes another tower just like this tower. Then he combines his towers.

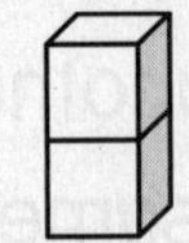

Which new shape could Bobby make?

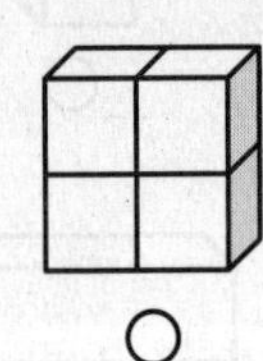
○

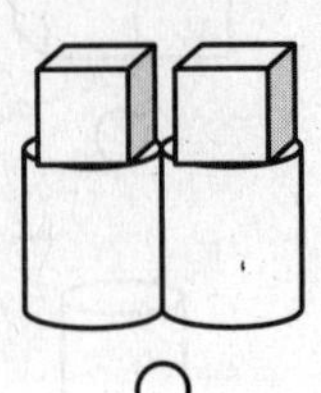
○

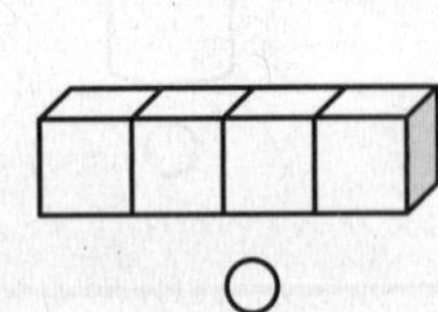
○

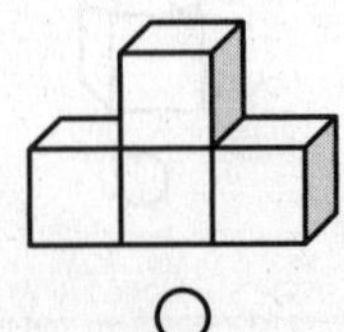
○

22. Raul makes another shape just like this. Then he combines the shapes.

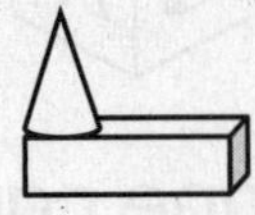

Which new shape could Raul make?

○

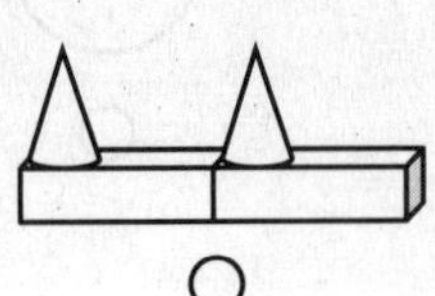
○

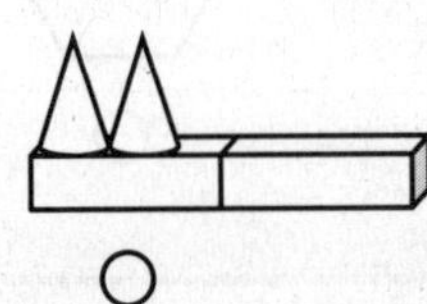
○

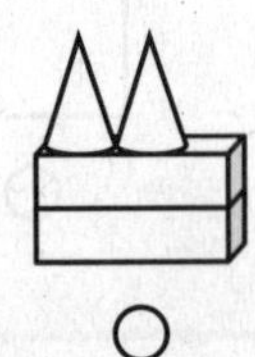
○

23. Nate combined two shapes to make this new shape.

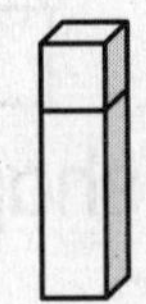

Which is another way to show the same shape?

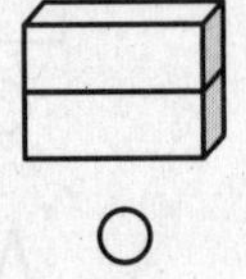
○

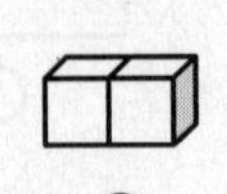
○

○

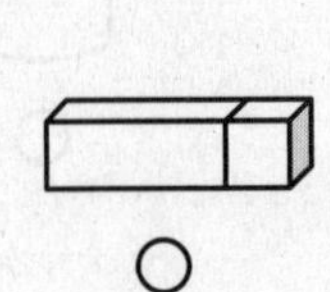
○

24. Angel combined two shapes to make this new shape.

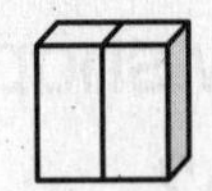

Which is another way to show the same shape?

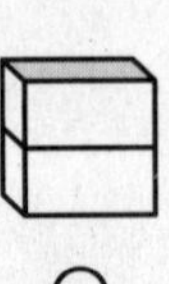
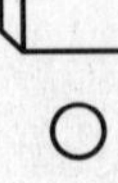
○

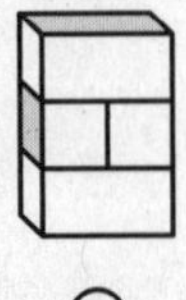
○

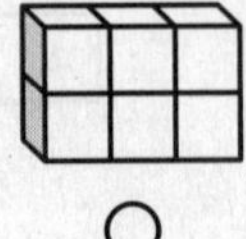
○

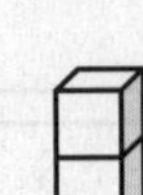
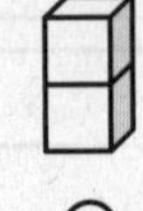
○

Choose the correct answer.

1. What is the name of the shape?

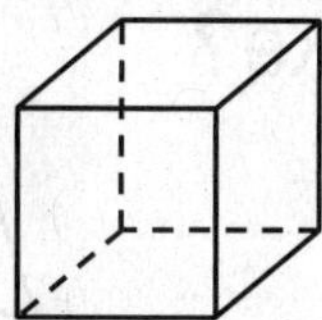

○ sphere ○ cylinder

○ cube ○ cone

2. What is the name of the shape?

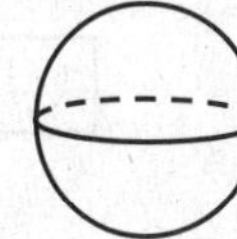

○ cone ○ cube

○ cylinder ○ sphere

3. Ami traces around the flat surfaces of a rectangular prism.

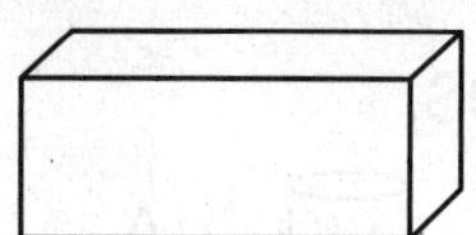

What shape can Ami draw?

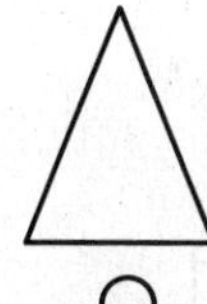
○

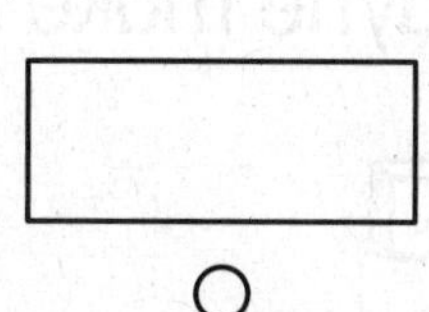
○

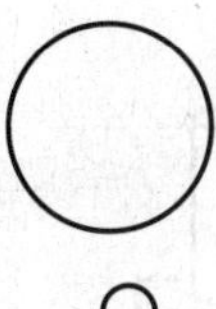
○

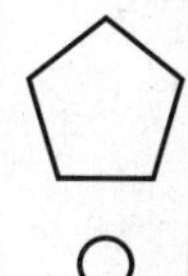
○

4. Rafi traces around the flat surface of a cylinder.

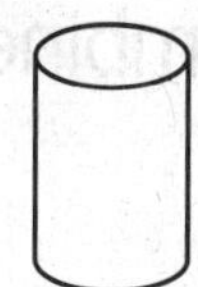

What shape can Rafi draw?

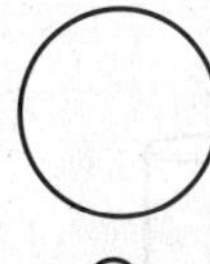
○

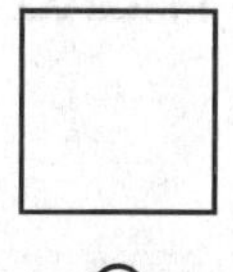
○

○

○

GO ON

5. Which flat surface does a cone have?

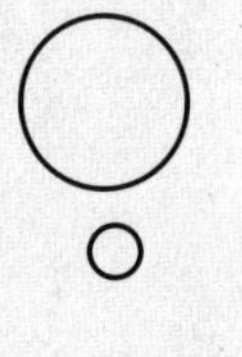 ○ 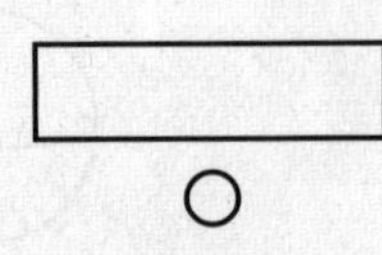 ○

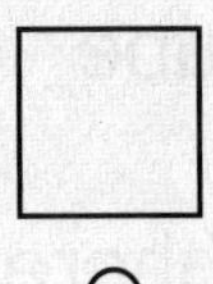 ○  ○

6. Lisa combines these shapes.

What new shape can Lisa make?

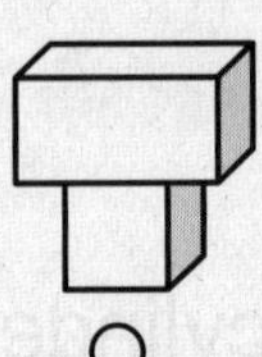 ○  ○

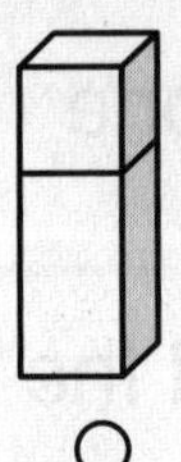 ○ 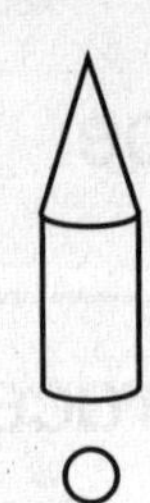 ○

7. Martin combines these shapes.

What new shape can Martin make?

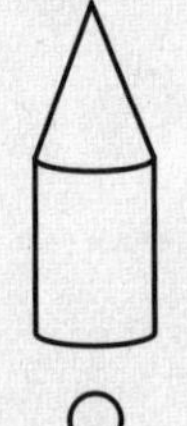 ○ 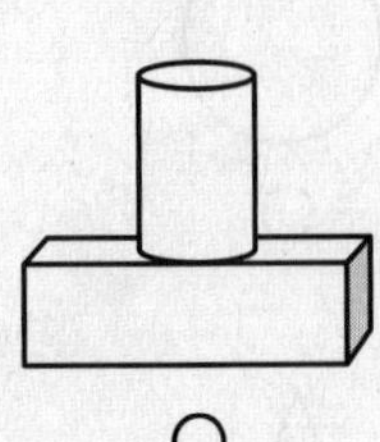 ○

 ○ 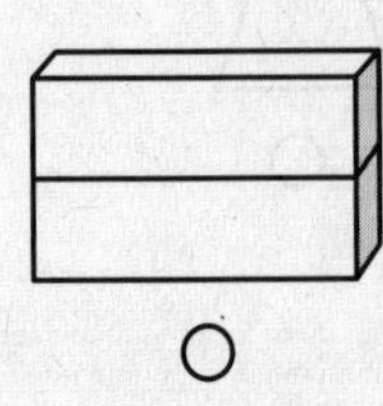 ○

8. Dwayne combines these shapes.

Which new shape can Dwayne make?

 ○  ○

 ○ 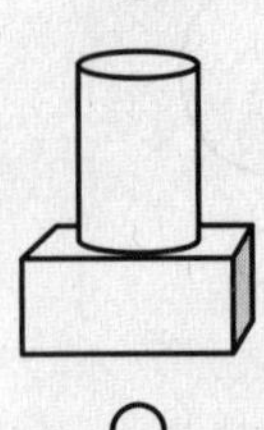 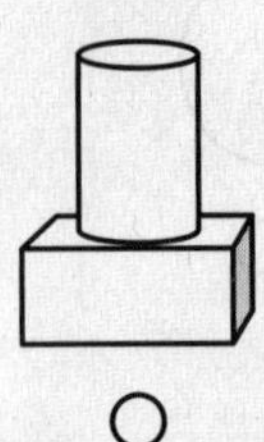 ○

GO ON

9. Mitch makes another tower just like this tower. Then he combines his towers.

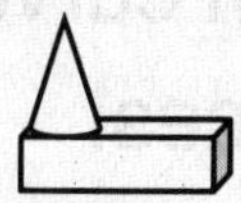

Which new shape could Mitch make?

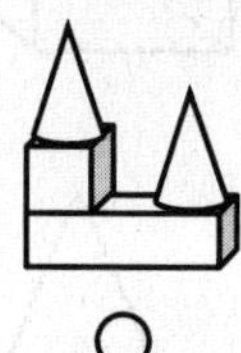

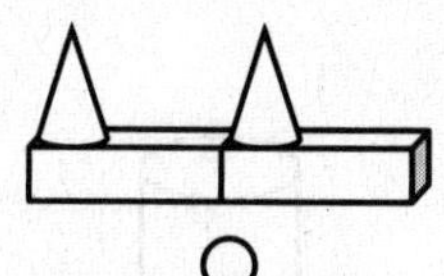

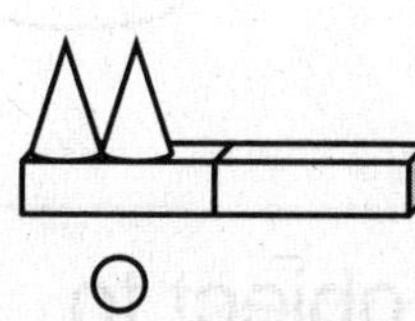

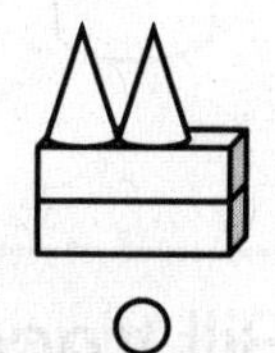

10. Look at the shape.

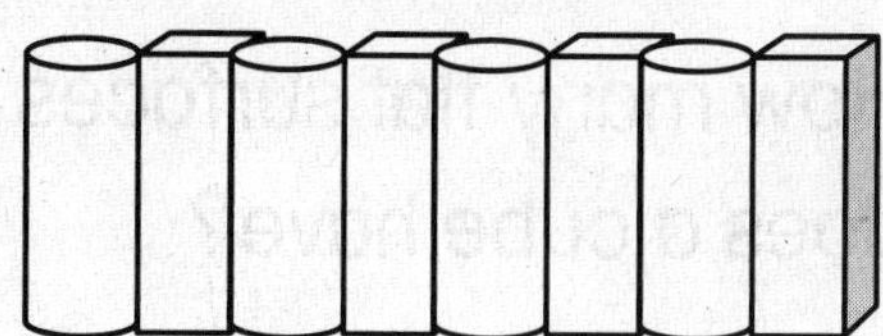

How many ▯ are used to make the shape?

○ 2
○ 3
○ 4
○ 5

11. Which shapes did Sally use to build this bridge?

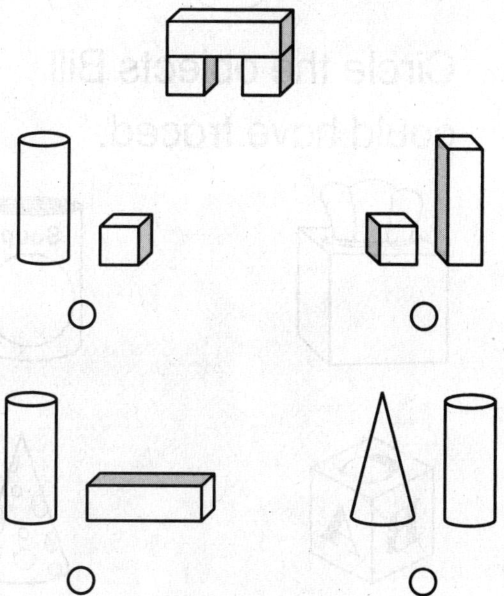

12. Clint uses shapes to build this gate. What shapes does Clint use?

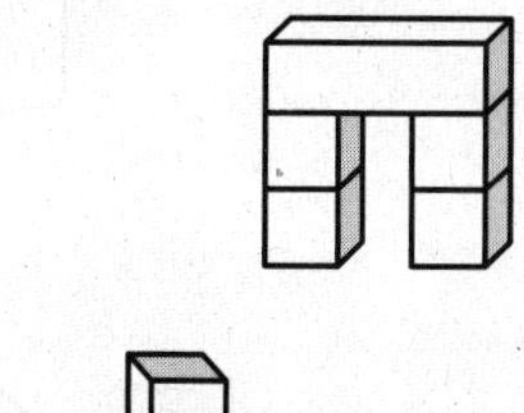

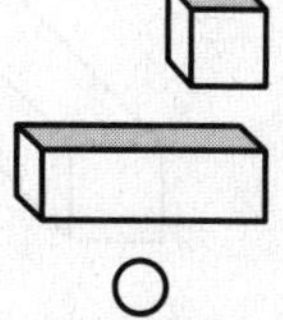

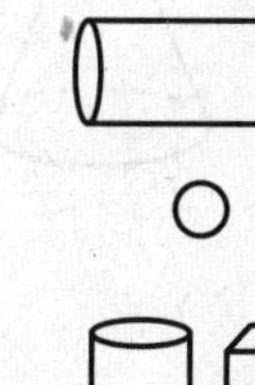

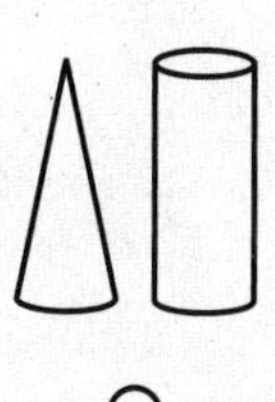

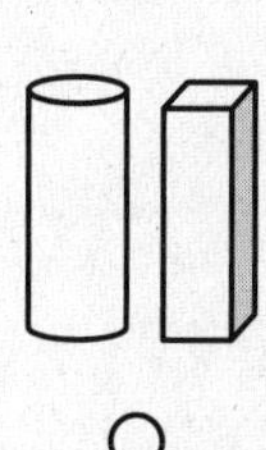

GO ON

Write the correct answer.

13. How many flat surfaces does a cube have?

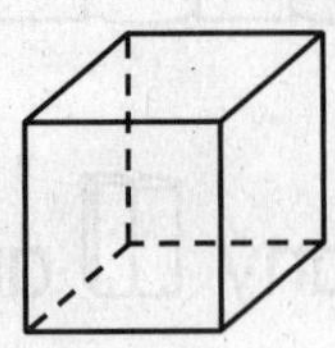

________ flat surfaces

14. Circle the shapes that have both curved and flat surfaces.

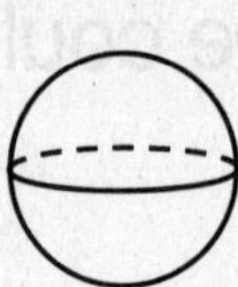
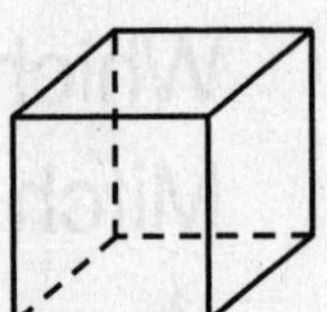
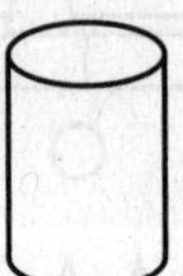
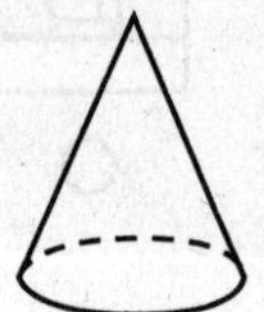

15. Circle the shapes that have this flat surface.

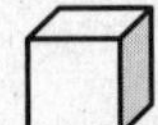
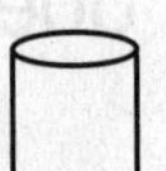

16. Bill traces an object to make this shape.

Circle the objects Bill could have traced.

17. Lee traces this box.

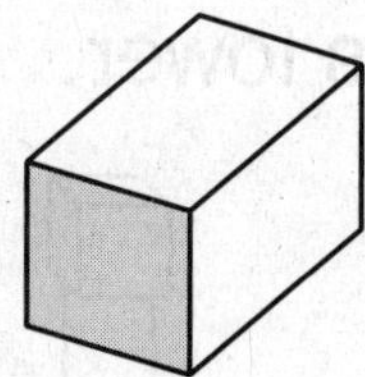

Circle the shapes that Lee can draw.

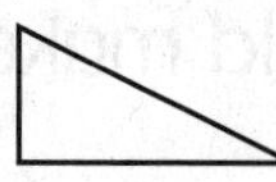

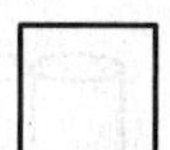
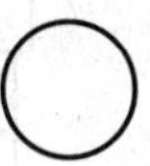

18. Circle the ways that show the same new shape.

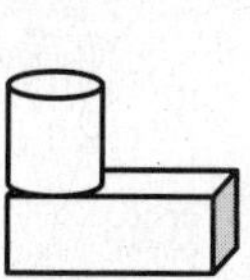
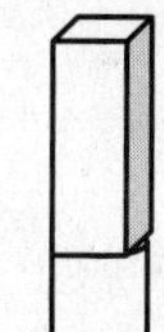
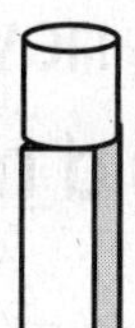
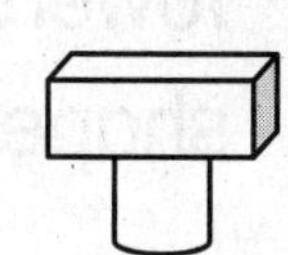

19. Eli combines these shapes.

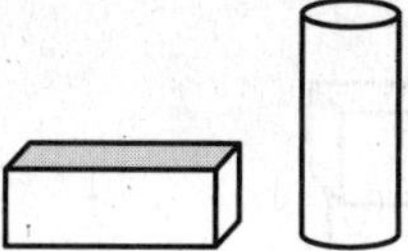

Circle the new shapes Eli could make.

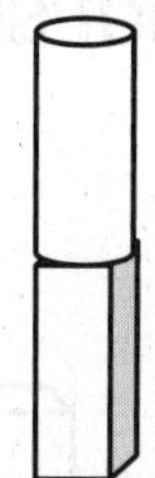
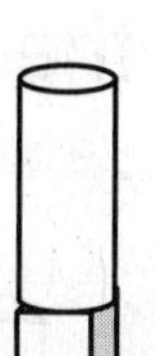
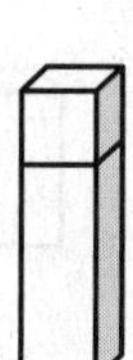
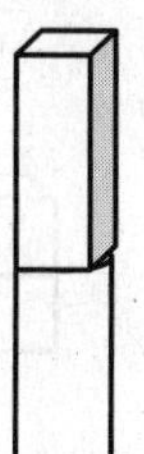

20. Kim combines these shapes.

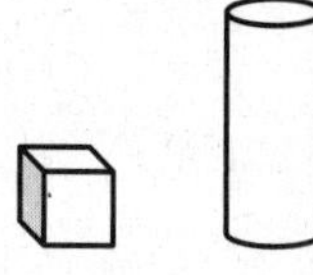

Circle the new shapes Kim could make.

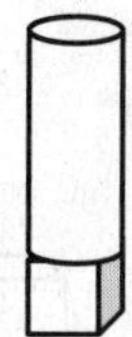
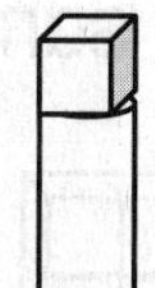

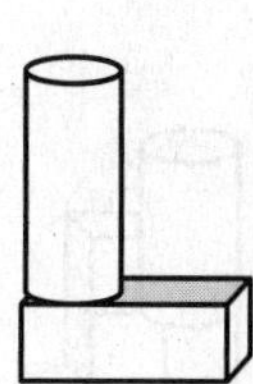

GO ON

Name ____________________

21. Marty makes another tower just like this tower.

Then he combines his towers. Circle the new shapes Marty could make.

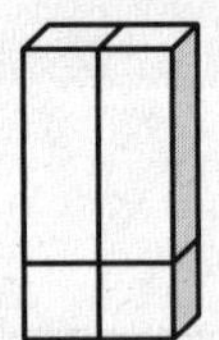
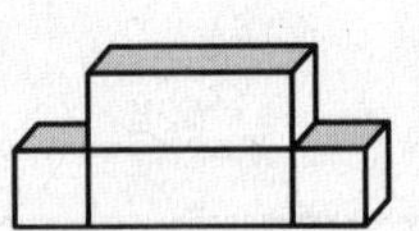
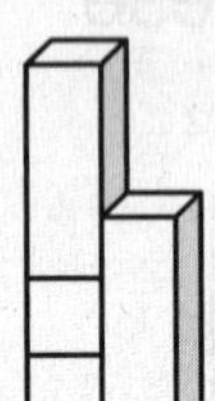
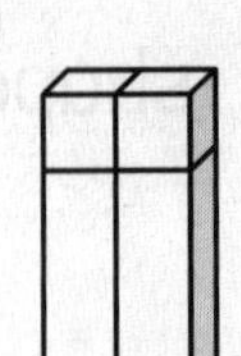

22. Tina builds towers just like this tower.

Then she combines her towers. Circle the new shapes Tina could make.

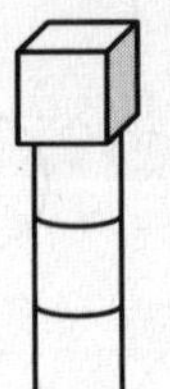
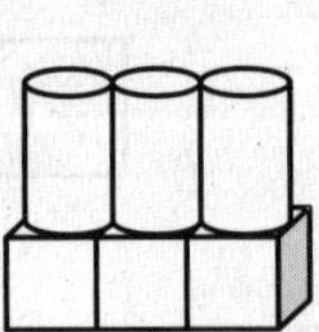
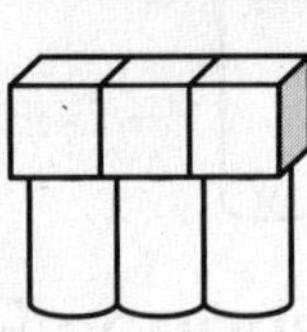
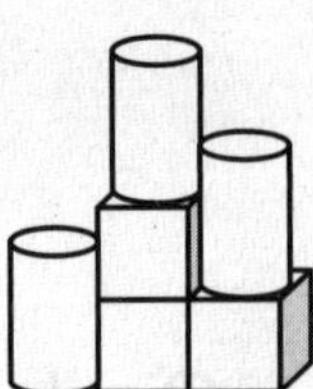

23. Circle the ways that show the same shape.

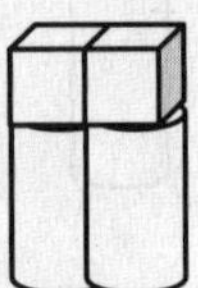
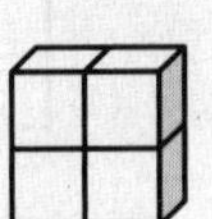
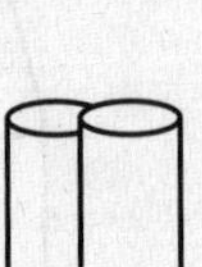

24. Circle the ways that show the same shape.

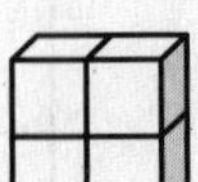
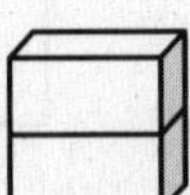

GO ON

Name ____

Extended Constructed Response

25. Ann has these blocks.

cone

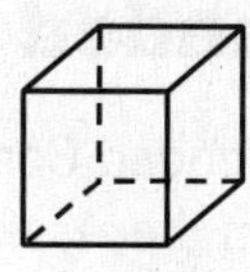

cube

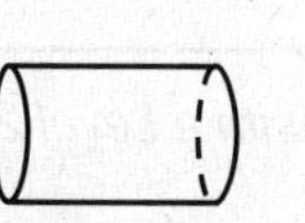

cylinder

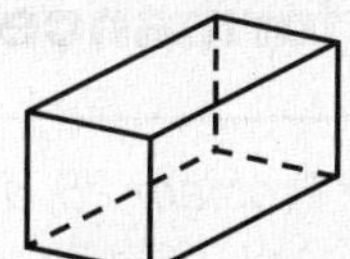

rectangular prism

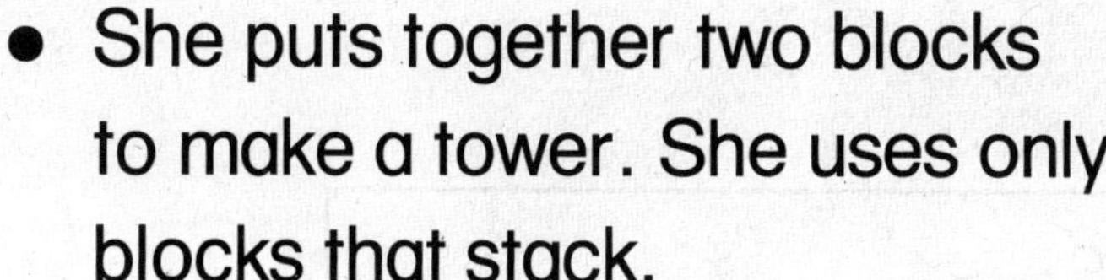

- She puts together two blocks to make a tower. She uses only blocks that stack.

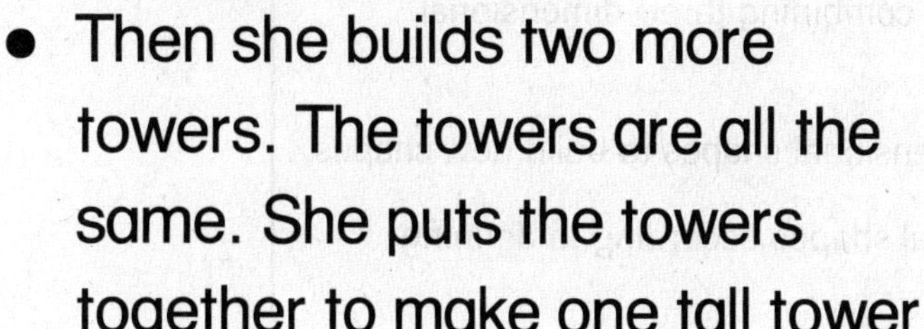

- Then she builds two more towers. The towers are all the same. She puts the towers together to make one tall tower.

Use blocks. Build a tower that Ann could make.
Draw your tower. Write the names of the two shapes you used.
Use words to tell how you decided which blocks to use.

Child's Name ______________________________

Extended Constructed Response

The Extended Constructed Response item is scored using the 3-point scoring rubric in the *Assessment Guide*. A child can receive partial credit for answers that are partially correct or partially completed.

Performance Indicators

For Problem 25, a child with a Level 2 paper:

_____ correctly composes a new shape by combining three-dimensional shapes with specified attributes.

_____ correctly uses composite three-dimensional shapes to build new shapes.

_____ correctly identifies three-dimensional shapes according to defining attributes.

_____ gives a reasonable explanation for choosing which type of block to use.

Choose the correct answer.

1. Which shows equal shares?

○ 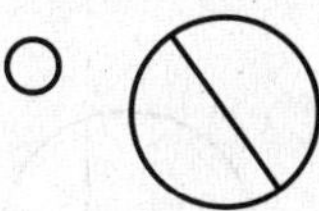 ○ 

○ 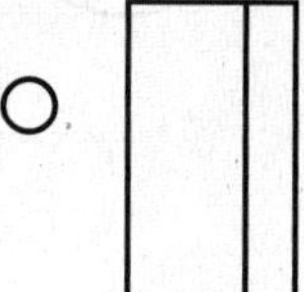 ○ 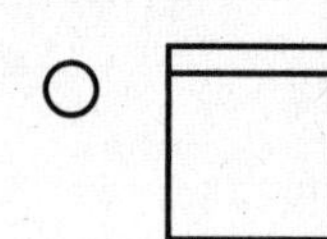

2. Which shows unequal parts?

○ 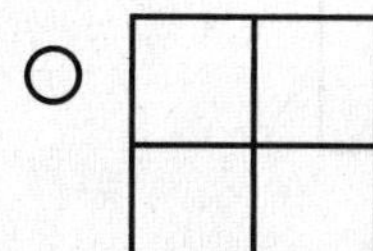 ○ 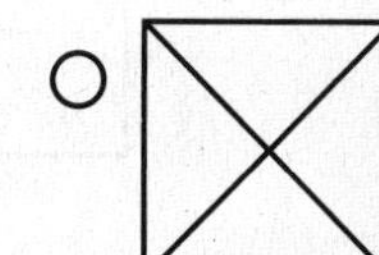

○ 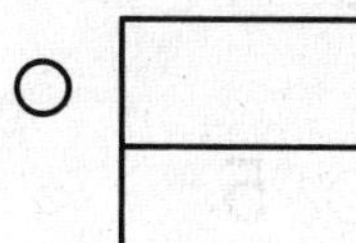 ○ 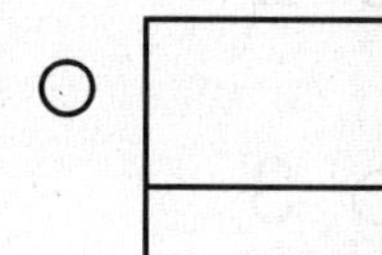

3. Ian draws a group of shapes with more than 3 sides. Which shape belongs in Ian's group?

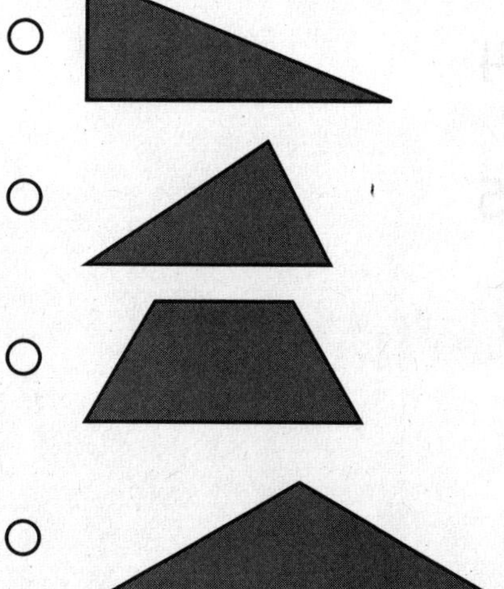

4. Look at the picture. What are the parts?

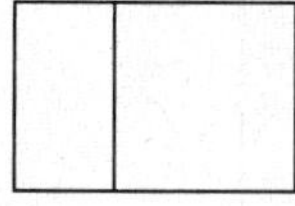

○ 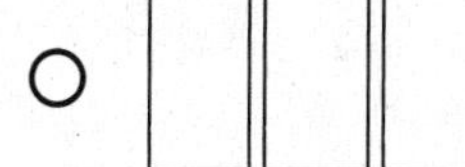

○ 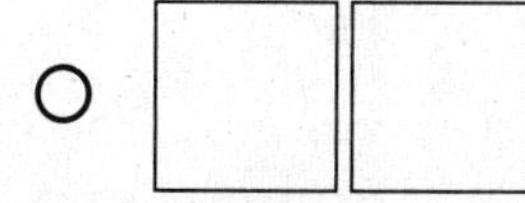

○ 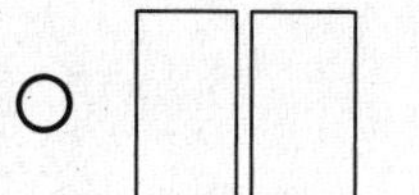

○ 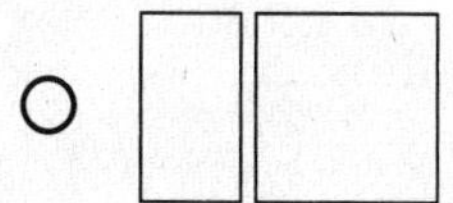

GO ON

5. How many vertices does a square have?

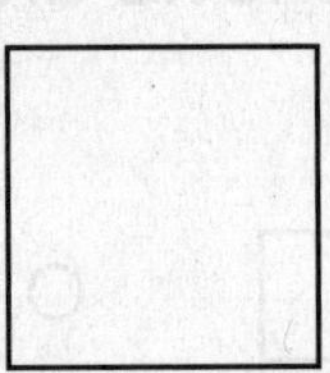

○ 2 ○ 4

○ 3 ○ 5

6. Which shows halves?

○ 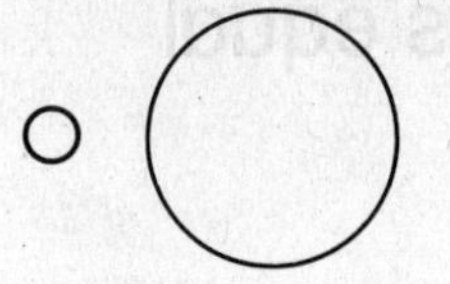 ○ 

○ 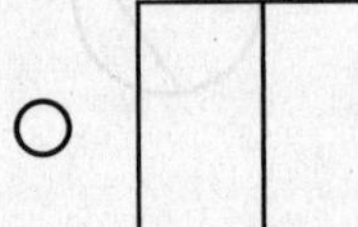 ○ 

7. Which shape has a half shaded?

○ 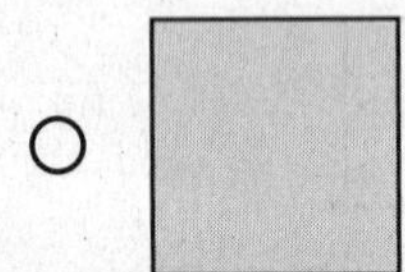

○ 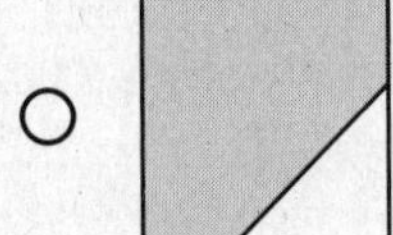

○ 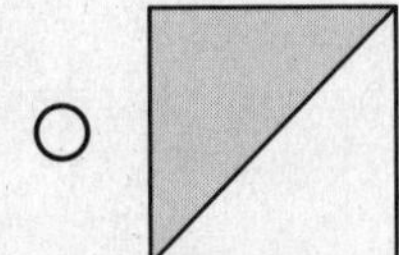

○ 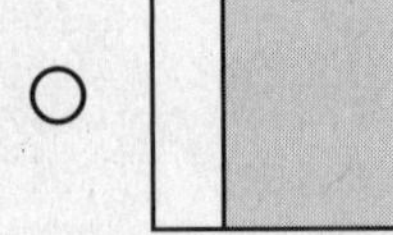

8. How many ⏢ do you use to make a ⬡?

○ 2

○ 3

○ 4

○ 5

GO ON

9. Which shape shows a fourth shaded?

○ 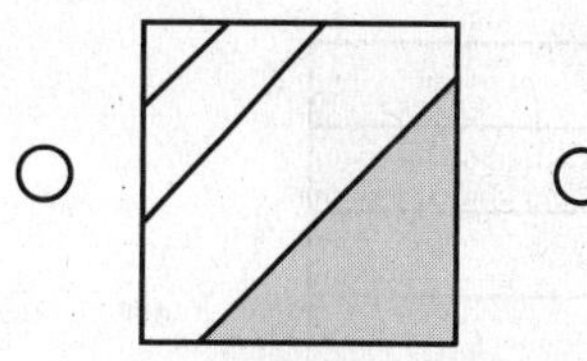
○ 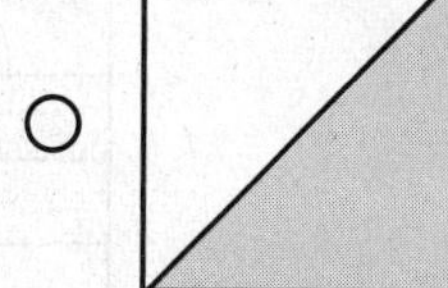
○ 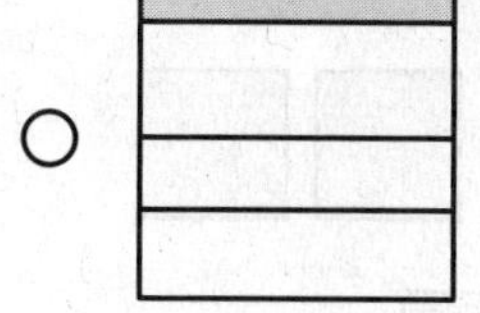
○ 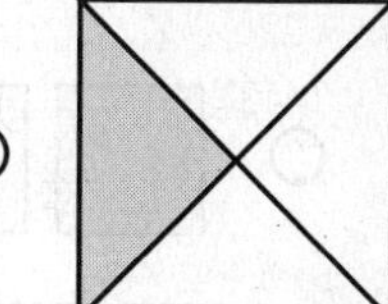

10. Which two pattern blocks can you use to make this shape?

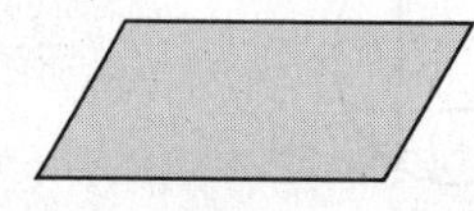

○ 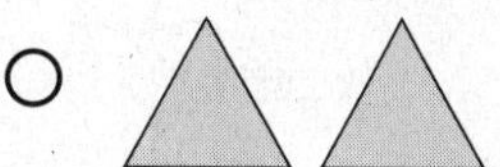
○ 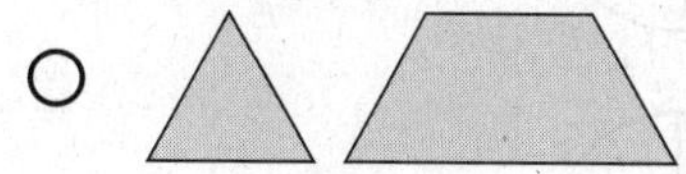
○ 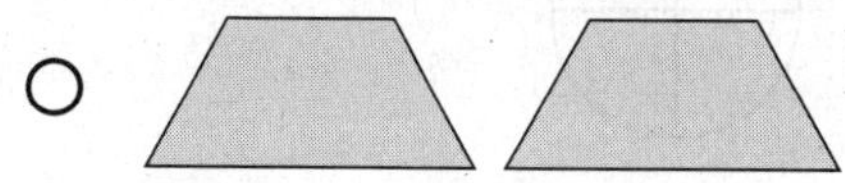
○ 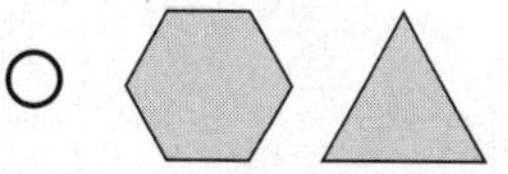

11. Which shapes can combine to make this new shape?

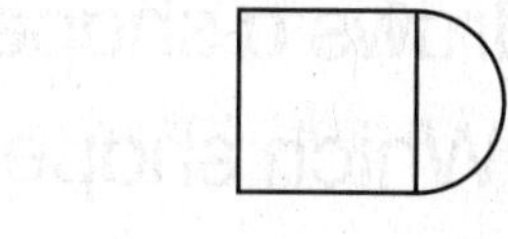

○ 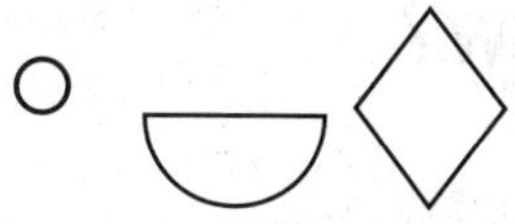
○ 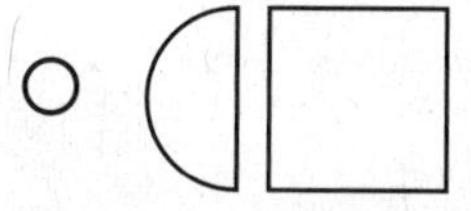
○ 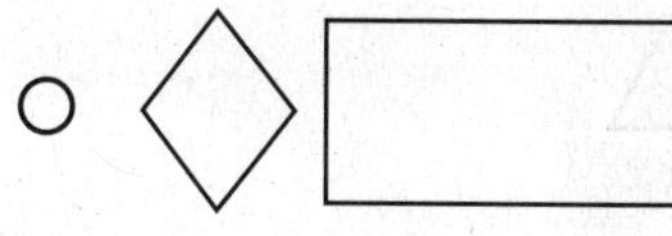
○ 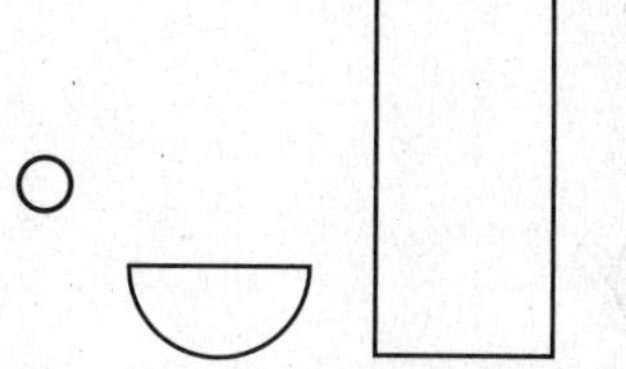

12. Which shape has 3 vertices?

○ 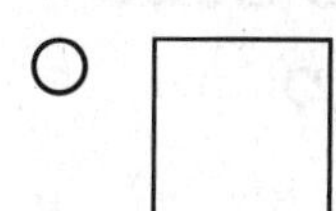
○ 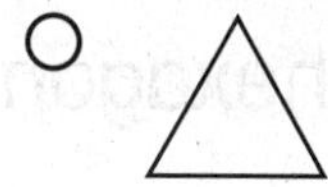
○ 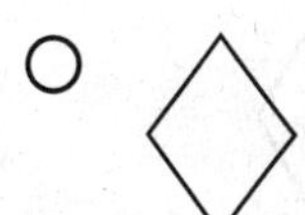
○ 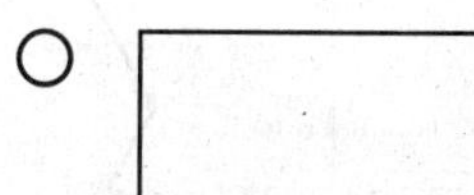

GO ON

13. Which shows equal shares?

○ 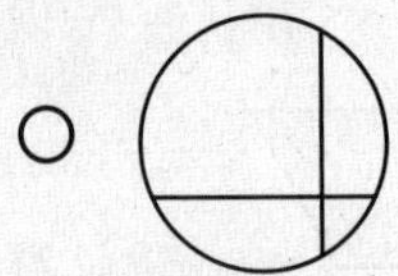

○ 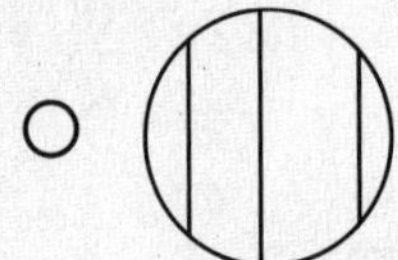

○ 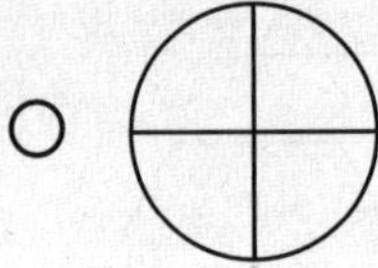

○ 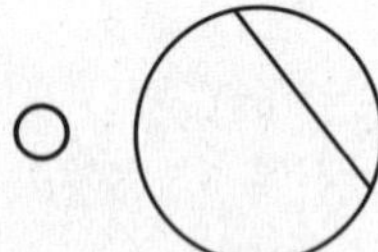

14. Look at the picture. What are the parts?

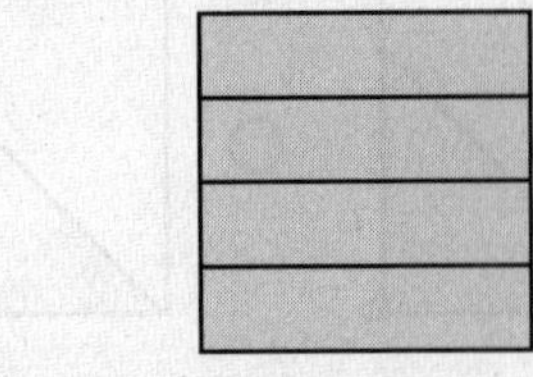

○ 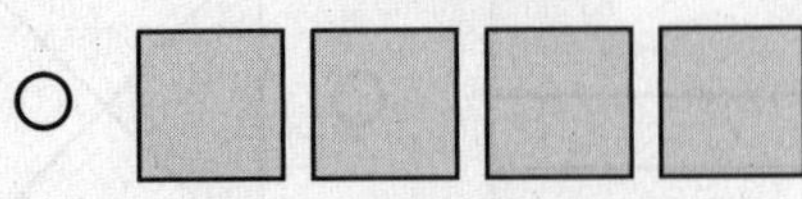

○ 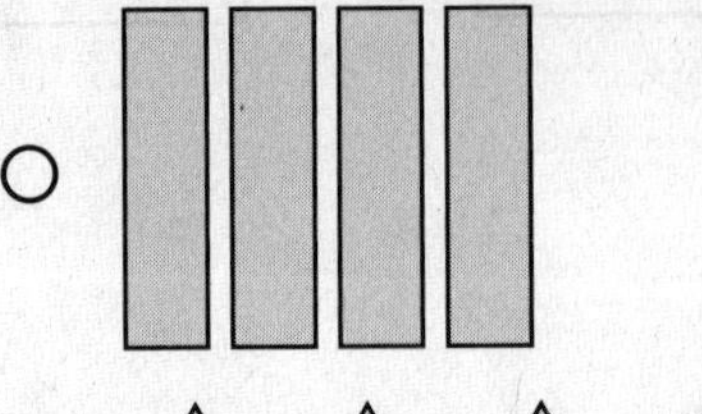

○ 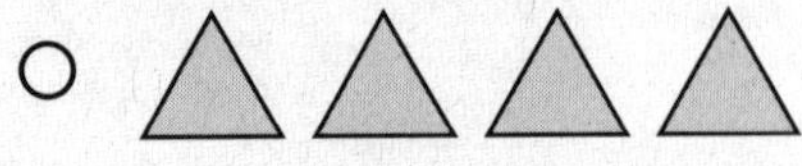

○ 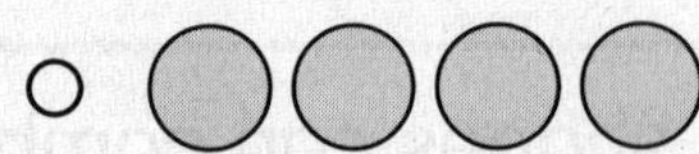

15. How many sides does a hexagon have?

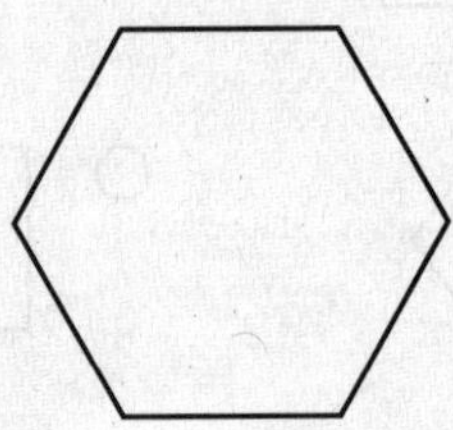

○ 3 ○ 4

○ 5 ○ 6

16. Marcie draws a shape with 3 sides. Which shape can Marcie draw?

○ 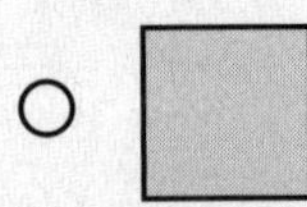

○ 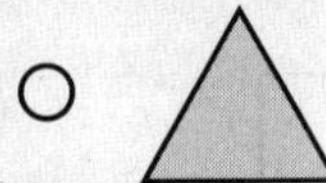

○ 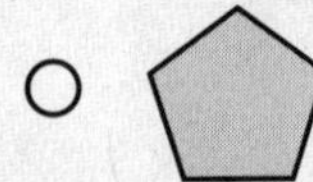

○ 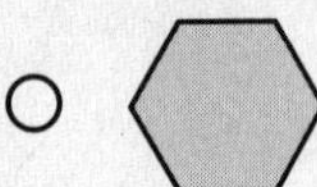

GO ON

Name ____________________

17. Which shows halves?

○ 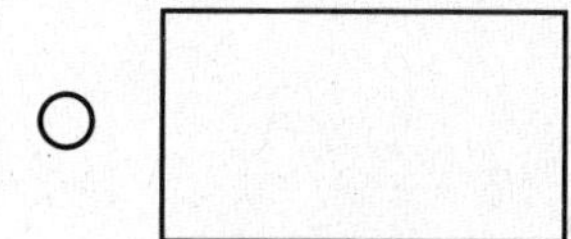

○ 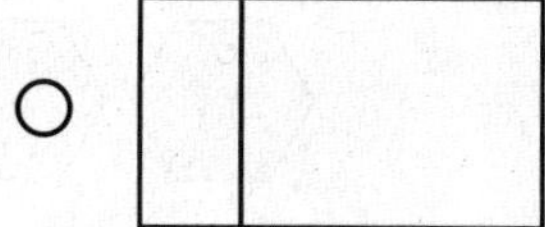

○ 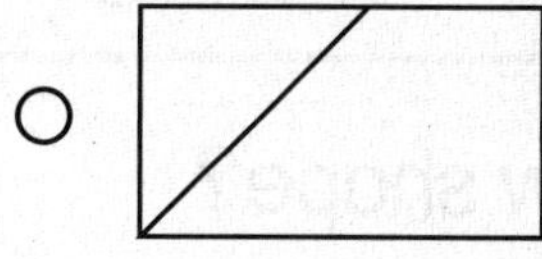

○

18. How many △ do you use to make a ⏢ ?

○ 2

○ 3

○ 4

○ 6

19. Which shape shows a quarter shaded?

○ 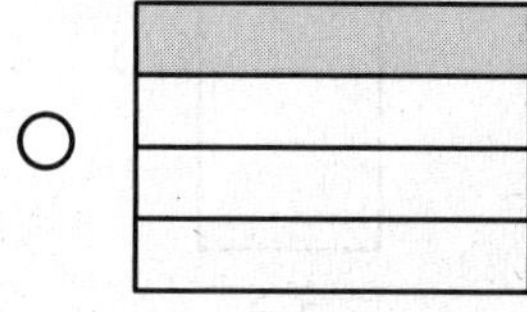

○ 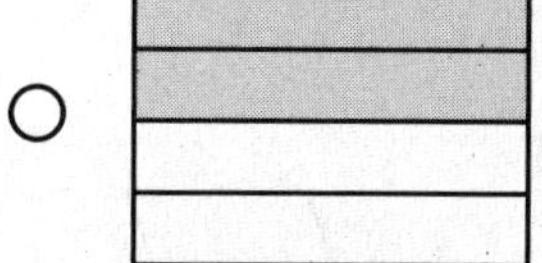

○ 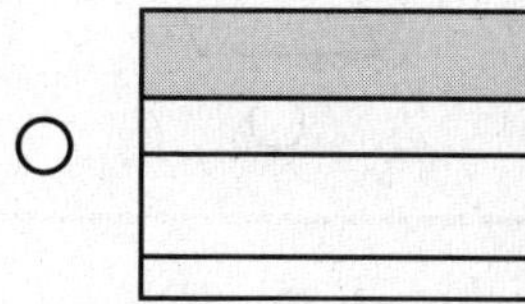

○ 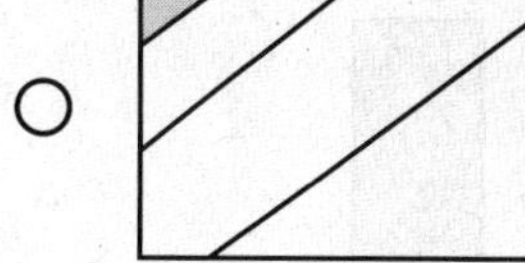

20. Which shows fourths?

○ 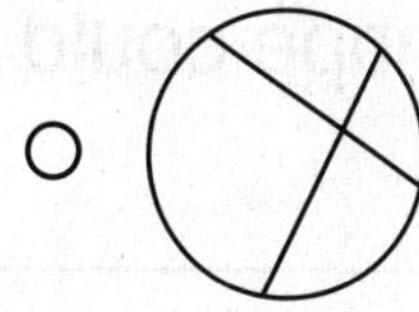

○ 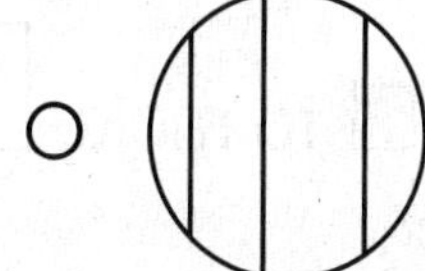

○ 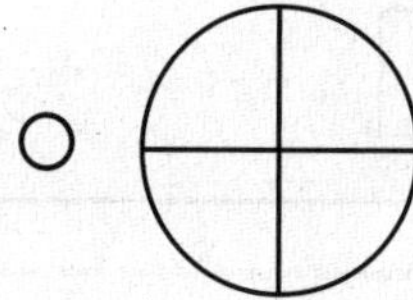

○ 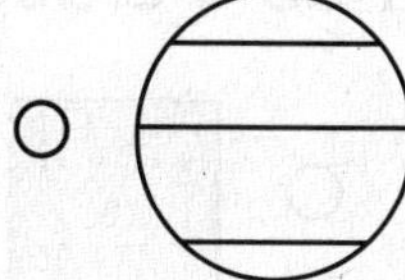

GO ON

Name ____________________

21. Which two pattern blocks can you use to make this shape?

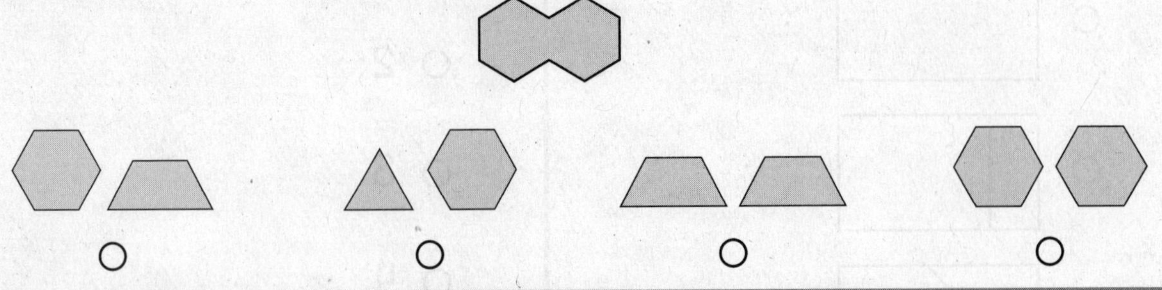

22. Which shapes can combine to make this new shape?

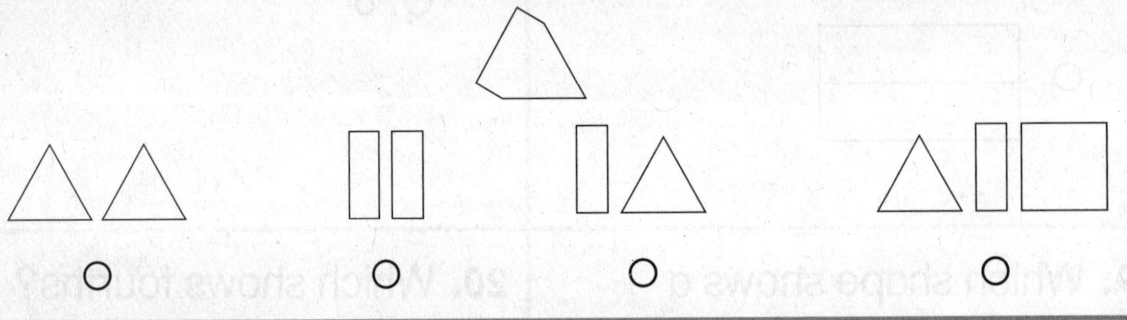

23. Which new shape could you make?

Step 1

Combine □ and □ to make ▯.

Step 2

Combine ▯ and ▯.

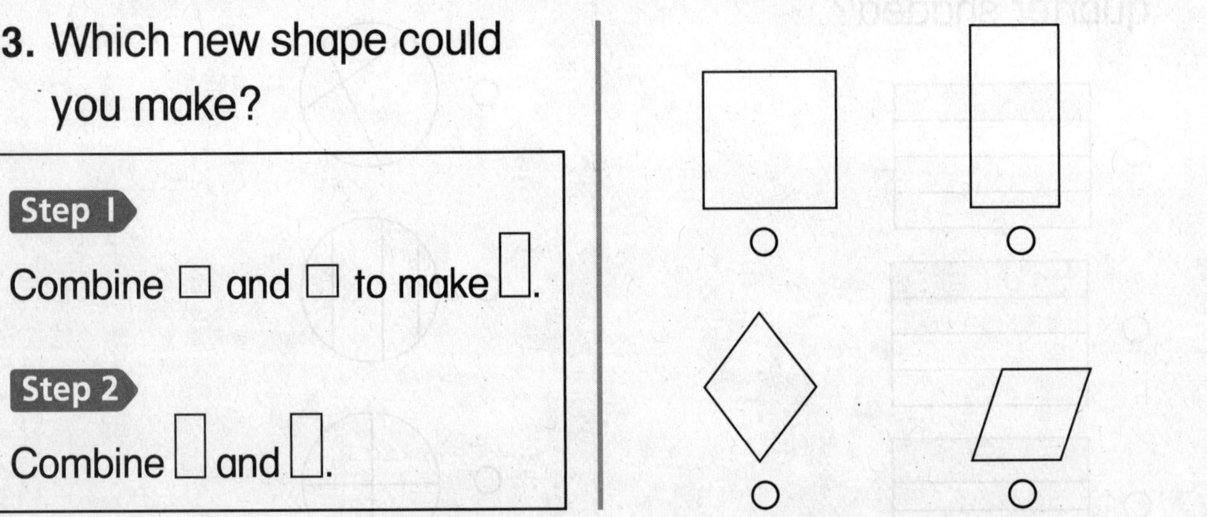

24. Which shape has 4 sides that are the same length?

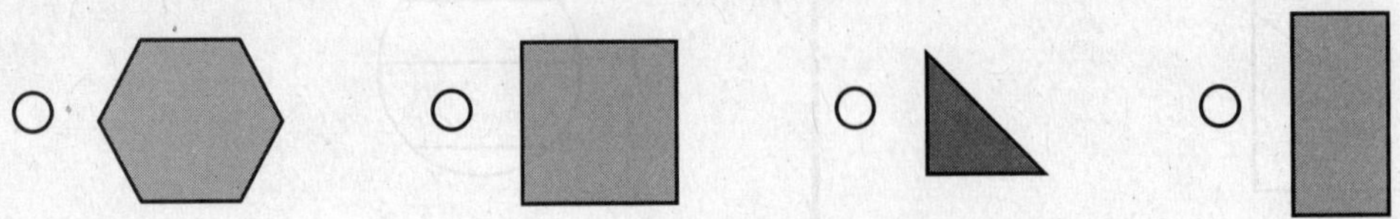

Name ____________________

Choose the correct answer.

1. Which shows equal shares?

○ 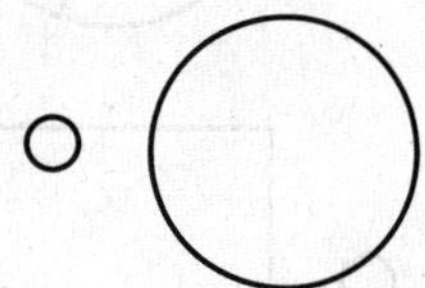

○ 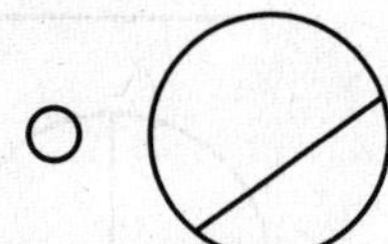

○ 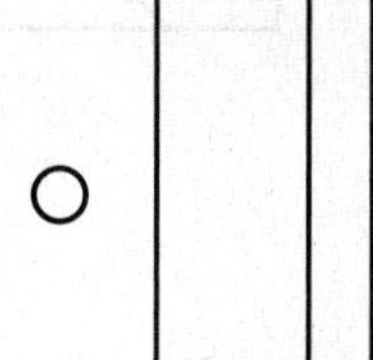

○ 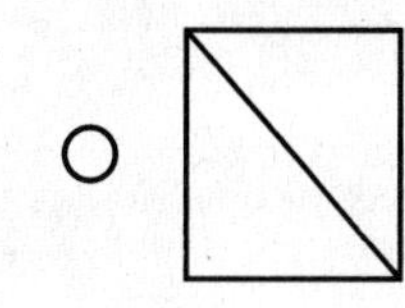

2. Which shows unequal parts?

○ 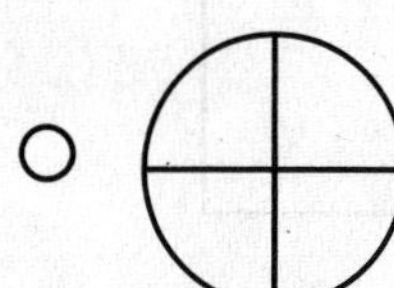

○ 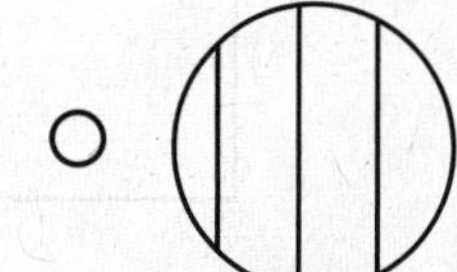

○ 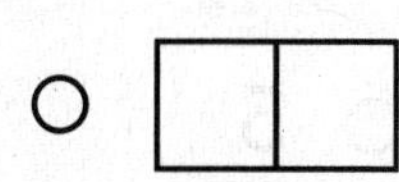

○ 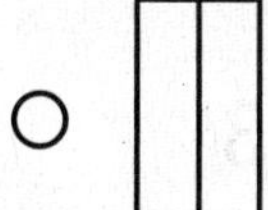

3. Which shape has 3 sides and 3 vertices?

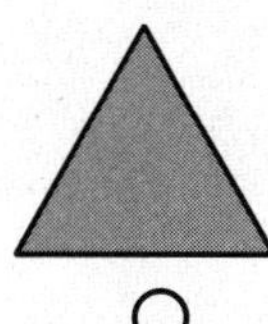
○

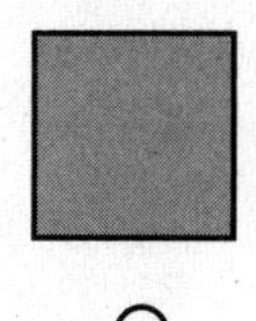
○

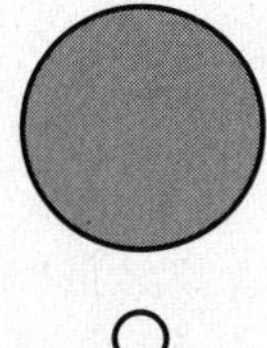
○

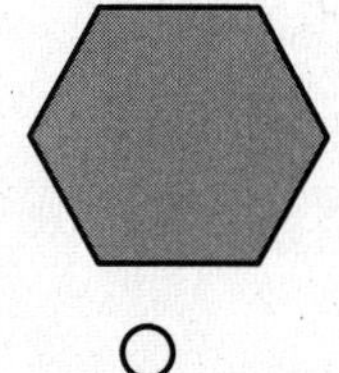
○

4. Look at the picture. What are the parts?

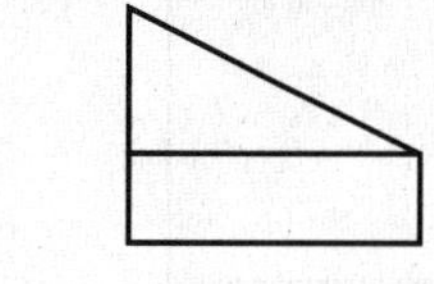

○ 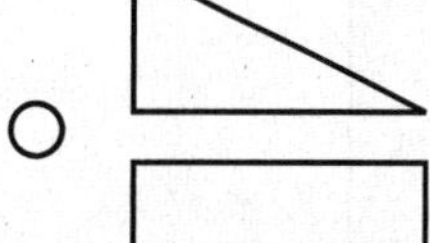

○ 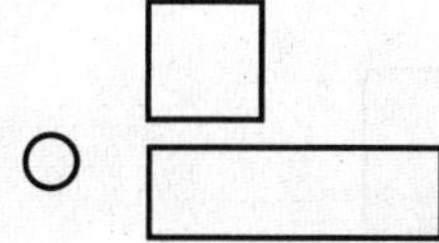

○ 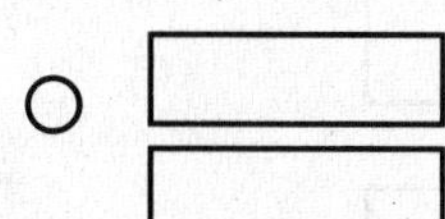

○ 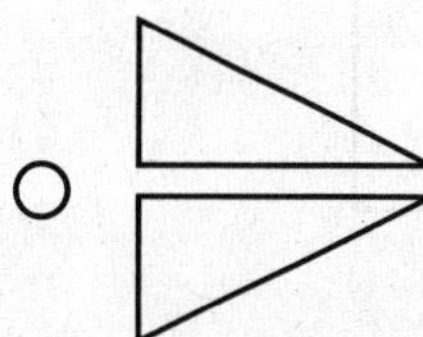

GO ON

Name ______________________________

5. How many vertices does a rectangle have?

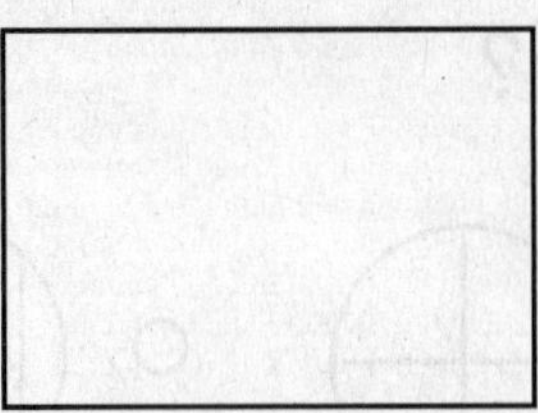

○ 2 ○ 4

○ 3 ○ 5

6. Which shows halves?

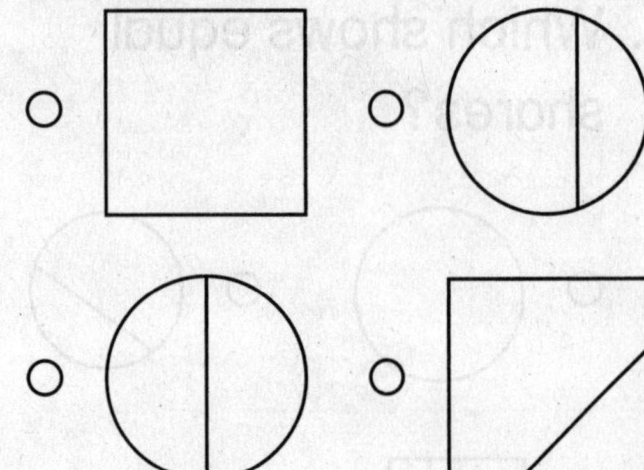

7. Which shape shows a half shaded?

○ 

○ 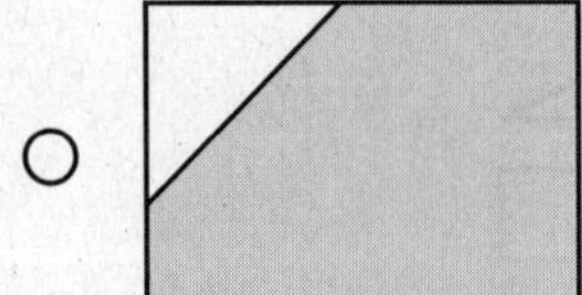

○ 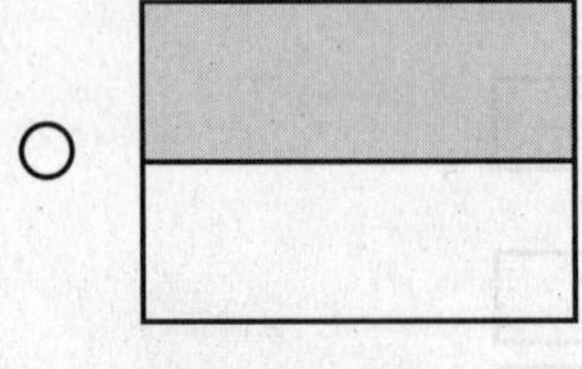

○ 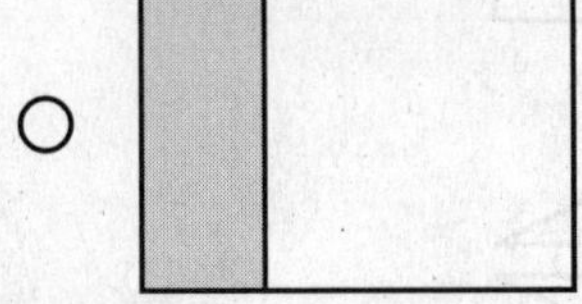

8. How many ◊ do you use to make a ⬡?

○ 2

○ 3

○ 4

○ 5

GO ON

Name ________________________________

9. Which shape shows a fourth shaded?

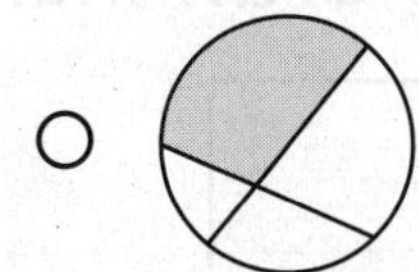
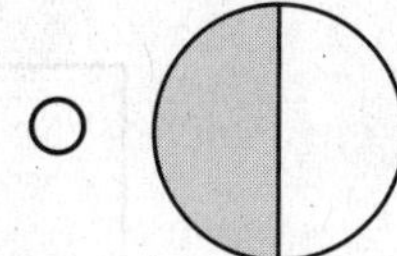
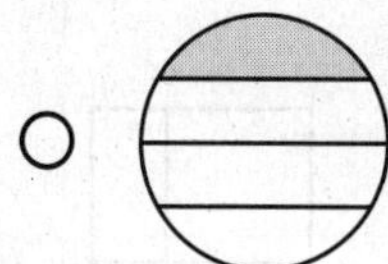
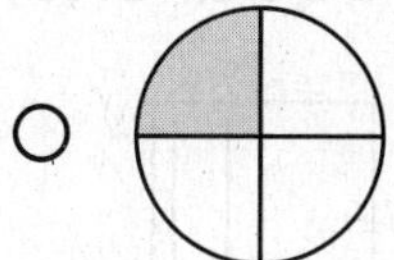

10. Which two pattern blocks can you use to make this shape?

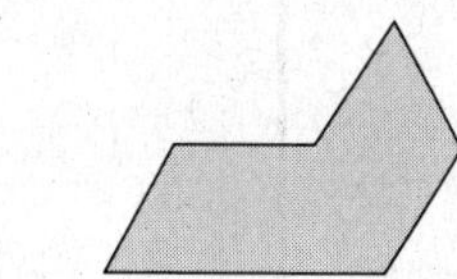

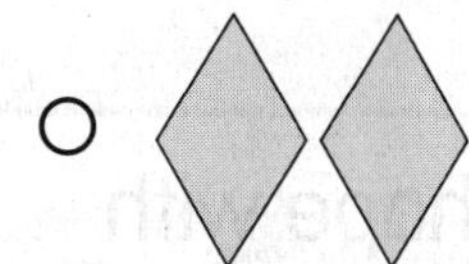
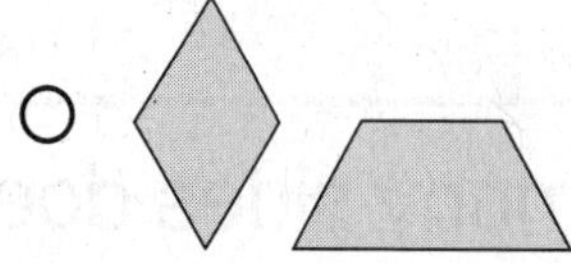
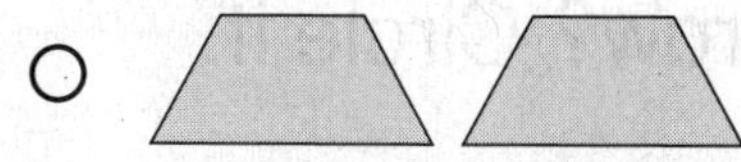
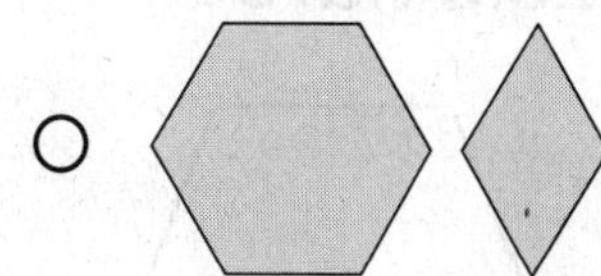

11. Which shapes can combine to make this new shape?

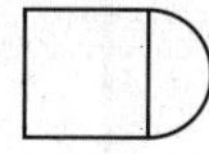

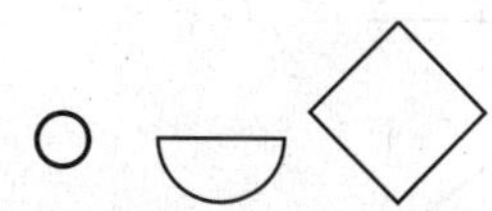

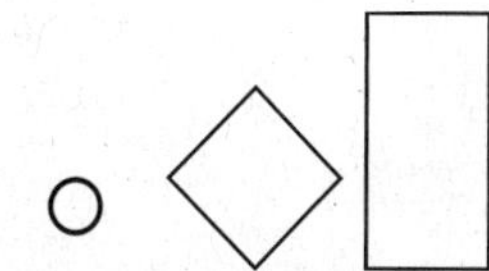

12. Which shape has four vertices?

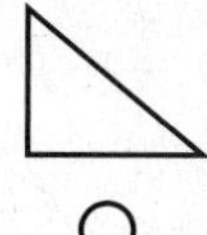
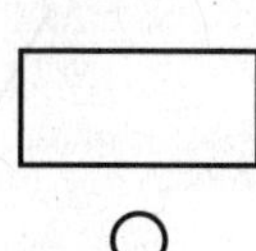

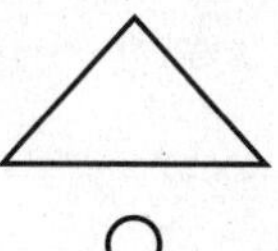

GO ON

Name ________________________________

13. Color the shape that shows equal shares.

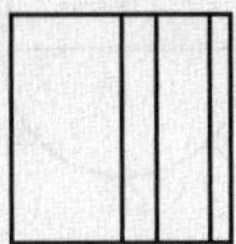

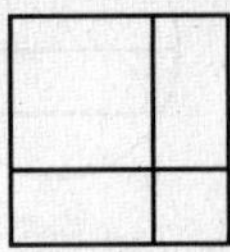

14. Look at the picture. What are the parts? Draw them.

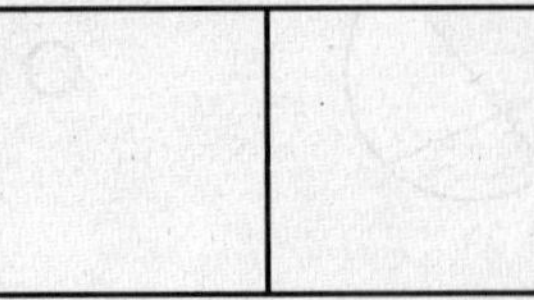

15. How many sides does a trapezoid have?

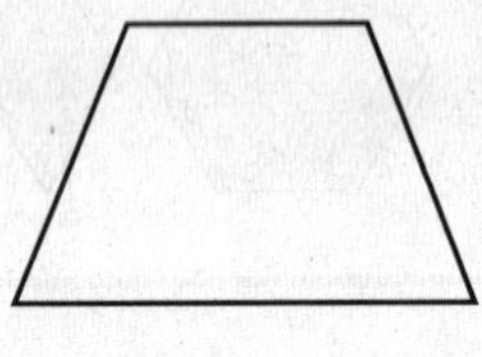

_______ sides

16. Mel drew a shape with 4 sides. Which shape did Mel draw? Circle it.

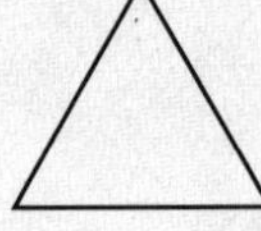

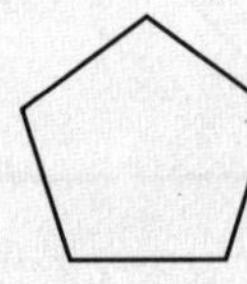

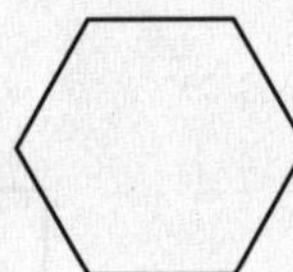

GO ON

17. Which shape shows halves? Circle it.

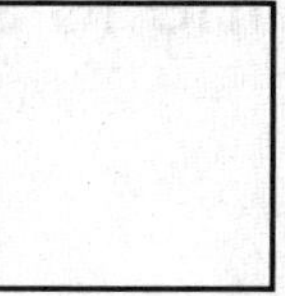
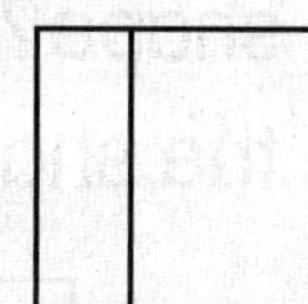
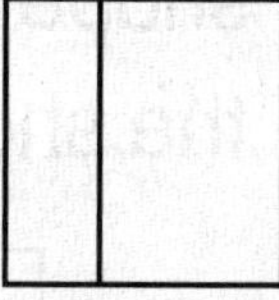
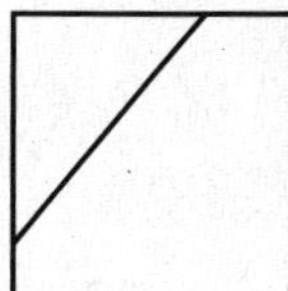
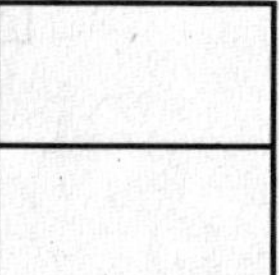

18. Draw to show how many △ make a .

19. Color the shape that shows fourths.

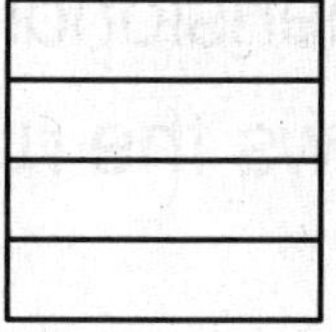
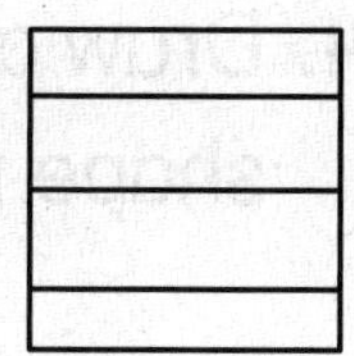
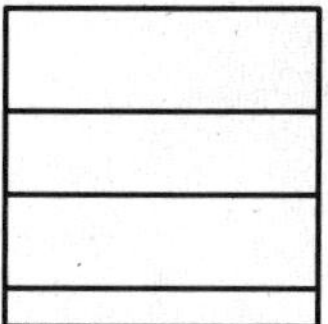
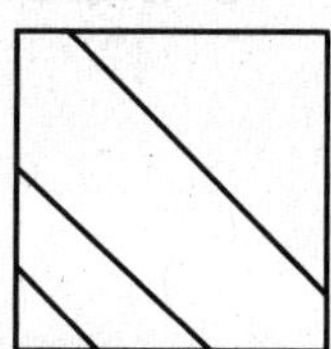

20. Which shape shows fourths? Circle it.

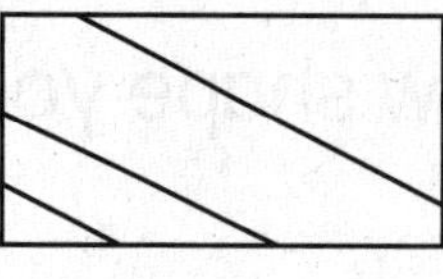
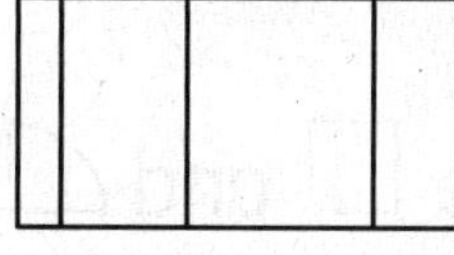
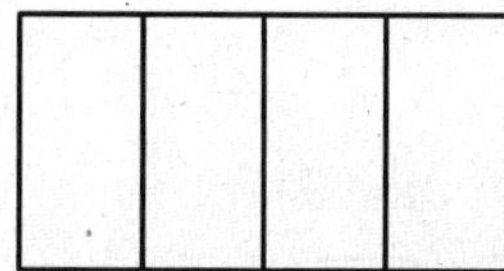
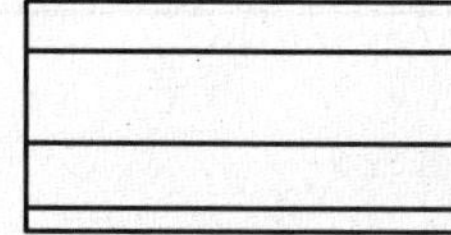

GO ON

21. Which two pattern blocks make this shape? Draw a line to show them.

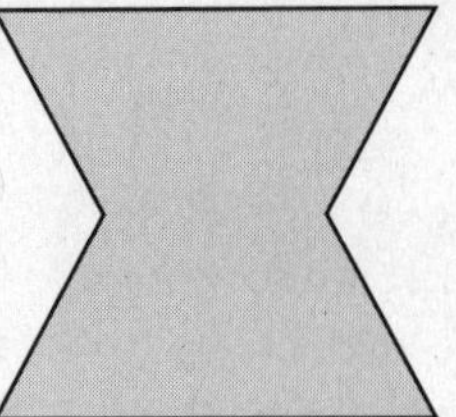

22. Which two shapes can combine to make this new shape? Draw a line to show the shapes.

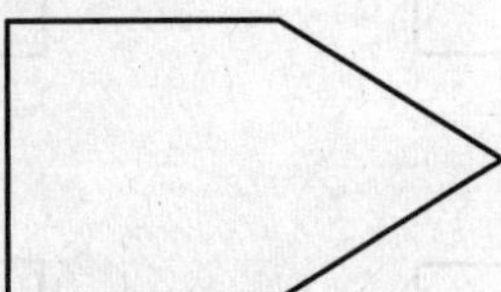

23. Use shapes to solve. Draw the new shape you could make.

Step 1

Combine □ and ◿ to make ◝.

Step 2

Then use ◝ and ◝.

24. Draw a two-dimensional shape that follows the rule.

6 sides and 6 vertices

Extended Constructed Response

25. Use pattern blocks to fill this shape.
Draw to show what you use.

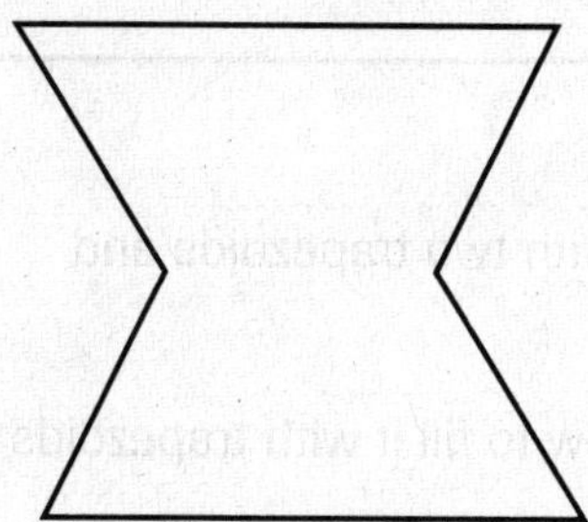

How many ⏢ do you use to fill the shape? ____

How many △ do you use to fill the shape? ____

Use numbers, pictures, or words to explain.

Extended Constructed Response

The Extended Constructed Response item is scored using the 3-point scoring rubric in the *Assessment Guide*. A child can receive partial credit for answers that are partially correct or partially completed.

Performance Indicators

For Problem 25, a child with a Level 2 paper:

_____ correctly demonstrates how to fill the shape with two trapezoids and six triangles.

_____ correctly draws lines on the shape to show how to fill it with trapezoids and triangles.

_____ shows work that is easy to follow and clearly supports the answers given.

Child's Name ______________________ Date ____________

Chapter 1 • Diagnostic Interview Assessment

Materials • two-color counters
• Dot Cards (1–10) (see *eTeacher Resources*)

Skill/Item	Assess
Explore Numbers 1 to 4 Show groups of 1, 2, 3, and 4 counters. Have the child tell how many there are in each group. Place a pile of Dot Cards facedown. Ask the child to choose a card and write the number it shows.	_____ tells how many in all _____ writes the number shown
Numbers 1 to 10 Choose a number from 1 to 10. Ask the child to draw a picture to show the number. Repeat for another card.	_____ draws a picture for a specified number
Numbers 0 to 10 Have the child write the numbers from 0 to 10. Choose three of the numbers and ask him or her to show the number with counters.	_____ writes the numbers from 0 to 10 _____ uses counters to show how many

For intervention options, see TE p. 10.

Child's Name ______________________ Date ____________

Chapter 2 • Diagnostic Interview Assessment

Materials • two-color counters
• connecting cubes

Skill/Item	Assess
Explore Numbers 1 to 4 Show random groups of 1, 2, 3, and 4 counters. Have the child point to the group that has 3 counters.	_____ identifies a group of 3
Numbers 1 to 10 Have the child use counters to show a group of 8 and a group of 5.	_____ identifies a group of 5 _____ identifies a group of 8
Use Pictures to Subtract Set out a row of 9 counters. Write 9 − 7 = _____. Have the child take counters away to show the subtraction and tell how many counters are left. Ask the child to connect 5 cubes. Write 5 − 2 = ______. Have the child show the subtraction using cubes and tell the difference.	_____ uses counters and connecting cubes to show subtraction _____ finds the differences

For intervention options, see TE p. 50.

Child's Name ______________________ Date __________

Chapter 3 • Diagnostic Interview Assessment

Materials • two-color counters
• red and blue connecting cubes
• Numeral Cards 0–7 (see *eTeacher Resources*)

Skill/Item	Assess
Model Addition Show 2 red cubes and 4 blue cubes. Ask the child to tell how many cubes there are in each group and how many total connecting cubes there are. Show the child Numeral Cards for 3 and 7. Ask the child to use cubes to make a set for each number. Then ask the child how many cubes there are altogether in the two groups.	_____ uses connecting cubes to identify how many in each group _____ uses connecting cubes to represent a given number _____ uses connecting cubes to identify how many in total
Use Symbols to Add Set out a group of 4 yellow counters and a group of 3 red counters. Have the child draw the counters, write an addition sentence to show joining these 2 groups, and find the sum.	_____ uses strategy of drawing a picture to show a number _____ uses a picture to represent an addition sentence _____ uses a picture to find the sum of an addition sentence
Add in Any Order Show a cube train: 3 blue cubes and 1 red cube. Next to it, show a cube train: 1 red cube and 3 blue cubes. Have the child write the addition sentence that represents each cube train. Ask the child to explain what is the same and different about their number sentences.	_____ uses connecting cubes to model addition with two addends _____ uses connecting cubes to model addition of two addends in a different order _____ writes the addition sentences represented by the cube models _____ describes how the number sentences are the same and different

For intervention options, see TE p. 94.

Child's Name ______________________________ Date ______________

Chapter 4 • Diagnostic Interview Assessment

Materials • two-color counters
• red connecting cubes
• Numeral Cards (0–7), sign cards (–, =) (see *eTeacher Resources*)

Skill/Item	Assess
Model Subtraction Set out a row of 6 counters. Ask the child to take away 2 counters and tell how many counters are left. Repeat using 5 counters, taking away 3 counters.	_____ uses counters to show "take away" _____ uses counters to show how many are left _____ identifies number of counters remaining
Use Symbols to Subtract Show 7 – 4 = _____. Have the child use connecting cubes to show the subtraction and find the difference. Have the child use the Numeral Cards and sign cards to show the number sentence and the difference.	_____ uses connecting cubes to show subtraction _____ uses connecting cubes to find the difference _____ uses Numeral Cards and sign cards to show the number sentence being modeled and the difference
Subtract All or Zero Show 2 – 2 = 0 and 2 – 0 = 2. Ask the child to point to the sentence that subtracts zero. Show 4 – 0 = 4 and 4 – 4 = 0. Ask the child to use cubes to model the number sentence that shows subtracting all.	_____ uses pictures to identify subtracting zero _____ uses counters to model subtracting all

For intervention options, see TE p. 150.

Child's Name ______________________ Date __________

Chapter 5 • Diagnostic Interview Assessment

Materials • red and blue connecting cubes
• number line to 10 (see eTeacher Resources)

Skill/Item	Assess
Add in Any Order Have the child join cube trains of 4 blue cubes and 2 red cubes to show how many in all. Repeat with cube trains of 2 red cubes and 4 blue cubes. Ask the child to describe what is the same and different about the two sets of cube trains.	_____ uses connecting cubes to join groups to show how many in all _____ adds in any order _____ describes how the 2 addition scenarios are the same and different
Count On Write 7 + 2 = _____. Set a red cube above each number 0–10 on the number line. Have the child start at 7 and count on with connecting cubes on the number line. Have the child write the sum to complete the number sentence.	_____ counts on using connecting cubes and the number line _____ writes the sum to complete an addition sentence
Count Back Write 10 − 3 = _____. Set a red cube above each number 0–10 on the number line. Have the child start at 10 and take away connecting cubes on the number line to show the subtraction. Have the child write the difference.	_____ counts back using connecting cubes and the number line _____ writes the difference to complete a subtraction sentence

For intervention options, see TE p. 182.

Child's Name ________________________ Date ____________

Chapter 6 • Diagnostic Interview Assessment

Materials • connecting cubes
• crayons
• prepared drawings

Skill/Item	Assess
Explore Numbers 6 to 9 Have the child use connecting cubes to show a group of 6 and a group of 9.	_____ identifies a group of 6 _____ identifies a group of 9
Count Groups to 20 Prepare a drawing to show groups of 10 squares, 13 triangles, 17 rectangles, and 20 circles. Ask the child to find a group of 13 shapes and circle it with a red crayon. Have the child write the number 13. Continue, using different color crayons for the groups of 10, 17, and 20.	_____ finds the group with a specified number of objects _____ writes the number of objects in a specified group
Make Groups of 10 Prepare a drawing that shows 7 flowers. Have the child draw more flowers to make a group showing 10 flowers total. Ask the child how many flowers were in the original drawing and how many they had to add to show 10 total.	_____ draws more objects to make a group of 10 objects _____ identifies the number of objects in a set and the number needed to increase the value of the set to 10

For intervention options, see TE p. 238.

Child's Name ______________________ Date ______________

Chapter 7 • Diagnostic Interview Assessment

Materials • red and blue connecting cubes
• two-color counters

Skill/Item	Assess
Model More Set out a group of 5 connecting cubes and a group of 3 connecting cubes. Have the child point to the group that has more. Set out a group of 6 counters. Ask the child to use counters to show a group with more.	_____ identifies the group with more _____ models a group with more objects than a given number
More, Fewer Set out a row of 8 blue cubes. Directly under, set a row of 4 red cubes. Ask "which row has more cubes?" Ask "which row has fewer cubes?"	_____ compares and identifies the group with more _____ compares and identifies the group with fewer
Draw Equal Groups Set out a row of 5 red cubes. Ask the child to make a group of blue cubes to show an equal number. Repeat with a group of 7 counters.	_____ makes a group to show an equal number

For intervention options, see TE p. 286.

Child's Name ______________________ Date ______________

Chapter 8 • Diagnostic Interview Assessment

Materials • two-color counters
• Workmat 8
• Hundred Chart (see *eTeacher Resources*)

Skill/Item	Assess
Add and Subtract Have the child use counters to show 3 + 2. Ask the child to name the sum of 3 + 2. Then have the child use the counters to show 5 – 2. Ask the child to name the difference for 5 – 2.	_____ uses counters to model addition _____ find the sum _____ uses counters to model subtraction _____ finds the difference
Count Groups to 20 Have the child draw counters on Workmat 8 to show 14. Have the child draw a circle around the group of ten and then write how many counters there are in all.	_____ identifies a group of 10 _____ counts a set of objects _____ write the number to show how many in all
Use a Hundred Chart to Count Display a Hundred Chart. Ask the child if they will say 20 when counting from 11 to 18. Repeat with more number sequences.	_____ counts using a hundred chart _____ identifies that they will not say 20 when counting from 11-18 _____ recognizes the order of numbers

For intervention options, see TE p. 314.

Child's Name ______________________ Date ______________

Chapter 9 • Diagnostic Interview Assessment

Materials • connecting cubes
• classroom objects (math book, pencil, crayon)

Skill/Item	Assess
Bigger and Smaller Show the child a connecting cube and a math book. Ask "which is bigger?" Ask the child to find an object in the classroom that is smaller than the math book.	_____ identifies the bigger object _____ identifies an object smaller than a given object
Compare Length Show the child a new pencil and a crayon. Ask "which is shorter?" Ask the child to find an object that is longer than the crayon.	_____ identifies the shorter object _____ identifies an object longer than a specified object
Numbers 1 to 10 Have the child say the counting sequence from 1 to 10 aloud as you write the numbers on the board. Make sure the child says one number for each number you write.	_____ recognizes the order of numbers _____ matches number name with numeral

For intervention options, see TE p. 366.

Child's Name ______________________ Date __________

Chapter 10 • Diagnostic Interview Assessment

Materials • two-color counters
• red and blue connecting cubes
• 1-inch Grid Paper (see *eTeacher Resources*)

Skill/Item	Assess
Make a Concrete Graph Have the child toss a handful of two-color counters on the table. Have the child sort the counters by color into two rows in the grid. Ask the child to find out how many counters there are of each color.	____ sorts counters by color into two rows on the grid ____ identifies how many counters there are of each color
More, Fewer Give the child a red 6-cube train and 8 loose blue connecting cubes. Have the child show *more* with the blue connecting cubes by making a 7- or 8-cube train and comparing it to the 6-cube train. Then have the child show *fewer* by making a cube train with 5 or fewer blue connecting cubes and comparing it to the 6-cube train.	____ uses connecting cubes to show *more* ____ uses connecting cubes to show *fewer*
Draw Equal Groups Display a row of 4 red counters. Have the child use yellow counters to show the same number as the number of red counters. Repeat the activity with 7 red counters.	____ uses counters to show equal groups

For intervention options, see TE p. 410.

Child's Name ______________________________ Date ______________

Chapter 11 • Diagnostic Interview Assessment

Materials • several short pencils and one long pencil
• models of three-dimensional shapes (sphere, cylinder, cube, cone, rectangular prism)

Skill/Item	Assess
Alike and Different Display one cylinder standing vertically on a flat surface, one cone positioned on its side, and one cone standing on its flat surface. Ask the child to identify the objects that are alike. Ask the child "which object is different? How do you know?"	_____ identifies objects that are alike _____ identifies an object that is different _____ describes how an object is different
Identify Three-Dimensional Shapes Display a sphere, cylinder, and cube. Ask the child to point to the cylinder. Repeat using other shapes.	_____ identifies the sphere _____ identifies the cylinder _____ identifies the cube _____ identifies other shapes
Sort by Size Display several short pencils and one long pencil. Ask the child to make two groups of pencils according to size.	_____ makes comparisons of longer and shorter objects _____ sorts items according to size

For intervention options, see TE p. 454.

Child's Name ______________________ Date ______________

Chapter 12 • Diagnostic Interview Assessment

Materials • two-dimensional shapes (see *eTeacher Resources*)

Skill/Item	Assess
Sort by Shape Provide a group of squares, triangles, and rectangles. Have the child put the shapes with 4 sides in one group and the shapes with 3 sides in another group.	_____ sorts two-dimensional shapes with 4 sides into a group _____ sorts two-dimensional shapes with 3 sides into a group
Sort Shapes Provide a group of circles and triangles. Ask the child to sort the shapes. Mix up the circles and triangles, and add squares and rectangles to the group. Ask the child to sort the shapes again. Ask the child to name each group of shapes.	_____ sorts circles, triangles, squares, and rectangles _____ identifies the groups into which the shapes have been sorted.
Identify Two-Dimensional Shapes Hold up a circle. Ask the child to name the shape. Repeat using the other shapes. Say the name of each two-dimensional shape. Have the child find the correct two-dimensional shape each time you say a shape name.	_____ identifies the circle _____ identifies the other two-dimensional shapes _____ identifies the shapes that match given shape names

For intervention options, see TE p. 482.

Child's Name ________________ Date ________

Performance Assessment • Chapters 1–5

Playing Games

The child performs tasks to show an understanding of the concepts, skills, and strategies covered for the Critical Area: developing understanding of addition, subtraction, and strategies for addition and subtraction within 20.

Task A  Tossing Bean Bags | Individual or pairs

Common Core State Standards: CC.1.OA.1, CC.1.OA.6, CC.1.OA.8

Objective: To assess the child's understanding of doubles and the ability to record doubles addition sentences

---

Task B  The Lost Checkers | Individual or pairs

Common Core State Standards: CC.1.OA.1, CC.1.OA.6, CC.1.OA.8

Objective: To assess the child's ability to model a subtraction situation and write a subtraction sentence

Materials: counters

Task C  Soccer Balls | Individual or pairs

Common Core State Standards: CC.1.OA.1, CC.1.OA.3, CC.1.OA.6

Objective: To assess the child's ability to write different addition sentences for ways to make 10

Task D  Number Cube Toss | Individual or pairs

Common Core State Standards: CC.1.OA.1, CC.1.OA.2, CC.1.OA.3, CC.1.OA.6

Objective: To assess the child's ability to add three one-digit numbers

Child's Name ______________________ Date __________

Performance Assessment • Chapters 1–5

Playing Games

Task	Performance Indicators	Score (One score per task)
A	_____ writes 2 different doubles facts _____ identifies a sum less than 18 _____ identifies a sum less than 18 and greater than 6	2 1 0
B	_____ draws a picture to show the story and writes a corresponding subtraction sentence _____ chooses 12 as the minuend _____ chooses a difference less than 8	2 1 0
C	_____ writes 6 different addition sentences _____ chooses 10 as the sum _____ does not include 4 + 6 = 10	2 1 0
D	_____ solves an addition problem with 3 addends _____ recognizes that no addend is greater than 6 _____ chooses a sum of 14	2 1 0
		Total Score _____ / 8

See p. AGxi for a 3-point scoring rubric.

Name ___________________________

Tossing Bean Bags

Glen and Brad are tossing beanbags.

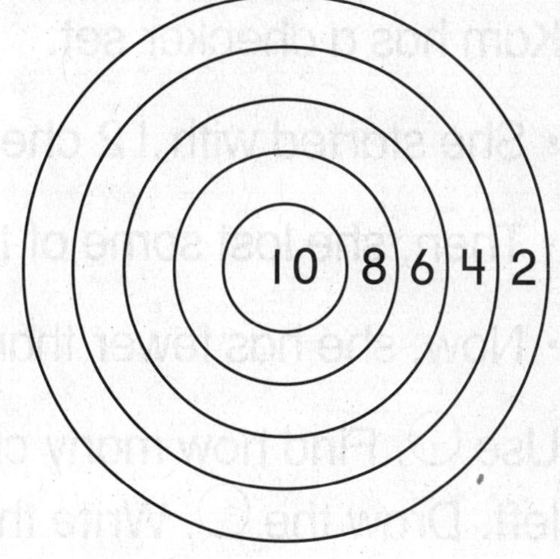

- Glen tosses two beanbags. They both land on the same number. His score is less than 18.

Write a doubles fact to show a score that Glen could get.

- Brad tosses two beanbags. They both land on the same number.
- Brad's score is greater than 6 and less than Glen's score.

Write a doubles fact to show a score that Brad could get.

Show your work.

Glen ___________________ Brad ___________________

Name ____

The Lost Checkers

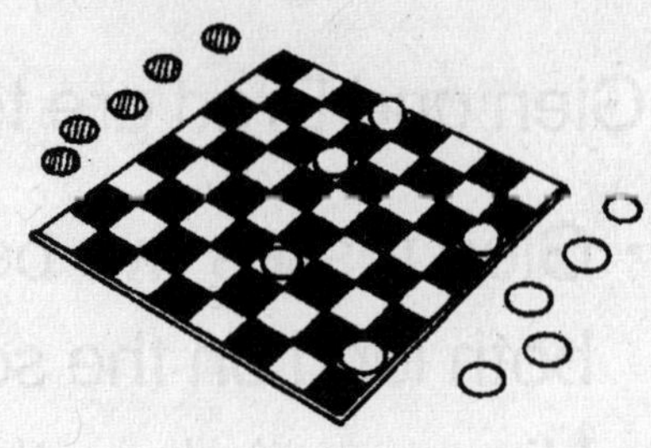

Kam has a checker set.

- She started with 12 checkers.
- Then, she lost some of them.
- Now, she has fewer than 8 checkers left.

Use ◯. Find how many checkers Kam could have left. Draw the ◯. Write the subtraction sentence.

Show your work.

Name ______________________________

Soccer Balls

Coach Adam puts 10 soccer balls on two shelves.

- He puts 4 soccer balls on the top shelf.
- He puts 6 soccer balls on the bottom shelf.
- Then he adds to make sure there are 10 soccer balls in all. $4 + 6 = 10$

Think of six other ways Coach Adam can put 10 soccer balls on the two shelves. Write an addition sentence for each way. You can draw pictures to help you.

Show your work.

1.

2.

3.

4.

5.

6.

Name ______________________________

Number Cube Toss

Jenny tosses a number cube three times. She adds the numbers tossed. Then she moves that number of spaces on a game board.

- The number cube has numbers 1 to 6.
- Jenny tosses the number cube three times.
- She moves a total of 14 spaces.

Write three numbers Jenny could have tossed. Add to make sure the sum is correct.

Show your work.

Child's Name ______________________ Date __________

Performance Assessment • Chapters 6–8

Number Puzzles

The child performs tasks to show an understanding of the concepts, skills, and strategies covered for the Critical Area: developing understanding of whole number relationships and place value, including grouping in tens and ones.

Task A  What Number Did You Say? | Individual or pairs

Common Core State Standard: CC.1.NBT.1

Objective: To assess the child's ability to count and write a range of numbers within 120

Task B  Number Show | Individual or pairs

Common Core State Standard: CC.1.NBT.2

Objective: To assess the child's understanding of a two-digit number as different amounts of tens and ones

---

Task C  What Is the Score? | Individual or pairs

Common Core State Standard: CC.1.NBT.3

Objective: To assess the child's ability to compare two-digit numbers and use the <, >, and = symbols

---

Task D  Page Number Puzzle | Individual or pairs

Common Core State Standards: CC.1.NBT.2, CC.1.NBT.5

Objective: To assess the child's ability to mentally add 10 to two-digit numbers

Child's Name _______________________ Date _______________

Performance Assessment • Chapters 6–8

Number Puzzles

Task	Performance Indicators	Score (One score per task)
A	_____ chooses 3 numbers excluding 98 to 112 _____ chooses 3 numbers from 98 to 112 _____ correctly writes numbers in order from 98 to 112	2 1 0
B	_____ chooses a two-digit number _____ shows 3 different ways to represent the two-digit number _____ draws or records the correct number of tens and ones	2 1 0
C	_____ writes three two-digit scores, each with 8 as the tens digit _____ includes 2 scores that match and one score that is greater than the matching scores _____ uses symbols to compare the scores in different ways	2 1 0
D	_____ writes a two-digit number with 2 as the ones digit _____ chooses any tens digit from 2 to 7 _____ writes a reasonable explanation of the mental math strategy of adding 10	2 1 0
		Total Score _______ / 8

See p. AGxi for a 3-point scoring rubric.

Name ______________________

What Number Did You Say?

Jeremy counts aloud from 98 to 112.

What are three numbers Jeremy should **not** say?

__________ __________ __________

What are three numbers Jeremy should say?

__________ __________ __________

Write all the numbers from 98 to 112.
Check your answers.

Show your work.

Number Show

Ken shows 34 in different ways.

3 tens 4 ones

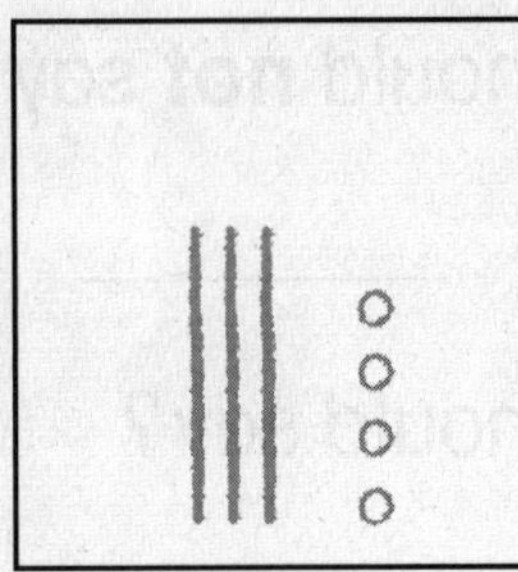

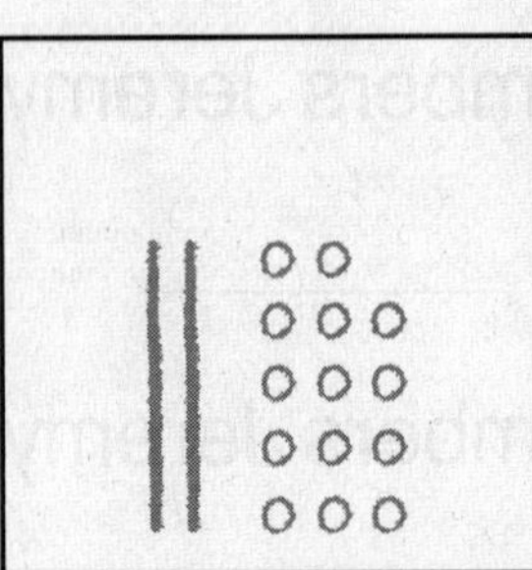

Choose a different two-digit number. ________

How could you show the number in three different ways?

Show your work.

Name ______________________________

What Is the Score?

Liz, Jose, and Brad play a video game. The scores are between 80 and 90 points.

- Brad's score is greater than Liz's score.
- Liz and Jose have the same score.

Write three scores that Brad, Liz, and Jose could have.

Brad ________ Liz ________ Jose ________

Use $<$, $>$, and $=$ to show 3 ways to compare the scores.

Show your work.

____ ◯ ____

____ ◯ ____

____ ◯ ____

Name ______________________________

Page Number Puzzle

Karen is reading a book.

- The book has 80 pages.
- On the first day, Karen stopped reading on page 12.
- Each day she reads 10 more pages.

On what page could Karen be at the end of a day?

Use mental math to solve the problem. Explain.

Show your work.

Child's Name ______________________ Date ____________

Performance Assessment • Chapters 9–10

Helping Out

The child performs tasks to show an understanding of the concepts, skills, and strategies covered for the Critical Area: developing understanding of linear measurement and measuring lengths as iterating length units.

Task A  Share with Jen | Individual or pairs

Common Core State Standard: CC.1.MD.1

Objective: To assess the child's understanding of comparing lengths indirectly by comparing to a third object

Materials: pencil

Task B  Heart to Heart | Individual or pairs

Common Core State Standard: CC.1.MD.2

Objective: To assess the child's ability to accurately measure with a nonstandard unit and record the measurement

Materials: tiles, blue crayon, red crayon

Task C  Fix the List | Individual or pairs

Common Core State Standard: CC.1.MD.3

Objective: To assess the child's ability to write and tell time to the hour and half hour

---

Task D  Juicy Tallies | Individual or pairs

Common Core State Standard: CC.1.MD.4

Objective: To assess the child's ability to represent and interpret data on a tally chart

Child's Name _______________________ Date ___________

Performance Assessment • Chapters 9–10

Helping Out

Task	Performance Indicators	Score (One score per task)
A	_____ draws a blue pencil that is shorter than the given pencil _____ draws a red pencil that is longer than the given pencil _____ writes a reasonable explanation	2 1 0
B	_____ traces and measures a line _____ records the measurement of the red and blue lines _____ writes a reasonable explanation of how to measure a line with tiles	2 1 0
C	_____ writes times that make sense _____ draws the hour hand shorter than the minute hand _____ positions the clock hands correctly for time to the hour and half hour	2 1 0
D	_____ chooses appropriate numbers for each juice _____ accurately completes the tally chart _____ accurately completes statements about the data	2 1 0
		Total Score _____ / 8

See p. AGxi for a 3-point scoring rubric.

Name ___

Share with Jen

Jen has three pencils to share.

- The pencils are different lengths.
- The blue pencil is shorter than the gray pencil.
- The red pencil is longer than the gray pencil.

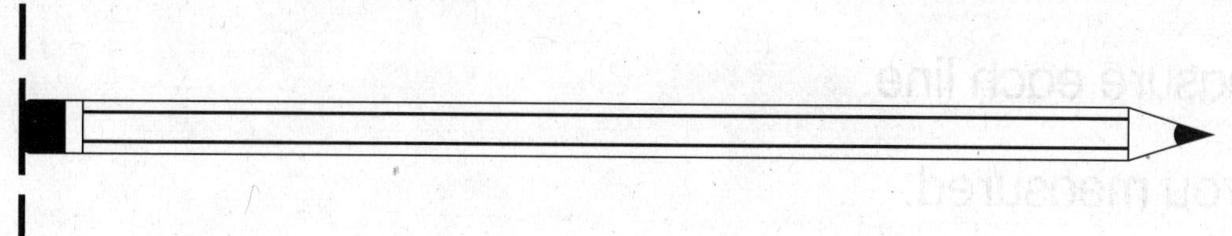

Draw the blue pencil.
Draw the red pencil.
Use words to explain how you ordered the pencils.

Show your work.

Name ____________________

Heart to Heart

Help Kate measure between the hearts.

- Use a red crayon. Trace a line between any 2 hearts.
- Use a blue crayon. Trace another line between 2 different hearts.

Use ■ to measure each line.

Explain how you measured.

Show your work.

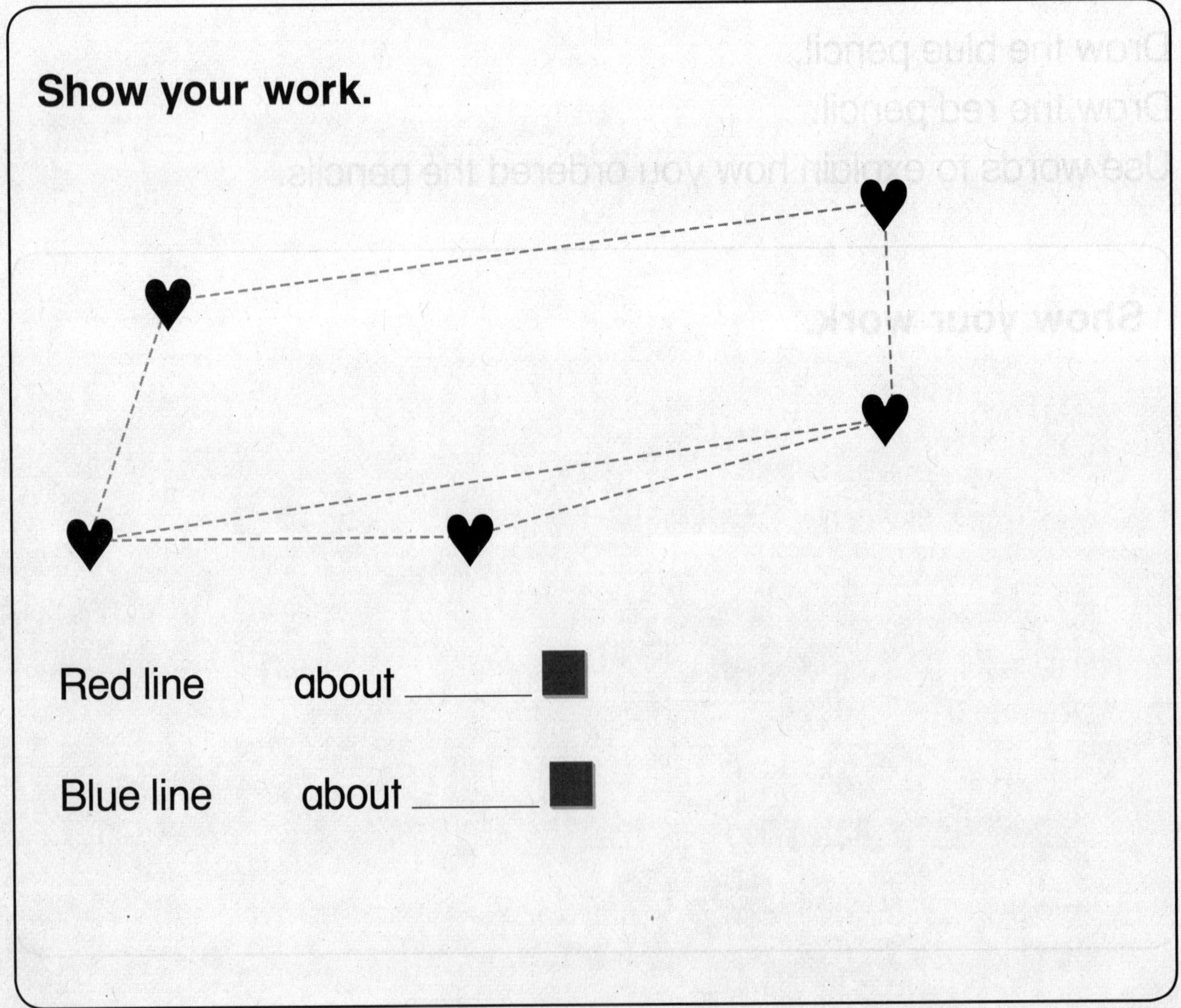

Red line about ______ ■

Blue line about ______ ■

Name ____________________

Fix the List

Dan makes a list of things he does Saturday afternoon.

Help Dan complete his list.

Activities	Time
Lunch	____ : 30
Chores	____ : 00
Play	____ : 30
Read	____ : 00

- Complete each time. Use times that make sense.
- Draw the hour hand and minute hand to show each time.

Show your work.

12 11 1 10 2 9 3 8 4 7 5 6
Lunch

12 11 1 10 2 9 3 8 4 7 5 6
Chores

12 11 1 10 2 9 3 8 4 7 5 6
Play

12 11 1 10 2 9 3 8 4 7 5 6
Read

Name ______________________

Juicy Tallies

Help Gina make a tally chart. First write a number for each kind of juice. →

Favorite Juices
____ orange
____ apple
____ grape

• Write a number from 5 to 10 for each juice.

• Write a different number for each juice.

• Then complete the tally chart.

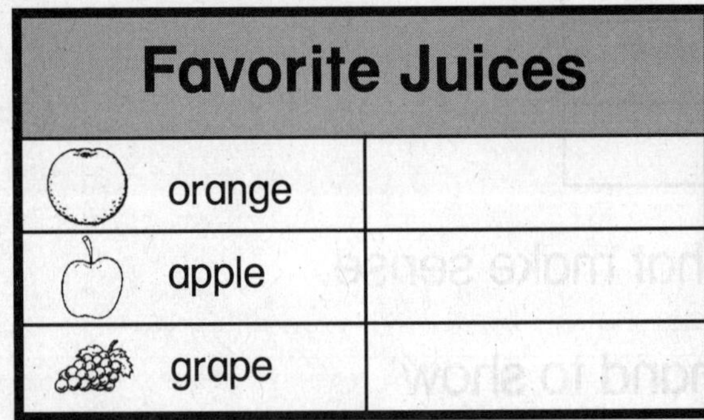

Favorite Juices	
orange	
apple	
grape	

Use the tally chart to complete each sentence.

1. ______ children chose orange juice.

2. Most children chose ______.

3. Fewer children chose ______ than ______.

Child's Name ______________________ Date ____________

Performance Assessment • Chapters 11–12

Getting in Shape

The child performs tasks to show an understanding of the concepts, skills, and strategies covered for the Critical Area: reasoning about attributes of, and composing and decomposing geometric shapes.

Task A  Shape Designs | Individual or pairs

Common Core State Standard: CC.1.G.1

Objective: To assess the child's ability to identify attributes of three-dimensional shapes, in particular the two-dimensional shapes that make up their flat surfaces

Materials: three-dimensional shapes

Task B  Build the Blocks | Individual or pairs

Common Core State Standard: CC.1.G.2

Objective: To assess the child's ability to create a composite shape and compose new shapes from the composite shape

Materials: three-dimensional shapes

Task C  Working Out | Individual or pairs

Common Core State Standard: CC.1.G.3

Objective: To assess the child's understanding of the relationship between the number of equal shares and their size

---

Task D  Sorting Shapes | Individual or pairs

Common Core State Standard: CC.1.G.1

Objective: To assess the child's ability to distinguish defining attributes and draw shapes that possess those attributes

Child's Name ______________________________ Date ______________

Performance Assessment • Chapters 11–12

Getting in Shape

Task	Performance Indicators	Score (One score per task)
A	_____ identifies a three-dimensional shape with a circular flat surface (cone or cylinder) _____ identifies a three-dimensional shape with a square flat surface (cube or rectangular prism) _____ creates a picture from the flat surfaces of three-dimensional shapes and identifies the three-dimensional shape(s)	2 1 0
B	_____ builds two copies of the composite shape in the illustration _____ uses the composite shapes to build a new shape _____ draws a picture that resembles the new shape	2 1 0
C	_____ illustrates halves as two equal parts _____ illustrates fourths as four equal parts _____ demonstrates understanding that a fourth of a shape is smaller than a half of the same shape	2 1 0
D	_____ correctly identifies a sorting rule for the given group of shapes _____ draws a group of shapes with different attributes than the given group of shapes _____ writes a sorting rule based on the attributes of the shapes drawn	2 1 0
		Total Score _______ / 8

See p. AGxi for a 3-point scoring rubric.

Name ___________________________

Shape Designs

Dee traces the flat surfaces of three-dimensional shapes.

- She makes this picture.
- She uses 2 different three-dimensional shapes.

What three-dimensional shapes did she trace?

____

____

Use three-dimensional shapes. Trace around them to draw a different picture Dee could make. Tell how to make it.

Show your work.

Name ____________________

Build the Blocks

Jenny likes to build with blocks.

- She puts two blocks together to build this shape.
- She makes another shape just like this one.
- Then she puts the two shapes together.

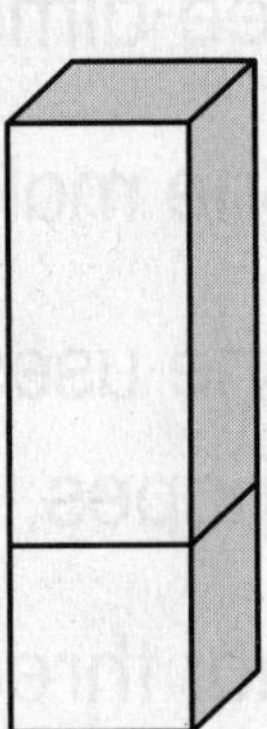

Use three-dimensional shapes. Build a new shape Jenny could make. Draw the new shape.

Show your work.

Name ________________

Working Out

Adam and Ben played soccer.

Now Adam is hungry!

- Adam wants a granola bar.
- He wants to share the bar with Ben.
- Adam asks if Ben wants a fourth or a half of the granola bar.

Does Ben choose a fourth or a half? Why? Draw to show the choices. Use the drawings to explain your answer.

Show your work.

Name ______________________________

Sorting Shapes

Reggie has some shapes.

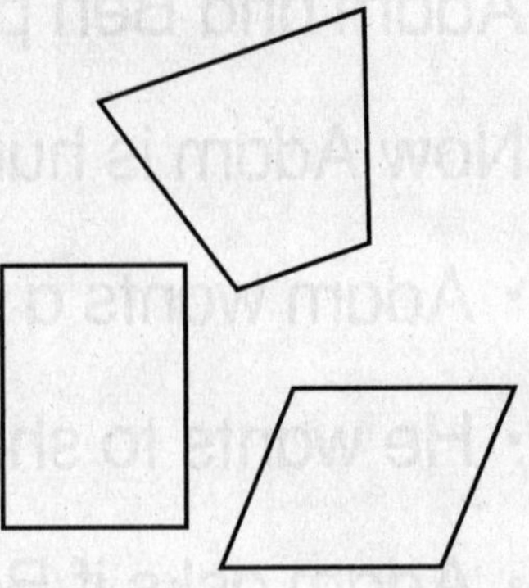

- He wants to sort them into 2 different groups.
- First Reggie makes this group of shapes.

What is the sorting rule for Reggie's group?

____

Draw another group of shapes that Reggie could make. Write the sorting rule.

Show your work.

Name ______________________________

Choose the correct answer.

1. What does the 2 in 352 mean?

- ○ 2 hundreds
- ○ 2 tens
- ○ 2 ones
- ○ 2 zeroes

2. There are 17 children at the playground. 2 more children join them. How many children are there now?

$$\begin{array}{r} 17 \\ +\ 2 \\ \hline \end{array}$$

- ○ 19 children
- ○ 18 children
- ○ 16 children
- ○ 15 children

3. What number does the model show?

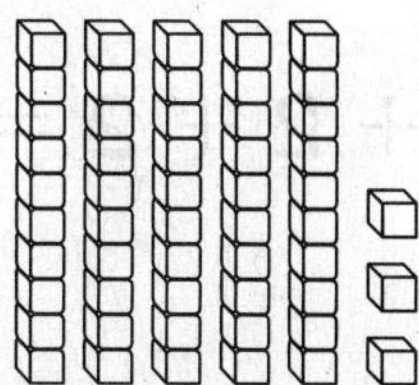

- ○ 30 + 5
- ○ 50 + 3
- ○ 50 + 0
- ○ 60 + 3

4. Ben has 4 star stickers, 5 balloon stickers, and 2 flower stickers. How many stickers does he have in all?

- ○ 12 stickers
- ○ 9 stickers
- ○ 11 stickers
- ○ 7 stickers

GO ON

5. What number completes the table?

Add 5	
5	10
6	11
7	12
8	?

○ 15 ○ 10

○ 13 ○ 5

6. There are 45 cars in the large parking lot. There are 21 cars in the small parking lot. How many cars are in both lots?

$$\begin{array}{r} 45 \\ +\ 21 \\ \hline \end{array}$$

○ 76 ○ 66

○ 68 ○ 64

7. What symbol correctly compares the numbers?

182 ◯ 192

○ >

○ +

○ =

○ <

8. Koto wrapped 3 presents. She put 2 bows on each present. How many bows did she use?

$$2 + 2 + 2 = ?$$

○ 8

○ 6

○ 4

○ 2

GO ON

9. What number completes the table?

Add 6	
9	15
7	13
5	?
3	9

○ 8 ○ 10

○ 9 ○ 11

10. Christy's address is 495 West Street. What does the 4 in 495 mean?

○ 4 hundreds

○ 4 tens

○ 4 ones

○ 4 zeros

11. Which is a way to model the problem?

Molly has 3 sisters. She wants to give 2 books to each of her sisters. How many books does she need?

○ 2 groups of 2 books

○ 2 groups of 3 books

○ 3 groups of 2 books

○ 3 groups of 3 books

12. What number completes the table?

Subtract 8	
12	4
14	6
16	?
17	9

○ 5 ○ 7

○ 6 ○ 8

GO ON

13. There are 3 children on the swings, 9 children on the monkey bars, and 1 child on the slide. How many children are there in all?

○ 10

○ 11

○ 12

○ 13

14. Kassidy made a table.

Subtract 3	
9	6
10	7
?	8
12	9

What number completes the table?

○ 15 ○ 13

○ 11 ○ 14

15. Kara has 16 red balloons and 12 green balloons. How many balloons does she have in all?

$$\begin{array}{r} 16 \\ +\ 12 \\ \hline \end{array}$$

○ 28

○ 18

○ 16

○ 4

16. Max makes 5 gift bags. He puts 3 pencils in each bag. How many pencils does he use?

$3 + 3 + 3 + 3 + 3 = ?$

○ 9

○ 15

○ 12

○ 18

GO ON

Name ________________________________

17. Jason uses tens and ones to show a number.

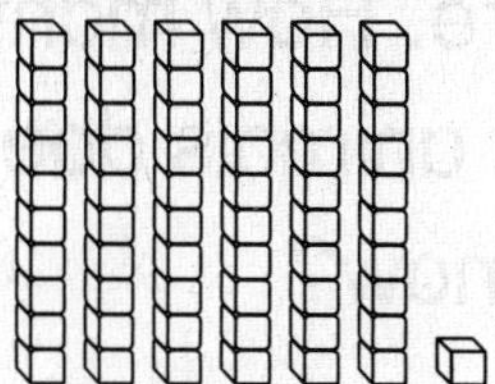

What number does Jason show?

○ 16 ○ 61

○ 51 ○ 65

18. Which is a way to model the problem?

Mrs. Lee makes 4 lunches. She puts 2 plums in each lunch. How many plums does she use in all?

○ 2 groups of 4 plums

○ 4 groups of 2 plums

○ 4 groups of 4 plums

○ 6 groups of 2 plums

19. What number completes the table?

Subtract 6	
7	1
9	?
11	5
13	7

○ 3 ○ 6

○ 8 ○ 12

20. Mr. Lowe worked 42 hours one week. He worked 36 hours the next week. How many hours did he work in all?

$$\begin{array}{r} 42 \\ +\ 36 \\ \hline \end{array}$$

○ 78 hours ○ 68 hours

○ 75 hours ○ 65 hours

GO ON

21. Which is a way to write the number?

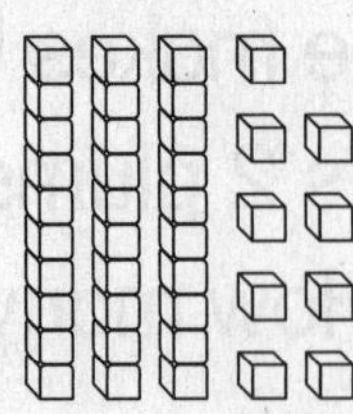

- ○ 20 + 5
- ○ 20 + 9
- ○ 30 + 5
- ○ 30 + 9

22. David has 23 books about animals. He gets 4 more. How many books about animals does he have now?

- ○ 29
- ○ 28
- ○ 27
- ○ 25

23. Which is a rule for the table?

?	
9	13
8	12
7	11
6	10

- ○ Add 4
- ○ Add 3
- ○ Subtract 5
- ○ Subtract 3

24. Jon compares 186 and 194. Which way to compare is correct?

- ○ 186 > 194
- ○ 194 < 186
- ○ 194 = 186
- ○ 194 > 186

STOP

Name ______________________________

Choose the correct answer.

1. Abby read a book with 124 pages. What does the 1 in 124 mean?

- ○ 1 hundred
- ○ 1 ten
- ○ 1 one
- ○ 1 zero

2. There are 14 children at the park. 4 more children join them. How many children are at the park now?

$$\begin{array}{r} 14 \\ +\ 4 \\ \hline \end{array}$$

- ○ 19
- ○ 18
- ○ 15
- ○ 14

3. What number does the model show?

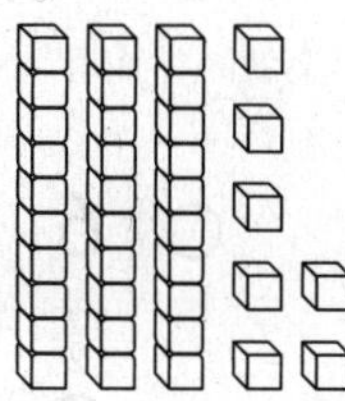

- ○ 70 + 3
- ○ 30 + 8
- ○ 30 + 9
- ○ 30 + 7

4. Jason has 5 fish, 5 turtles, and 1 dog. How many pets does Jason have in all?

- ○ 15
- ○ 11
- ○ 13
- ○ 10

GO ON

5. What number completes the table?

Add 4	
6	10
8	12
10	14
12	?

○ 18 ○ 14

○ 16 ○ 4

6. Mrs. Burns sold 16 pies in the morning. She sold 32 pies in the afternoon. How many pies did she sell in all?

$$\begin{array}{r} 16 \\ +\ 32 \\ \hline \end{array}$$

○ 58 ○ 48

○ 49 ○ 44

7. What symbol correctly compares the numbers?

506 ○ 560

○ >

○ +

○ =

○ <

8. Jamal has 3 red fish, 3 blue fish, and 3 green fish. How many fish does he have altogether?

$3 + 3 + 3 = ?$

○ 9 ○ 6

○ 8 ○ 3

GO ON

Name ____________________

9. What number completes the table?

Add 2	
5	?
6	8
7	9
8	10

- ○ 7
- ○ 5
- ○ 6
- ○ 4

10. The library has 350 books about animals. What does the 5 mean in 350?

- ○ 5 hundreds
- ○ 5 tens
- ○ 5 ones
- ○ 5 zeros

11. Which is a way to model the problem?

Sean plays with 3 friends. He wants to give each friend 4 stickers. How many stickers does he need?

- ○ 2 groups of 3 stickers
- ○ 3 groups of 2 stickers
- ○ 3 groups of 4 stickers
- ○ 4 groups of 3 stickers

12. What number completes the table?

Subtract 5	
12	7
11	6
10	?
9	4

- ○ 2
- ○ 4
- ○ 3
- ○ 5

GO ON

Name ______________________________

Write the correct answer.

13. Mrs. Abbot sells 6 yellow shirts, 2 red shirts, and 3 black shirts. How many shirts does she sell in all?

____ + ____ + ____ = ____

______ shirts

14. Claire made a table. What number completes the table?

Subtract 4	
13	9
12	8
11	____
10	6

15. Sara has 15 large photos and 13 small photos. How many photos does she have in all?

$$\begin{array}{r} 15 \\ +\ 13 \\ \hline \end{array}$$

______ photos

16. Jenny makes 3 fruit baskets. She puts 2 bananas in each basket. How many bananas does she use?

____ + ____ + ____ = ____

______ bananas

GO ON

Name ______________________________

17. Sam uses tens and ones to show a number.

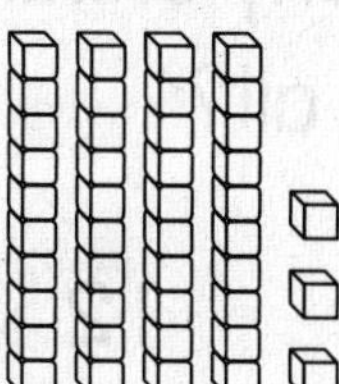

What number does the model show?

_____ tens _____ ones

18. Which is a way to model the problem?

Morgan has 3 boxes. She puts 4 crayons in each box. How many crayons are there in all?

_____ groups of _____ crayons

19. Emma made this table. What number completes the table?

Subtract 3	
12	9
10	7
8	?
6	3

_____

20. Ray has 34 pennies and 34 dimes. How many coins does Ray have in all?

$$\begin{array}{r} 34 \\ +\ 34 \\ \hline \end{array}$$

_____ coins

GO ON

21. How many tens and ones does the model show?

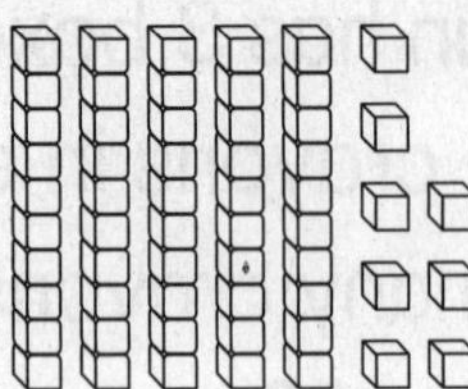

_____ tens _____ ones

22. There are 12 boys in the class. There are 5 girls. How many children are there in all?

$$\begin{array}{r} 12 \\ +\ 5 \\ \hline \end{array}$$

_____ children

23. What is a rule for the table?

?	
3	6
6	9
9	12
12	15

_____

24. Compare 130 and 125. Write >, <, or =.

130 ◯ 125

GO ON

Name ______________________________

Extended Constructed Response

25. Evie makes 6 muffins. She puts 2 strawberries on the top of each muffin. How many strawberries does she use?

Draw a picture to show the story.

Explain how you knew what to draw.

____

____

How many strawberries does she use?

________ strawberries

Name ____________________

Extended Constructed Response

The Extended Constructed Response item is scored using the 3-point scoring rubric in the *Assessment Guide.* A child can receive partial credit for answers that are partially correct or partially completed.

Performance Indicators

For Problem 25, a child with a Level 2 paper:

_____ correctly draws a picture to show equal groups.

_____ understands the difference between number of groups and number in each group.

_____ correctly finds the total number.

_____ shows work that is easy to follow and clearly supports the answers given.

Choose the correct answer.

1. Use the paper clip ruler to measure.

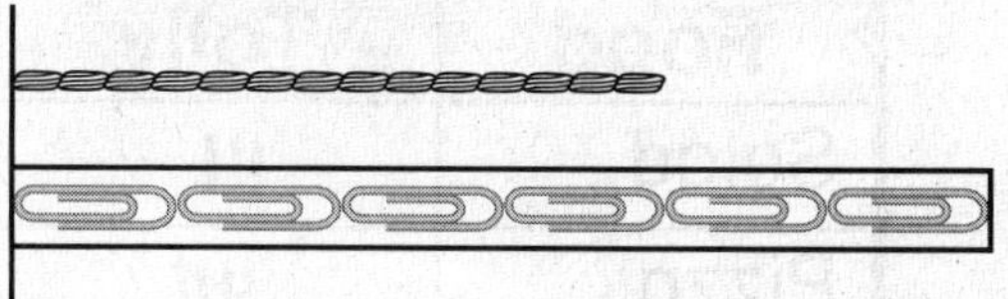

How long is the yarn?

- ○ about 6
- ○ about 5
- ○ about 4
- ○ about 3

2. The clock shows when Macy wakes up.

What time is it?

- ○ 7:00
- ○ 8:00
- ○ 7:30
- ○ 12:00

3. Which shape shows 2 equal shares?

○ 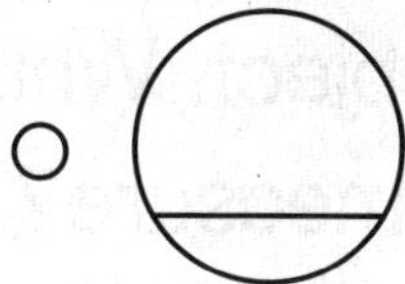

○ 

○ 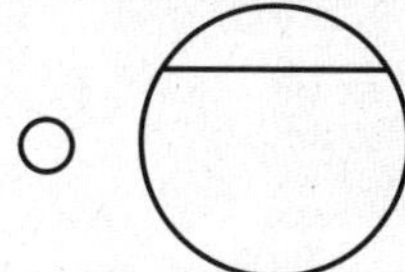

○ 

4. Ellen uses [paper clip] to measure the length of an object. Which object did she measure?

- ○ a bed
- ○ a stapler
- ○ a door
- ○ a printer

GO ON

Name ____________________

5. Which yarn is the **longest**?

- ○
- ○
- ○
- ○

6. Use the tally chart to answer the question.

Favorite Lunches	
Food	**Tally**
Salad	III
Pizza	~~IIII~~
Sandwich	II

How many children chose pizza?

○ 10 ○ 3

○ 5 ○ 2

7. Use the paper clip ruler to measure.

How long is the stick?

- ○ about 2 paper clips
- ○ about 3 paper clips
- ○ about 4 paper clips
- ○ about 5 paper clips

8. Parker uses a pencil to measure an object. Which object did he measure?

- ○ an eraser
- ○ a glue stick
- ○ a desk
- ○ a marker

GO ON

9. Use the picture graph to answer the question.

Favorite Fruits						
apple	웃	웃	웃	웃		
orange	웃	웃	웃	웃	웃	웃

Each 웃 stands for 1 child.

How many children chose oranges?

○ 3 ○ 5

○ 4 ○ 6

10. Use the bar graph to answer the question.

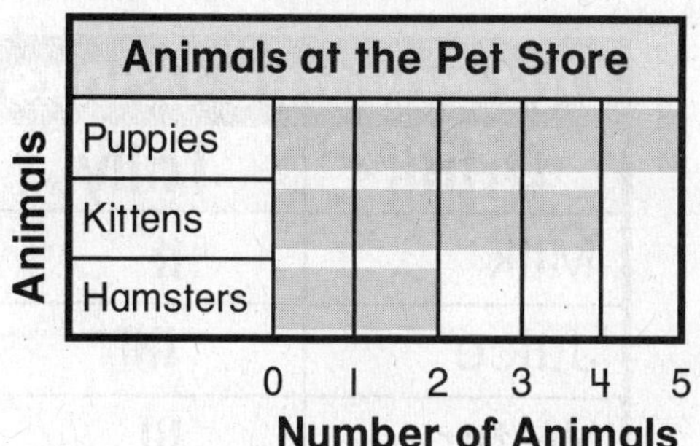

How many more puppies than kittens are there?

○ 1 more ○ 3 more

○ 2 more ○ 4 more

11. Which shape has 3 sides?

○ 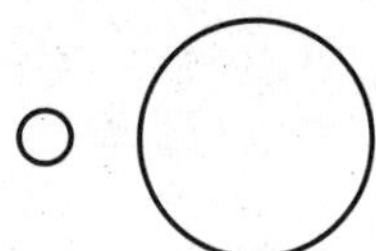

○ 

○ 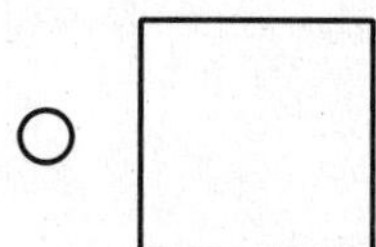

○ 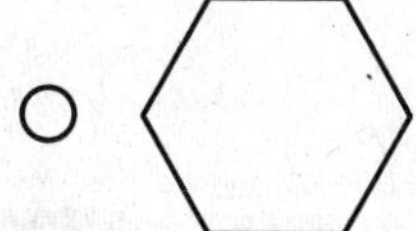

12. The clock shows when Zoe gets home.

What time is it?

○ 3:00 ○ 4:00

○ 3:30 ○ 4:30

GO ON

Name ______________________________

13. Use the tally chart to answer the question.

Our Favorite Drinks	
Drink	**Tally**
Milk	||
Juice	𝍸
Water	|||

How many children chose juice?

○ 3 ○ 5

○ 4 ○ 6

14. Which shape has 4 vertices?

○  

○ 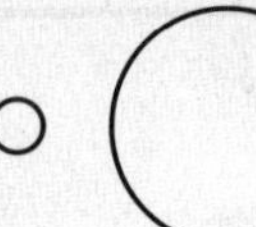

○ 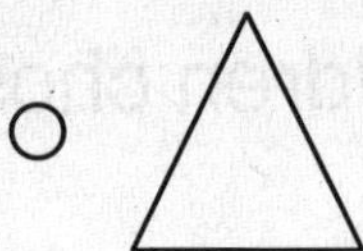

○ 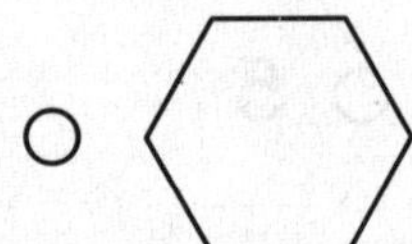

15. Which string is the **shortest**?

○ 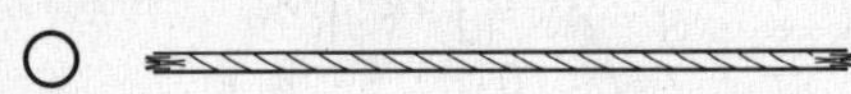

○ 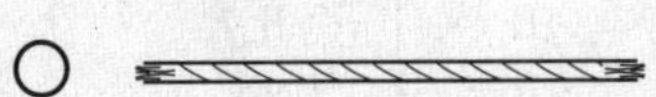

○ 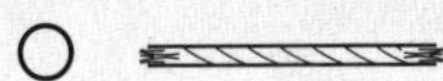

○ 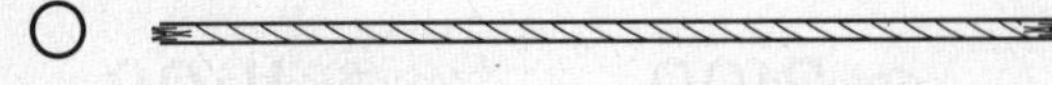

16. Which shape shows 4 equal shares?

○ 

○ 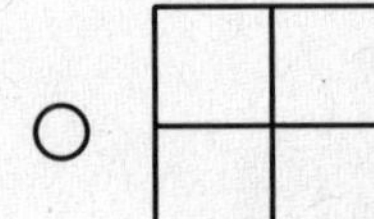

○ 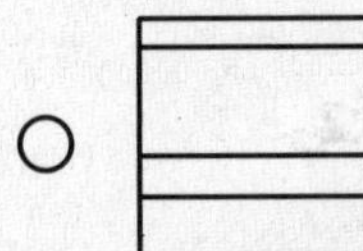

○ 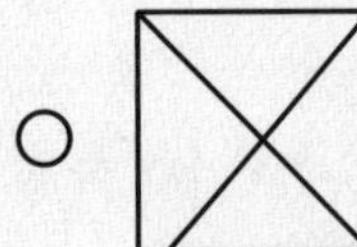

GO ON

Name ______________________________

17. Use the picture graph to answer the question.

Favorite Zoo Animals							
lion	웃	웃	웃	웃	웃		
tiger	웃	웃	웃				
bear	웃	웃	웃	웃	웃	웃	웃

Each 웃 stands for 1 child.

What animal did the most children choose?

○ lion ○ bear

○ tiger ○ elephant

18. Use the bar graph to answer the question.

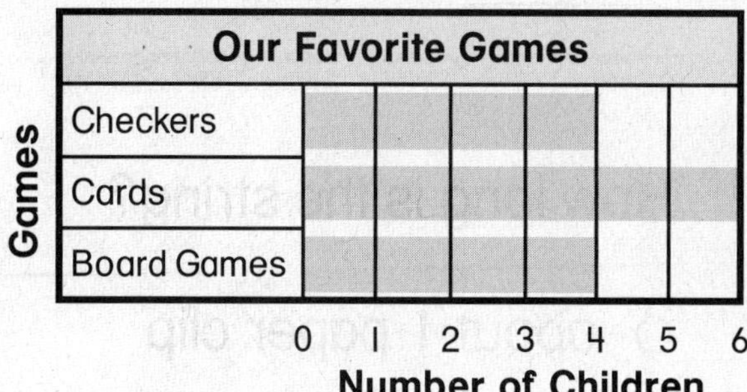

How many children chose cards?

○ 3 ○ 5

○ 4 ○ 6

19. Deakin uses a [unit cube] to measure an object. Which object did he measure?

○ a stove

○ a table

○ a shoe

○ a bookcase

20. The clock shows when Jasmine eats lunch.

What time is it?

○ 6:00 ○ 10:00

○ 8:00 ○ 12:00

GO ON

21. Use the paper clip ruler to measure.

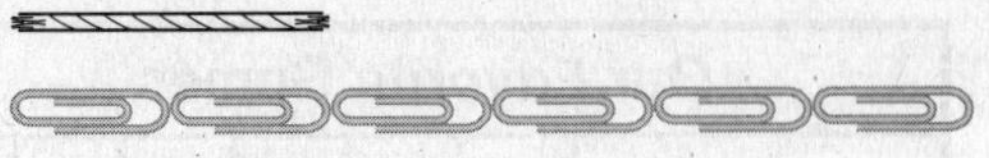

How long is the string?

- ○ about 1 paper clip
- ○ about 2 paper clips
- ○ about 4 paper clips
- ○ about 5 paper clips

22. Which shape has 6 vertices?

○ 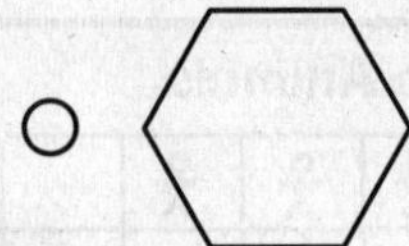

○ 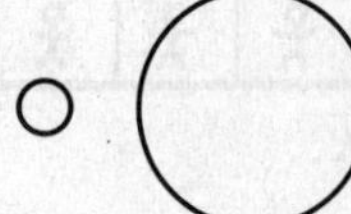

○ 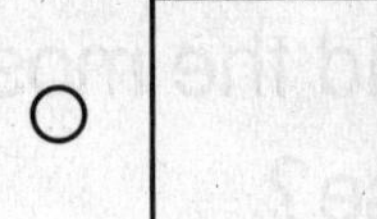

○ 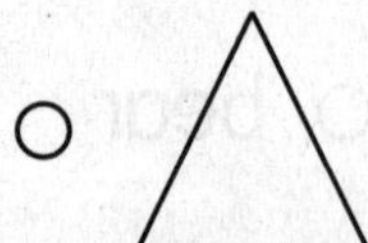

23. Which shape shows 4 equal shares?

○ 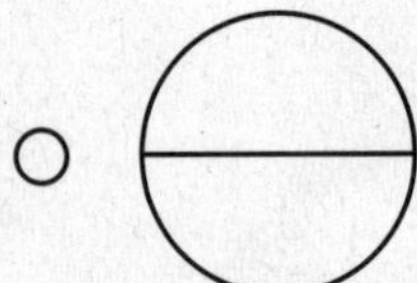

○ 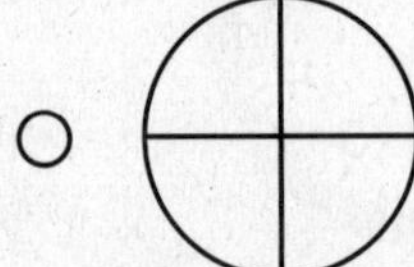

○ 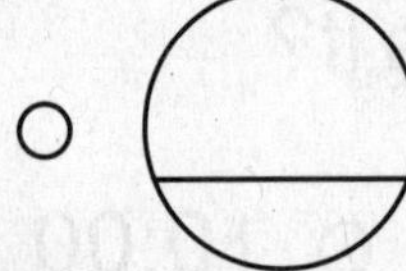

○ 

24. Which ribbon is the **shortest**?

○ 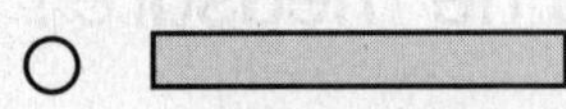

○ 

○ 

○ 

STOP

Choose the correct answer.

1. Use the paper clip ruler to measure.

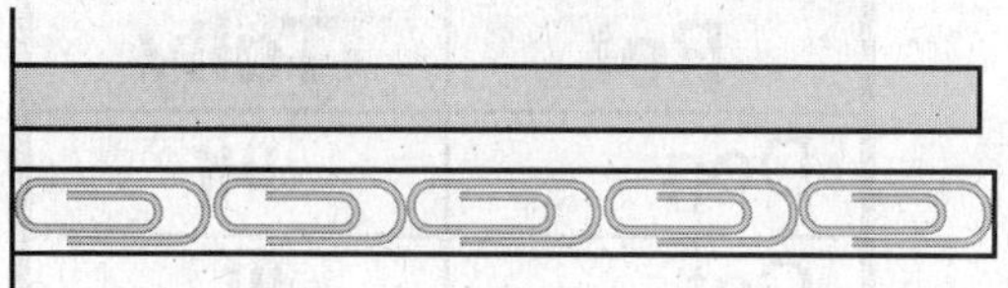

How long is the ribbon?

- ○ about 6
- ○ about 5
- ○ about 4
- ○ about 3

2. The clock shows when school starts.

What time is it?

- ○ 8:00
- ○ 9:00
- ○ 8:30
- ○ 12:00

3. Which shape shows 4 equal shares?

- ○ 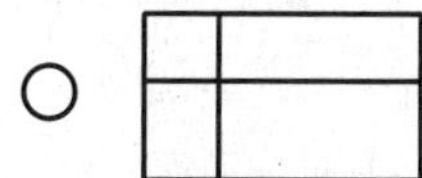
- ○ 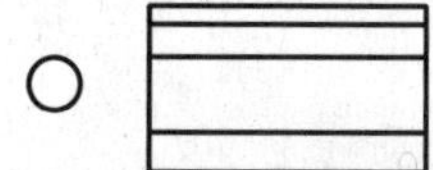
- ○ 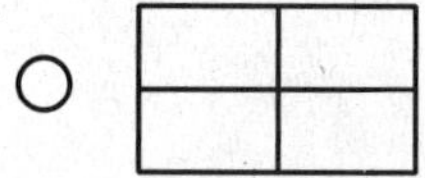
- ○

4. Kylie uses to measure the length of an object. Which object did she measure?

- ○ a car
- ○ a juice box
- ○ a bathtub
- ○ a bicycle

GO ON

Name ____________________

5. Which string is the **shortest**?

- ○
- ○
- ○
- ○

6. Use the tally chart to answer the question.

Our Favorite Pets	
Pet	**Tally**
Dog	~~IIII~~
Cat	III
Fish	II

How many children chose cat?

○ 5 ○ 3

○ 4 ○ 2

7. Use the paper clip ruler to measure.

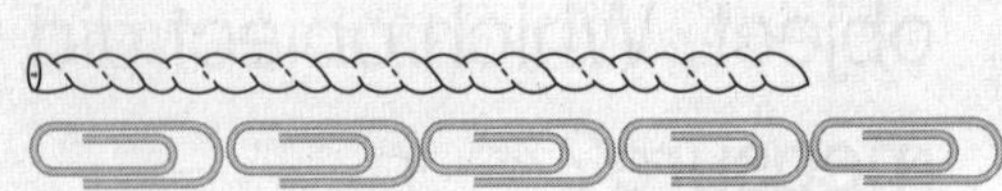

How long is the rope?

- ○ about 3 paper clips
- ○ about 4 paper clips
- ○ about 5 paper clips
- ○ about 6 paper clips

8. Josh uses [paper clip] to measure the length of an object. Which object did he measure?

- ○ book shelf
- ○ washing machine
- ○ wallet
- ○ park bench

GO ON

9. Use the picture graph to answer the question.

Favorite Instruments							
guitar	웃	웃	웃	웃	웃		
piano	웃	웃	웃	웃	웃	웃	웃

Each 웃 stands for 1 child.

How many children chose piano?

○ 7 children ○ 5 children

○ 6 children ○ 4 children

10. Use the bar graph to answer the question.

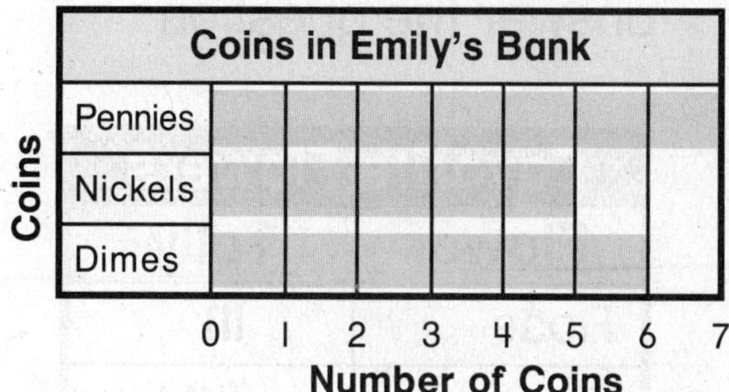

How many more pennies than nickels are there?

○ 4 more ○ 2 more

○ 3 more ○ 1 more

11. Which shape has 4 sides?

○ 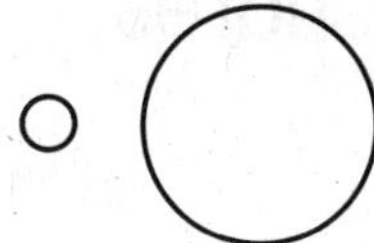

○ 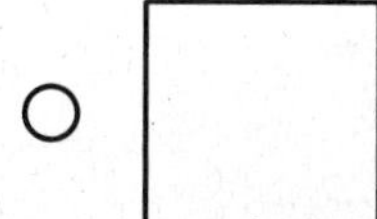

○ 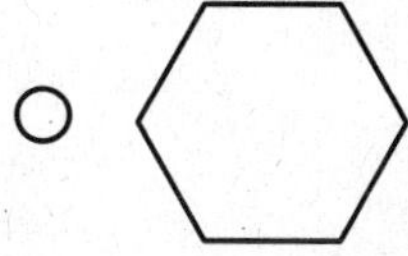

○ 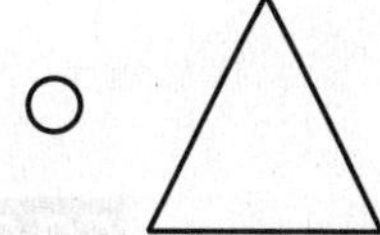

12. The clock shows when Mason gets to the park.

What time is it?

○ 5:00 ○ 6:00

○ 5:30 ○ 6:30

GO ON

Write the correct answer.

13. Use the tally chart to answer the question.

Favorite Flowers	
Flower	**Tally**
Rose	III
Daisy	𝍸 I
Tulip	𝍸

How many children chose tulip?

_______ children

14. Circle the shape that has 6 vertices.

15. Write 1, 2, and 3 to order the strings from **shortest** to **longest**.

____

____

____

16. Circle the shape that shows 4 equal shares.

GO ON

Name ____________________

17. Use the picture graph to answer the question.

Favorite Birds							
robin	🯅	🯅	🯅	🯅			
seagull	🯅	🯅	🯅				
blue jay	🯅	🯅	🯅	🯅	🯅	🯅	🯅

Each 🯅 stands for 1 child.

What bird did the most children choose?

____

18. Use the bar graph to answer the question.

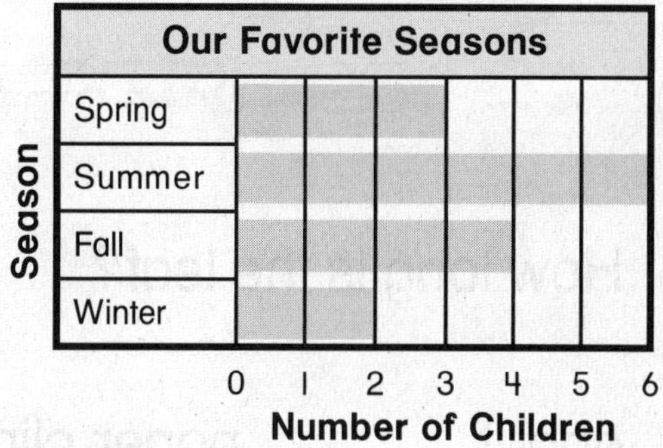

How many children chose fall?

_______ children

19. Use a cube to measure the length of a crayon. What is the measurement?

about _______ cubes

20. The clock shows when Owen gets to the playground.

What time is it? _______

GO ON

Name ____________________

21. Use the paper clip ruler to measure.

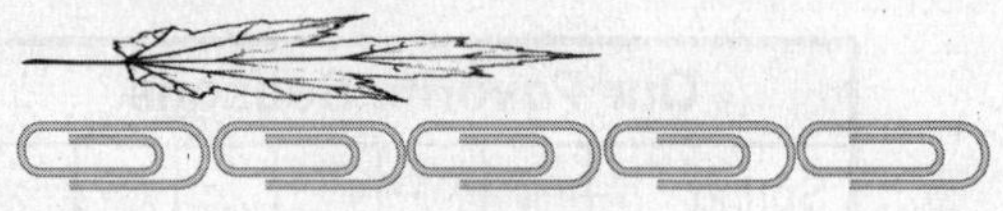

How long is the leaf?

about ________ paper clips

22. Circle the shape that has four sides.

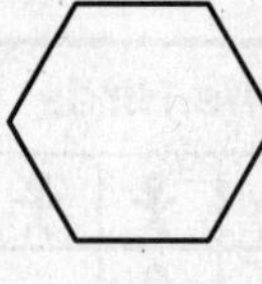

23. Circle the shape that shows equal shares. Write to name the equal shares.

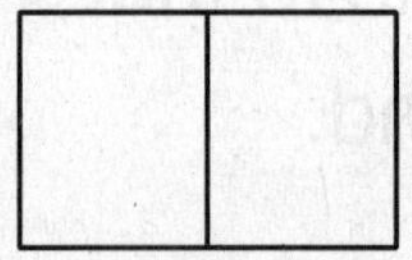

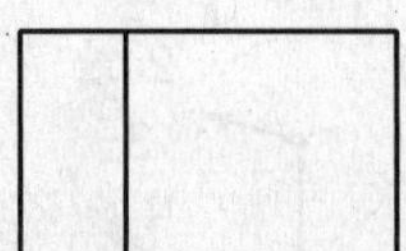

________ equal shares

24. Write 1, 2, and 3 to order the strings from **longest** to **shortest**.

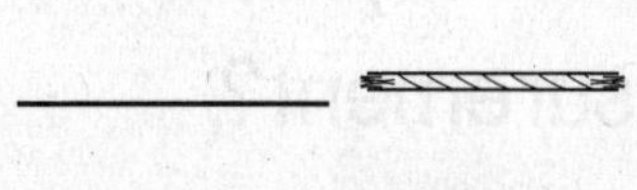

GO ON

Name ______________________________

Extended Constructed Response

25. Kia wants to cut a square pizza into four equal shares. Draw two ways to show fourths.

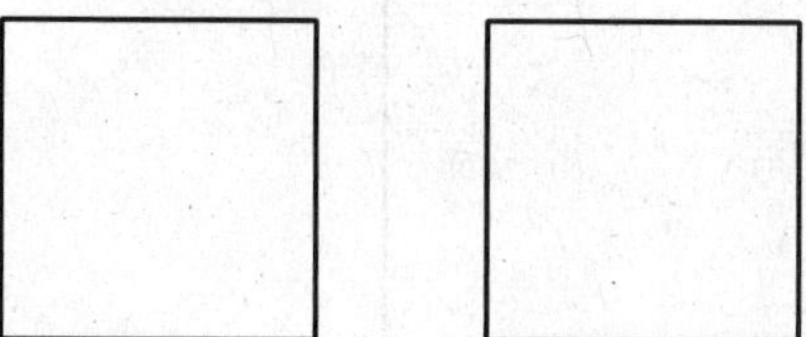

Explain why each square shows fourths.

____

____

Name ____

Extended Constructed Response

The Extended Constructed Response item is scored using the 3-point scoring rubric in the *Assessment Guide.* A child can receive partial credit for answers that are partially correct or partially completed.

Performance Indicators

For Problem 25, a child with a Level 2 paper:

_____ correctly shows fourths.

_____ understands the concept of equal parts.

_____ shows work that is easy to follow and clearly supports the answers given.

Child's Name ______________________ Date ______________

Beginning-of-Year/Middle-of-Year/End-of-Year Test

Item	Lesson	*CCSS	Common Error	Intervene with	Soar to Success Math
1	4.1	CC.1.OA.5	May count back incorrectly	**R**—4.1 **TE**—p. 153B	11.13
2	4.3	CC.1.OA.4	May not recognize which addition sentence can be used to help solve the subtraction	**R**—4.3 **TE**—p. 161B	29.21
3	4.5	CC.1.OA.6	May not understand how to make a ten to subtract	**R**—4.5 **TE**—p. 169B	
4	9.1	CC.1.MD.1	May not understand how to order objects by length using the terms *shortest* and *longest*	**R**—9.1 **TE**—p. 369B	41.05
5	9.3	CC.1.MD.2	May not measure length correctly with nonstandard units	**R**—9.3 **TE**—p. 377B	41.06
6	9.8	CC.1.MD.3	May not identify time to the hour or half hour	**R**—9.8 **TE**—p. 397B	51.08, 51.10
7	6.2	CC.1.NBT.1	May not count by tens	**R**—6.2 **TE**—p. 245B	28.14
8	6.10	CC.1.NBT.1	May incorrectly count the number of tens and ones	**R**—6.10 **TE**—p. 277B	2.20
9	6.6	CC.1.NBT.2	May confuse tens and ones	**R**—6.6 **TE**—p. 261B	1.14, 1.15
10	11.1	CC.1.G.1	May not correctly count flat surfaces	**R**—11.1 **TE**—p.457B	39.17, 39.26
11	11.2	CC.1.G.2	May have difficulty combining three-dimensional shapes	**R**—11.2 **TE**—p. 461B	39.28
12	11.5	CC.1.G.1	May have difficulty recognizing the two-dimensional shapes on three-dimensional shapes	**R**—11.5 **TE**—p. 473B	39.33
13	1.3	CC.1.OA.1	May not identify the number of counters correctly	**R**—1.3 **TE**—p. 21B	
14	1.5	CC.1.OA.3	May not understand the value of zero	**R**—1.5 **TE**—p. 29B	10.07
15	1.6	CC.1.OA.3	May not understand the meaning of the term *addend*	**R**—1.6 **TE**—p. 33B	10.08
16	1.7	CC.1.OA.1	May not correctly identify ways to make numbers to 10	**R**—1.7 **TE**—p. 37B	10.13
17	5.2	CC.1.OA.6	May not understand the meaning of *related facts*	**R**—5.2 **TE**—p. 189B	29.21, 29.32

***CCSS**—Common Core State Standards

Key: R—Reteach Book, **TE**—RtI Activities

Child's Name ______________________ Date ______________

Beginning-of-Year/Middle-of-Year/End-of-Year Test

Item	Lesson	*CCSS	Common Error	Intervene with	Soar to Success Math
18	5.7	CC.1.OA.1	May not know whether to add or subtract to solve the problem	**R**—5.7 **TE**—p. 209B	66.01
19	5.5	CC.1.OA.8	May have difficulty determining the missing number	**R**—5.5 **TE**—p. 201B	
20	5.9	CC.1.OA.7	May not understand what makes a number sentence *true* or *false*	**R**—5.9 **TE**—p. 217B	
21	8.3	CC.1.NBT.6	May have difficulty subtracting tens	**R**—8.3 **TE**—p. 325B	11.18
22	8.6	CC.1.NBT.4	May add the ones to the tens	**R**—8.6 **TE**—p. 337B	
23	8.7	CC.1.NBT.4	May incorrectly identify the tens and ones to add	**R**—8.7 **TE**—p. 341B	10.30
24	12.2	CC.1.G.1	May not be able to identify the attributes of two-dimensional shapes	**R**—12.2 **TE**—p. 489B	38.12
25	12.7	CC.1.G.2	May not understand how to take apart two-dimensional shapes	**R**—12.7 **TE**—p. 509B	38.19
26	12.10	CC.1.G.3	May not understand the concept of fourths or quarters	**R**—12.10 **TE**—p. 521B	5.05
27	2.3	CC.1.OA.1	May not understand how to take apart to subtract	**R**—2.3 **TE**—p. 61B	11.03
28	2.4	CC.1.OA.1	May not understand how to use the bar model to subtract	**R**—2.4 **TE**—p. 65B	11.03
29	2.5	CC.1.OA.8	May not understand the terms *more* or *fewer*	**R**—2.5 **TE**—p. 69B	11.11
30	2.7	CC.1.OA.8	May subtract all instead of subtracting 0	**R**—2.7 **TE**—p. 77B	11.06
31	10.3	CC.1.MD.4	May misread bars, or incorrectly add or subtract	**R**—10.3 **TE**—p. 421B	54.06
32	10.4	CC.1.MD.4	May not understand how to make a bar graph	**R**—10.4 **TE**—p. 425B	
33	10.5	CC.1.MD.4	May miscount the tally marks	**R**—10.5 **TE**—p. 429B	54.03
34	7.4	CC.1.NBT.3	May not understand the terms *is greater than* and *is less than*	**R**—7.4 **TE**—p. 301B	

***CCSS**—Common Core State Standards

Key: R—Reteach Book, **TE**—RtI Activities

Child's Name ______________________ Date ____________

Beginning-of-Year/Middle-of-Year/End-of-Year Test

Item	Lesson	*CCSS	Common Error	Intervene with	Soar to Success Math
35	7.3	CC.1.NBT.3	May not know the difference between *is greater than, is less than,* and *is equal to* symbols	**R**—7.3 **TE**—p. 297B	7.15
36	7.5	CC.1.NBT.5	May not correctly find 10 more or 10 less	**R**—7.5 **TE**—p. 305B	28.14
37	3.2	CC.1.OA.5	May not count on correctly	**R**—3.2 **TE**—p. 101B	10.2
38	3.5	CC.1.OA.6	May not use the correct doubles fact	**R**—3.5 **TE**—p. 113B	10.19
39	3.9	CC.1.OA.6	May not understand how to make a ten to add	**R**—3.9 **TE**—p. 129B	10.20
40	3.11	CC.1.OA.3	May add only two of the addends	**R**—3.11 **TE**—p. 137B	10.18, 10.19, 10.20

***CCSS**—Common Core State Standards

Key: R—Reteach Book, **TE**—RtI Activities

Child's Name ______________________ Date ______________

Chapter 1 Test • Forms A and B

Item	Lesson	*CCSS	Common Error	Intervene with	Soar to Success Math
1, 2, 13	1.5	CC.1.OA.3	May not understand the value of zero	**R**—1.5 **TE**—p. 29B	10.07
3, 14	1.2	CC.1.OA.1	May not understand how to model adding to a group	**R**—1.2 **TE**—p. 17B	10.03, 10.09
4	1.2	CC.1.OA.1	May count incorrectly	**R**—1.2 **TE**—p. 17B	10.03, 10.09
5, 15, 16	1.6	CC.1.OA.3	May not understand the meaning of the term *addend*	**R**—1.6 **TE**—p. 33B	10.08
6, 7, 19	1.7	CC.1.OA.1	May not correctly identify ways to make numbers to 10	**R**—1.7 **TE**—p. 37B	10.13
8, 17, 18	1.1	CC.1.OA.1	May not correctly use the pictures to find the sum	**R**—1.1 **TE**—p. 13B	
9, 20, 21	1.3	CC.1.OA.1	May count the counters incorrectly	**R**—1.3 **TE**—p. 21B	
10, 11, 22	1.8	CC.1.OA.6	May subtract instead of add	**R**—1.8 **TE**—p. 41B	10.11, 10.12
12, 23, 24	1.4	CC.1.OA.1	May not understand the bar model	**R**—1.4 **TE**—p. 25B	

***CCSS**—Common Core State Standards

Key: R—Reteach Book, **TE**—RtI Activities

Item	DOK Level	Rubric Level
25	2	2 1 0

Child's Name ______________________ Date ____________

Chapter 2 Test • Forms A and B

Item	Lesson	*CCSS	Common Error	Intervene with	Soar to Success Math
1, 13, 14	2.2	CC.1.OA.1	May miscount the cubes	**R**—2.2 **TE**—p. 57B	11.07
2, 15	2.9	CC.1.OA.6	May subtract incorrectly	**R**—2.9 **TE**—p. 85B	11.03, 11.10
3, 4, 16	2.5	CC.1.OA.8	May not understand the terms *more* or *fewer*	**R**—2.5 **TE**—p. 69B	11.11
5, 17	2.1	CC.1.OA.1	May miscount the items	**R**—2.1 **TE**—p. 53B	11.04
6, 18	2.6	CC.1.OA.1	May not understand how to use a bar model to compare	**R**—2.6 **TE**—p. 73B	11.11
7, 19, 20	2.4	CC.1.OA.1	May not understand how to use a bar model to subtract	**R**—2.4 **TE**—p. 65B	11.03
8, 9, 21	2.8	CC.1.OA.1	May not understand the phrase *take apart*	**R**—2.8 **TE**—p. 81B	11.03
10, 23	2.7	CC.1.OA.8	May subtract all instead of subtracting 0	**R**—2.7 **TE**—p. 77B	11.06
11, 12, 22	2.3	CC.1.OA.1	May not understand how to take apart to subtract	**R**—2.3 **TE**—p. 61B	11.03
24	2.7	CC.1.OA.8	May subtract 0 instead of subtracting all	**R**—2.7 **TE**—p. 77B	11.06

*CCSS—Common Core State Standards

Key: R—Reteach Book, **TE**—RtI Activities

Item	DOK Level	Rubric Level
25	2	2 1 0

Child's Name ______________________ Date ______________

Chapter 3 Test • Forms A and B

Item	Lesson	*CCSS	Common Error	Intervene with	Soar to Success Math
1, 13	3.3	CC.1.OA.6	May not identify the correct doubles fact	**R**—3.3 **TE**—p. 105B	10.04
2, 15	3.10	CC.1.OA.3	May add only two of the addends	**R**—3.10 **TE**—p. 133B	10.24
3, 14	3.1	CC.1.OA.3	May not know what the term *addend* means	**R**—3.1 **TE**—p. 97B	10.08
4, 16	3.9	CC.1.OA.6	May not understand how to make a ten to add	**R**—3.9 **TE**—p. 129B	10.20
5, 17	3.12	CC.1.OA.2	May add only two of the addends	**R**—3.12 **TE**—p. 141B	10.05
6, 18	3.7	CC.1.OA.6	May not count all of the counters shown	**R**—3.7 **TE**—p. 121B	10.17
7, 19	3.11	CC.1.OA.3	May add only two of the addends	**R**—3.11 **TE**—p. 137B	10.18, 10.19, 10.20, 10.24
8, 20	3.2	CC.1.OA.5	May not count on correctly	**R**—3.2 **TE**—p. 101B	10.02
9	3.6	CC.1.OA.6	May not correctly use the addition strategies *doubles plus one* or *doubles minus one*	**R**—3.6 **TE**—p. 117B	10.02, 10.04
10, 22	3.4	CC.1.OA.6	May not understand how to use doubles facts to solve addition problems	**R**—3.4 **TE**—p. 109B	10.04
11	3.5	CC.1.OA.6	May not use the correct doubles fact	**R**—3.5 **TE**—p. 113B	10.04
12, 24	3.8	CC.1.OA.6	May not understand how to make a ten to add	**R**—3.8 **TE**—p. 125B	10.20
21	3.6	CC.1.OA.6	May not correctly use the addition strategy *count on 1, 2, or 3*	**R**—3.6 **TE**—p. 117B	10.02, 10.04
23	3.5	CC.1.OA.6	May not understand the addition strategy *doubles minus one*	**R**—3.5 **TE**—p. 113B	10.04

***CCSS**—Common Core State Standards

Key: R—Reteach Book, **TE**—RtI Activities

Item	DOK Level	Rubric Level
25	2	2 1 0

Child's Name ______________________ Date ____________

Chapter 4 Test • Forms A and B

Item	Lesson	*CCSS	Common Error	Intervene with	Soar to Success Math
1, 2, 13, 14	4.1	CC.1.OA.5	May count back incorrectly	**R**—4.1 **TE**— p. 153B	11.13
3, 4, 23	4.5	CC.1.OA.6	May not understand how to make a ten to subtract	**R**—4.5 **TE**—p. 169B	
5, 6, 22	4.6	CC.1.OA.1	May subtract incorrectly	**R**—4.6 **TE**—p. 173B	60.02
7, 8	4.3	CC.1.OA.4	May not recognize which subtraction sentence the addition sentence can help solve	**R**—4.3 **TE**—p. 161B	29.21
9, 10, 15, 16	4.2	CC.1.OA.4	May not understand how to use addition to subtract	**R**— 4.2 **TE**—p. 157B	29.21
11, 12, 24	4.4	CC.1.OA.6	May not know how to make a ten to subtract	**R**—4.4 **TE**—p. 165B	
17, 18	4.6	CC.1.OA.1	May not know which operation to use	**R**—4.6 **TE**—p. 173B	60.02
19, 20	4.3	CC.1.OA.4	May not recognize which addition sentence can be used to help solve the subtraction	**R**— 4.3 **TE**—p. 161B	29.21
21	4.6	CC.1.OA.1	May not know which operation to use	**R**—4.6 **TE**—p. 173B	60.02

***CCSS**—Common Core State Standards

Key: R—Reteach Book, **TE**—RtI Activities

Item	DOK Level	Rubric Level
25	2	2 1 0

Child's Name ______________________ Date __________

Chapter 5 Test • Forms A and B

Item	Lesson	*CCSS	Common Error	Intervene with	Soar to Success Math
1, 2	5.7	CC.1.OA.1	May not know whether to add or subtract to solve the problem	**R**—5.7; **TE**—p. 209B	66.01
3, 4	5.3	CC.1.OA.6	May not understand how to identify related facts	**R**—5.3; **TE**—p. 193B	29.31
5	5.2	CC.1.OA.6	May not understand the relationship among the numbers in a set of related facts	**R**—5.2; **TE**—p. 189B	29.21, 29.32
6, 7, 8	5.2	CC.1.OA.6	May not understand the meaning of related facts	**R**—5.2; **TE**—p. 189B	29.21, 29.32
9, 10	5.1	CC.1.OA.1	May not understand the bar model	**R**—5.1; **TE**—p. 185B	29.33
11, 12	5.5	CC.1.OA.8	May have difficulty determining the missing number	**R**—5.5; **TE**—p. 201B	
13, 14, 15	5.9	CC.1.OA.7	May not understand what makes a number sentence true or false	**R**—5.9; **TE**—p. 217B	
16, 17	5.6	CC.1.OA.8	May not understand related facts	**R**—5.6; **TE**—p. 205B	29.23
18, 19	5.8	CC.1.OA.6	May not understand how to make numbers in different ways	**R**—5.8; **TE**—p. 213B	1.12
20, 21	5.4	CC.1.OA.6	May not understand how to use a related addition fact to check subtraction	**R**—5.4; **TE**—p. 197B	
22	5.10	CC.1.OA.6	May not know whether to add or subtract to solve the problem	**R**—5.10; **TE**—p. 221B	29.29, 29.30
23, 24	5.10	CC.1.OA.6	May not add or subtract correctly	**R**—5.10; **TE**—p. 221B	29.29, 29.30

***CCSS**—Common Core State Standards

Key: R—Reteach Book, **TE**—RtI Activities

Item	DOK Level	Rubric Level
25	2	2 1 0

Child's Name ______________________ Date ______________

Chapter 6 Test • Forms A and B

Item	Lesson	*CCSS	Common Error	Intervene with	Soar to Success Math
1, 13, 14	6.6	CC.1.NBT.2	May confuse tens and ones	**R**—6.6 **TE**—p. 261B	1.14, 1.15
2, 15	6.1	CC.1.NBT.1	May not count forward by ones	**R**—6.1 **TE**—p. 241B	28.12
3, 16	6.7	CC.1.NBT.2	May confuse tens and ones	**R**—6.7 **TE**—p. 265B	1.15
4, 17	6.2	CC.1.NBT.1	May not count by tens	**R**—6.2 **TE**—p. 245B	28.14
5, 18	6.8	CC.1.NBT.2a CC.1.NBT.3	May incorrectly group ones in order to make numbers	**R**—6.8 **TE**—p. 269B	2.19
6, 19, 20	6.9	CC.1.NBT.1	May incorrectly count the number of tens and ones	**R**—6.9 **TE**—p. 273B	2.20
7, 8, 21	6.3	CC.1.NBT.2b	May miscount cubes	**R**—6.3 **TE**—p. 249B	1.13
9, 22	6.10	CC.1.NBT.1	May incorrectly count the number of tens and ones	**R**—6.10 **TE**—p. 277B	2.20
10, 23	6.4	CC.1.NBT.2b	May not understand naming a group of ten and ones	**R**—6.4 **TE**—p. 253B	1.13
11, 12, 24	6.5	CC.1.NBT.2a CC.1.NBT.2c	May not understand that each group of cubes is a ten	**R**—6.5 **TE**—p. 257B	1.16

***CCSS**—Common Core State Standards

Key: R—Reteach Book, **TE**—RtI Activities

Item	DOK Level	Rubric Level
25	2	2 1 0

Child's Name ______________________ Date __________

Chapter 7 Test • Forms A and B

Item	Lesson	*CCSS	Common Error	Intervene with	Soar to Success Math
1–4	7.1	CC.1.NBT.3	May not understand the term *is greater than*	**R**—7.1; **TE**—p. 289B	7.17
5, 6	7.3	CC.1.NBT.3	May miscount numbers shown with quick pictures	**R**—7.3; **TE**—p. 297B	7.15
7–9, 11, 12	7.2	CC.1.NBT.3	May not understand the term *is less than*	**R**—7.2; **TE**—p. 293B	7.17
10, 16, 18, 19	7.3	CC.1.NBT.3	May not know the difference between *is greater than*, *is less than*, and *is equal to* symbols	**R**—7.3; **TE**—p. 297B	7.15
13, 15, 20	7.5	CC.1.NBT.5	May not correctly find 10 more	**R**—7.5; **TE**—p. 305B	28.14
14, 17	7.5	CC.1.NBT.5	May not correctly find 10 less	**R**—7.5; **TE**—p. 305B	28.14
21	7.4	CC.1.NBT.3	May not correctly compare tens when determining if numbers are greater or lesser	**R**—7.4; **TE**—p. 301B	
22	7.4	CC.1.NBT.3	May not correctly compare ones when determining if numbers are greater or lesser	**R**—7.4; **TE**—p. 301B	
23, 24	7.4	CC.1.NBT.3	May not understand the terms *is greater than* and *is less than*	**R**—7.4; **TE**—p. 301B	

***CCSS**—Common Core State Standards

Key: R—Reteach Book, **TE**—RtI Activities

Item	DOK Level	Rubric Level
25	2	2 1 0

Child's Name ______________________ Date __________

Chapter 8 Test • Forms A and B

Item	Lesson	*CCSS	Common Error	Intervene with	Soar to Success Math
1–3	8.2	CC.1.NBT.4	May have difficulty adding tens	R—8.2; TE—p. 321B	10.28
4, 6	8.1	CC.1.OA.6	May have difficulty adding within 20	R—8.1; TE—p. 317B	10.21, 11.15
5	8.1	CC.1.OA.6	May have difficulty subtracting within 20	R—8.1; TE—p. 317B	10.21, 11.15
7–9	8.3	CC.1.NBT.6	May have difficulty subtracting tens	R—8.3; TE—p. 325B	11.18
10, 12	8.5	CC.1.NBT.4	May not add the correct number of tens	R—8.5; TE—p. 333B	10.25
11	8.5	CC.1.NBT.4	May not add the correct number of ones	R—8.5; TE—p. 333B	10.25
13, 14	8.7	CC.1.NBT.4	May incorrectly identify the tens and ones to add	R—8.7; TE—p. 341B	10.30
15, 16	8.8	CC.1.NBT.4	May not recognize addition in the word problem	R—8.8; TE—p. 345B	
17	8.4	CC.1.NBT.4	May not add the correct number of ones	R—8.4; TE—p. 329B	
18	8.4	CC.1.NBT.4	May not add the correct number of tens	R—8.4; TE—p. 329B	
19, 20, 21	8.6	CC.1.NBT.4	May add the ones to the tens	R—8.6; TE—p. 337B	
22, 24	8.9	CC.1.NBT.4, CC.1.NBT.6	May not add the correct number of ones or tens	R—8.9; TE—p. 349B	10.25, 10.28, 10.30, 11.18
23	8.9	CC.1.NBT.4, CC.1.NBT.6	May not subtract the correct number of ones or tens	R—8.9; TE—p. 349B	10.25, 10.28, 10.30, 11.18

***CCSS**—Common Core State Standards

Key: R—Reteach Book, **TE**—RtI Activities

Item	DOK Level	Rubric Level
25	2	2 1 0

Child's Name ______________________ Date ______________

Chapter 9 Test • Forms A and B

Item	Lesson	*CCSS	Common Error	Intervene with	Soar to Success Math
1, 2, 12	9.6	CC.1.MD.3	May incorrectly identify the position of the hour hand on the hour	**R**—9.6 **TE**—p. 389B	51.08
3, 13, 14	9.8	CC.1.MD.3	May not identify time to the hour or half hour	**R**—9.8 **TE**—p. 397B	51.08, 51.10
4, 15, 16	9.7	CC.1.MD.3	May incorrectly identify the position of the hour hand on the half hour	**R**—9.7 **TE**—p. 393B	51.10
5, 6, 17	9.2	CC.1.MD.1	May not understand how to order lengths using indirect measurement	**R**—9.2 **TE**—p. 373B	41.02, 41.05
7, 18	9.1	CC.1.MD.1	May not understand how to order objects by length using the terms *shortest* and *longest*	**R**—9.1 **TE**—p. 369B	41.05
8, 9, 19, 20	9.3	CC.1.MD.2	May not measure length correctly with nonstandard units	**R**—9.3 **TE**—p. 377B	41.06
10, 11, 21	9.9	CC.1.MD.3	May not identify time to the hour or half hour	**R**—9.9 **TE**—p. 401B	51.08, 51.10

***CCSS**—Common Core State Standards **Key: R**—Reteach Book, **TE**—RtI Activities

Item	DOK Level	Rubric Level
22	2	2 1 0

Child's Name ______________________ Date __________

Chapter 10 Test • Forms A and B

Item	Lesson	*CCSS	Common Error	Intervene with	Soar to Success Math
1, 2, 13, 14	10.5	CC.1.MD.4	May miscount the tally marks	**R**—10.5 **TE**—p. 429B	54.03
3, 4, 15, 16	10.6	CC.1.MD.4	May not understand how to use tally marks correctly	**R**—10.6 **TE**—p. 433B	54.10
5, 6, 17, 18	10.3	CC.1.MD.4	May misread bars, or incorrectly add or subtract	**R**—10.3 **TE**—p. 421B	54.06
7, 8, 19, 20	10.4	CC.1.MD.4	May not understand how to make a bar graph	**R**—10.4 **TE**—p. 425B	
9, 10, 21, 22	10.1	CC.1.MD.4	May miscount the pictures or incorrectly add or subtract	**R**—10.1 **TE**—p. 413B	54.05
11, 12, 23, 24	10.2	CC.1.MD.4	May not understand how to complete a row of a picture graph	**R**—10.2 **TE**—p. 417B	

***CCSS**—Common Core State Standards

Key: R—Reteach Book, **TE**—RtI Activities

Item	DOK Level	Rubric Level
25	2	2 1 0

Child's Name ______________________ Date ______________

Chapter 11 Test • Forms A and B

Item	Lesson	*CCSS	Common Error	Intervene with	Soar to Success Math
1, 2	11.1	CC.1.G.1	May not know the names of three-dimensional shapes	**R**—11.1 **TE**—p. 457B	39.17, 39.26
13	11.1	CC.1.G.1	May not correctly count flat surfaces	**R**—11.1 **TE**—p. 457B	39.17, 39.26
14	11.1	CC.1.G.1	May not correctly identify flat and curved surfaces	**R**—11.1 **TE**—p. 457B	39.17, 39.26
3–5, 15–17	11.5	CC.1.G.1	May have difficulty recognizing the two-dimensional shapes on three-dimensional shapes	**R**—11.5 **TE**—p. 473B	39.33
6–8, 19, 20	11.2	CC.1.G.2	May have difficulty combining three-dimensional shapes	**R**—11.2 **TE**—p. 461B	39.28
9, 21, 22	11.3	CC.1.G.2	May have difficulty combining combined shapes	**R**—11.3 **TE**—p. 465B	
10–12	11.4	CC.1.G,2	May have difficulty taking apart shapes	**R**—11.4 **TE**—p. 469B	39.26
18, 23, 24	11.4	CC.1.G.2	May not recognize shapes in a different orientation	**R**—11.4 **TE**—p. 469B	39.26

***CCSS**—Common Core State Standards

Key: R—Reteach Book, **TE**—RtI Activities

Item	DOK Level	Rubric Level
25	2	2 1 0

Child's Name ______________________ Date ______________

Chapter 12 Test • Forms A and B

Item	Lesson	*CCSS	Common Error	Intervene with	Soar to Success Math
1, 2, 13	12.8	CC.1.G.3	May not understand that equal shares are the same size or that unequal parts are not the same size	**R**—12.8 **TE**—p. 513B	5.03
3, 12, 24	12.1	CC.1.G.1	May not know the term *vertices* or *sides*	**R**—12.1 **TE**—p. 485B	38.11
4, 14	12.7	CC.1.G.2	May not understand how to take apart two-dimensional shapes	**R**—12.7 **TE**—p. 509B	38.19
5, 15, 16	12.2	CC.1.G.1	May incorrectly count the number of sides and vertices.	**R**—12.2 **TE**—p. 489B	38.12
6, 7, 17	12.9	CC.1.G.3	May not understand the concept of halves	**R**—12.9 **TE**—p. 517B	5.03
8, 18	12.3	CC.1.G.2	May not be able to visualize how to combine two-dimensional shapes to make a new two-dimensional shape	**R**—12.3 **TE**—p. 493B	38.17
9, 19, 20	12.10	CC.1.G.3	May not understand the concept of fourths or quarters	**R**—12.10 **TE**—p. 521B	5.05
10, 21	12.6	CC.1.G.2	May not understand how two-dimensional shapes are made with other two-dimensional shapes	**R**—12.6 **TE**—p. 505B	38.17
11, 22	12.4	CC.1.G.2	May not understand how to combine two-dimensional shapes in order to make a new two-dimensional shape	**R**—12.4 **TE**—p. 497B	38.17
23	12.5	CC.1.G.2	May not understand how to build with two-dimensional shapes in order to make a new two-dimensional shape	**R**—12.5 **TE**—p. 501B	38.17

***CCSS**—Common Core State Standards

Key: R—Reteach Book, **TE**—RtI Activities

Item	DOK Level	Rubric Level
25	2	2 1 0

Child's Name ______________________ Date ______________

Prerequisite Skills Inventory

Item	Grade K *CCSS	Common Error	Soar to Success Math
1	CC.K.OA.1	May have difficulty completing an addition sentence for a word problem	10.03
2	CC.K.OA.1	May have difficulty completing a subtraction sentence for a word problem	11.03
3	CC.K.OA.1	May add instead of subtract	11.03
4	CC.K.OA.2	May have difficulty completing an addition sentence for a word problem	10.09
5	CC.K.OA.4	May not recognize number pairs that have the sum of ten	10.04
6	CC.K.OA.3	May not recognize number pairs that have the sum of ten	10.09
7	CC.K.CC.1	May not be able to count to 100 using a hundred chart	28.11
8	CC.K.NBT.1	May have difficulty counting to 17	1.09
9	CC.K.NBT.1	May have difficulty counting to 14	1.08
10	CC.K.CC.7	May not understand the vocabulary *greater than*	7.08
11	CC.K.CC.7	May not understand the vocabulary *less than*	7.08
12	CC.K.OA.3	May not use pictures to decompose numbers	10.09
13	CC.K.MD.2	May confuse the terms *shorter than* and *taller than*	41.03
14	CC.K.MD.2	May confuse the terms *lighter than* and *heavier than*	42.02
15, 16	CC.K.MD.2	May confuse the terms *shorter* and *longer*	41.02
17	CC.K.G.4	May not correctly describe a square	38.02
18	CC.K.MD.3	May sort by an attribute other than shape	53.01, 1.03

***CCSS**—Common Core State Standards

Child's Name ______________________ Date ______________

Prerequisite Skills Inventory

Item	Grade K *CCSS	Common Error	Soar to Success Math
19	CC.K.MD.3	May sort by an attribute other than size	53.01, 1.03
20	CC.K.G.4	May not correctly describe triangles	38.02
21	CC.K.G.4	May not correctly describe hexagons	38.02
22	CC.K.G.1	May not understand the term beside	35.07
23	CC.K.G.2	May not correctly identify the triangle	38.02, 38.07
24	CC.K.G.2	May have difficulty identifying a cylinder	39.13, 39.26

***CCSS**—Common Core State Standards

Child's Name ______________________ Date ____________

Getting Ready Test: Lessons 1–11 • Forms A and B

Item	Lesson	Common Error	Intervene with
1, 10	2	May confuse place value	**R**—p. GRR2
2, 22	8	May incorrectly add the ones	**R**—p. GRR8
3, 17, 21	1	May confuse tens and ones	**R**—p. GRR1
4, 13	7	May not understand how to use strategies to add three numbers	**R**—p. GRR7
5, 23	4	May not understand which numbers to add	**R**—p. GRR4
6, 15, 20	9	May incorrectly add ones or tens	**R**—p. GRR9
7, 24	3	May confuse comparison symbols	**R**—p. GRR3
8, 16	10	May not understand how to recognize equal groups and find the total number	**R**—p. GRR10
9, 14	6	May not understand whether to add or subtract, or which numbers to use	**R**—p. GRR6
11, 18	11	May confuse the number of equal groups and the number in each group	**R**—p. GRR11
12, 19	5	May subtract incorrectly	**R**—p. GRR5

Key: R—Online Reteach Book

Item	DOK Level	Rubric Level
25	2	2 1 0

Child's Name ______________________ Date ______________

Getting Ready Test: Lessons 12–20 • Forms A and B

Item	Lesson	Common Error	Intervene with
1, 7, 21	13	May not understand how to use a ruler	**R**—p. GRR13
2, 12, 20	15	May confuse the hour hand and the minute hand on an analog clock	**R**—p. GRR15
3, 16, 23	20	May not recognize 2 or 4 equal shares	**R**—p. GRR20
4, 8, 19	12	May not understand how to choose non-standard units to measure	**R**—p. GRR12
5, 15, 24	14	May confuse the longest and shortest lengths	**R**—p. GRR14
6, 13	18	May not understand how to count tally marks	**R**—p. GRR18
9, 17	16	May not understand how to find information on a picture graph	**R**—p. GRR16
10, 18	17	May look at the wrong bars on the graph for information	**R**—p. GRR17
11, 14, 22	19	May confuse attributes of plane shapes	**R**—p. GRR19

Key: R—Online Reteach Book

Item	DOK Level	Rubric Level
25	2	2 1 0

Diagnostic Interview Assessment GO MATH!

Chapter	Skill	Child's Name														
1	Explore Numbers 1 to 4															
	Numbers 1 to 10															
	Numbers 0 to 10															
2	Explore Numbers 1 to 4															
	Numbers 1 to 10															
	Use Pictures to Subtract															
3	Model Addition															
	Use Symbols to Add															
	Add in Any Order															
4	Model Subtraction															
	Use Symbols to Subtract															
	Subtract All or Zero															

Diagnostic Interview Assessment GO MATH!

Chapter	Skill	Child's Name														
5	Add in Any Order															
	Count On															
	Count Back															
6	Explore Numbers 6 to 9															
	Count Groups to 20															
	Make Groups of 10															
7	Model More															
	More, Fewer															
	Draw Equal Groups															
8	Add and Subtract															
	Count Groups to 20															
	Use a Hundred Chart to Count															

Diagnostic Interview Assessment GO MATH!

Chapter	Skill	Child's Name														
9	Bigger and Smaller															
	Compare Length															
	Numbers 1 to 10															
10	Make a Concrete Graph															
	More, Fewer															
	Draw Equal Groups															
11	Alike and Different															
	Identify Three-Dimensional Shapes															
	Sort by Size															
12	Sort by Shape															
	Sort Shapes															
	Identify Two-Dimensional Shapes															

Performance Assessment GO MATH!

Teacher	Chapters 1–5				Chapters 6–8			
Name/Date	Task A	Task B	Task C	Task D	Task A	Task B	Task C	Task D

Performance Assessment GO MATH!

Grade 1
Class Record Form

Teacher	Chapters 9–10				Chapters 11–12			
Name/Date	Task A	Task B	Task C	Task D	Task A	Task B	Task C	Task D

Correlations

	Lesson Objectives	Test/Item Numbers
1.1	Use pictures to "add to" and find sums.	Chapter 1 Test: 8, 17, 18
1.2	Use concrete objects to solve "adding to" addition problems.	Chapter 1 Test: 3, 4, 14
1.3	Use concrete objects to solve "putting together" addition problems.	Chapter 1 Test: 9, 20, 21 Beginning/Middle/End-of-Year Test: 13
1.4	Solve adding to and putting together situations using the strategy *make a model.*	Chapter 1 Test: 12, 23, 24
1.5	Understand and apply the Additive Identity Property for Addition.	Chapter 1 Test: 1, 2, 13 Beginning/Middle/End-of-Year Test: 14
1.6	Explore the Commutative Property of Addition.	Chapter 1 Test: 5, 15, 16 Beginning/Middle/End-of-Year Test: 15
1.7	Model and record all the ways to put together numbers within 10.	Chapter 1 Test: 6, 7, 19 Beginning/Middle/End-of-Year Test: 16
1.8	Build fluency for addition within 10.	Chapter 1 Test: 10, 11, 22
2.1	Use pictures to show "taking from" and find differences.	Chapter 2 Test: 5, 17
2.2	Use concrete objects to solve "taking from" subtraction problems.	Chapter 2 Test: 1, 13, 14
2.3	Use concrete objects to solve "taking apart" subtraction problems.	Chapter 2 Test: 11, 12, 22 Beginning/Middle/End-of-Year Test: 27
2.4	Solve taking from and taking apart subtraction problems using the strategy *make a model.*	Chapter 2 Test: 7, 19, 20 Beginning/Middle/End-of-Year Test: 28
2.5	Compare pictorial groups to understand subtraction.	Chapter 2 Test: 3, 4, 16 Beginning/Middle/End-of-Year Test: 29
2.6	Model and compare groups to show the meaning of subtraction.	Chapter 2 Test: 6, 18
2.7	Identify how many are left when subtracting all or 0.	Chapter 2 Test: 10, 23, 24 Beginning/Middle/End-of-Year Test: 30
2.8	Model and record all of the ways to take apart numbers within 10.	Chapter 2 Test: 8, 9, 21
2.9	Build fluency for subtraction within 10.	Chapter 2 Test: 2, 15
3.1	Understand and apply the Commutative Property of Addition for sums within 20.	Chapter 3 Test: 3, 14
3.2	Use count on 1, 2, or 3 as a strategy to find sums within 20.	Chapter 3 Test: 8, 20 Beginning/Middle/End-of-Year Test: 37

	Lesson Objectives	Test/Item Numbers
3.3	Use doubles as a strategy to solve addition facts with sums within 20.	Chapter 3 Test: 1, 13
3.4	Use doubles to create equivalent but easier sums.	Chapter 3 Test: 10, 22
3.5	Use doubles plus 1 and doubles minus 1 as strategies to find sums within 20.	Chapter 3 Test: 11, 23 Beginning/Middle/End-of-Year Test: 38
3.6	Use the strategies count on, doubles, doubles plus 1, and doubles minus 1 to practice addition facts within 20.	Chapter 3 Test: 9, 21
3.7	Use a ten frame to add 10 and an addend less than 10.	Chapter 3 Test: 6, 18
3.8	Use make a ten as a strategy to find sums within 20.	Chapter 3 Test: 12, 24
3.9	Use numbers to show how to use the make a ten strategy to add.	Chapter 3 Test: 4, 16 Beginning/Middle/End-of-Year Test: 39
3.10	Use the Associative Property of Addition to add three addends.	Chapter 3 Test: 2, 15
3.11	Understand and apply the Associative Property or Commutative Property of Addition to add three addends.	Chapter 3 Test: 7, 19 Beginning/Middle/End-of-Year Test: 40
3.12	Solve adding to and putting together situations using the strategy *draw a picture*.	Chapter 3 Test: 5, 17
4.1	Use count back 1, 2, or 3 as a strategy to subtract.	Chapter 4 Test: 1, 2, 13, 14 Beginning/Middle/End-of-Year Test: 1
4.2	Recall addition facts to subtract numbers within 20.	Chapter 4 Test: 9, 10, 15, 16
4.3	Use addition as a strategy to subtract numbers within 20.	Chapter 4 Test: 7, 8, 19, 20 Beginning/Middle/End-of-Year Test: 2
4.4	Use make a 10 as a strategy to subtract.	Chapter 4 Test: 11, 12, 24
4.5	Subtract by breaking apart to make a ten.	Chapter 4 Test: 3, 4, 23 Beginning/Middle/End-of-Year Test: 3
4.6	Solve subtraction problem situations using the strategy *act it out*.	Chapter 4 Test: 5, 6, 17, 18, 21, 22
5.1	Solve addition and subtraction problem situations using the strategy *make a model*.	Chapter 5 Test: 9, 10
5.2	Record related facts within 20.	Chapter 5 Test: 5–8 Beginning/Middle/End-of-Year Test: 17
5.3	Identify related addition and subtraction facts within 20.	Chapter 5 Test: 3, 4
5.4	Apply the inverse relationship of addition and subtraction.	Chapter 5 Test: 20, 21

Lesson Objectives		Test/Item Numbers
5.5	Use related facts to determine unknown numbers.	Chapter 5 Test: 11, 12 Beginning/Middle/End-of-Year Test: 19
5.6	Use a related fact to subtract.	Chapter 5 Test: 16, 17
5.7	Choose an operation and strategy to solve an addition or subtraction word problem.	Chapter 5 Test: 1, 2 Beginning/Middle/End-of-Year Test: 18
5.8	Represent equivalent forms of numbers using sums and differences within 20.	Chapter 5 Test: 18, 19
5.9	Determine if an equation is true or false.	Chapter 5 Test: 13–15 Beginning/Middle/End-of-Year Test: 20
5.10	Add and subtract facts within 20 and demonstrate fluency for addition and subtraction within 10.	Chapter 5 Test: 22–24
6.1	Count by ones to extend a counting sequence up to 120.	Chapter 6 Test: 2, 15
6.2	Count by tens from any number to extend a counting sequence up to 120.	Chapter 6 Test: 4, 17 Beginning/Middle/End-of-Year Test: 7
6.3	Use models and write to represent equivalent forms of ten and ones.	Chapter 6 Test: 7, 8, 21
6.4	Use objects, pictures, and numbers to represent a ten and some ones.	Chapter 6 Test: 10, 23
6.5	Use objects, pictures, and numbers to represent tens.	Chapter 6 Test: 11, 12, 24
6.6	Group objects to show numbers to 50 as tens and ones.	Chapter 6 Test: 1, 13, 14 Beginning/Middle/End-of-Year Test: 9
6.7	Group objects to show numbers to 100 as tens and ones.	Chapter 6 Test: 3, 16
6.8	Solve problems using the strategy *make a model.*	Chapter 6 Test: 5, 18
6.9	Read and write numerals to represent a number of 100 to 110 objects.	Chapter 6 Test: 6, 19, 20
6.10	Read and write numerals to represent a number of 110 to 120 objects.	Chapter 6 Test: 9, 22 Beginning/Middle/End-of-Year Test: 8
7.1	Model and compare two-digit numbers to determine which is greater.	Chapter 7 Test: 1–4
7.2	Model and compare two-digit numbers to determine which is less.	Chapter 7 Test: 7–9, 11, 12
7.3	Use symbols for *is less than* "<", *is greater than* ">", and *is equal to* "=" to compare numbers.	Chapter 7 Test: 5, 6, 10, 16, 18, 19 Beginning/Middle/End-of-Year Test: 35
7.4	Solve problems using the strategy *make a model.*	Chapter 7 Test: 21–24 Beginning/Middle/End-of-Year Test: 34

	Lesson Objectives	Test/Item Numbers
7.5	Identify numbers that are 10 less or 10 more than a given number.	Chapter 7 Test: 13–15, 17, 20 Beginning/Middle/End-of-Year Test: 36
8.1	Add and subtract within 20.	Chapter 8 Test: 4–6
8.2	Draw a model to add tens.	Chapter 8 Test: 1–3
8.3	Draw a model to subtract tens.	Chapter 8 Test: 7–9 Beginning/Middle/End-of-Year Test: 21
8.4	Use a hundred chart to find sums.	Chapter 8 Test: 17, 18
8.5	Use concrete models to add ones or tens to a two-digit number.	Chapter 8 Test: 10–12
8.6	Make a ten to add a two-digit number and a one-digit number.	Chapter 8 Test: 19–21 Beginning/Middle/End-of-Year Test: 22
8.7	Use tens and ones to add two-digit numbers.	Chapter 8 Test: 13, 14 Beginning/Middle/End-of-Year Test: 23
8.8	Solve and explain two-digit addition word problems using the strategy *draw a picture.*	Chapter 8 Test: 15, 16
8.9	Add and subtract within 100, including continued practice with facts within 20.	Chapter 8 Test: 22–24
9.1	Order objects by length.	Chapter 9 Test: 7, 18 Beginning/Middle/End-of-Year Test: 4
9.2	Use the Transitivity Principle to measure indirectly.	Chapter 9 Test: 5, 6, 17
9.3	Measure length using nonstandard units.	Chapter 9 Test: 8, 9, 19, 20 Beginning/Middle/End-of-Year Test: 5
9.4	Make a nonstandard measuring tool to measure length.	
9.5	Solve measurement problems using the strategy *act it out.*	
9.6	Write times to the hour shown on analog clocks.	Chapter 9 Test: 1, 2, 12
9.7	Write times to the half hour shown on analog clocks.	Chapter 9 Test: 4, 15, 16
9.8	Tell times to the hour and half hour using analog and digital clocks.	Chapter 9 Test: 3, 13, 14 Beginning/Middle/End-of-Year Test: 6
9.9	Use the hour hand to draw and write times on analog and digital clocks.	Chapter 9 Test: 10, 11, 21
10.1	Analyze and compare data shown in a picture graph where each symbols represents one.	Chapter 10 Test: 9, 10, 21, 22

	Lesson Objectives	Test/Item Numbers
10.2	Make a picture graph where each symbol represents one and interpret the information.	Chapter 10 Test: 11, 12, 23, 24
10.3	Analyze and compare data shown in a bar graph.	Chapter 10 Test: 5, 6, 17, 18 Beginning/Middle/End-of-Year Test: 31
10.4	Make a bar graph and interpret the information.	Chapter 10 Test: 7, 8, 19, 20 Beginning/Middle/End-of-Year Test: 32
10.5	Analyze and compare data shown in a tally chart.	Chapter 10 Test: 1, 2, 13, 14 Beginning/Middle/End-of-Year Test: 33
10.6	Make a tally chart and interpret the information.	Chapter 10 Test: 3, 4, 15, 16
10.7	Solve problem situations using the strategy *make a graph*.	
11.1	Identify and describe three-dimensional shapes according to defining attributes.	Chapter 11 Test: 1, 2, 13, 14 Beginning/Middle/End-of-Year Test: 10
11.2	Compose a new shape by combining three-dimensional shapes.	Chapter 11 Test: 6–8, 19, 20 Beginning/Middle/End-of-Year Test: 11
11.3	Use composite three-dimensional shapes to build new shapes.	Chapter 11 Test: 9, 21, 22
11.4	Identify three-dimensional shapes used to build a composite shape using the strategy *act it out*.	Chapter 11 Test: 10–12, 18, 23, 24
11.5	Identify two-dimensional shapes on three-dimensional shapes.	Chapter 11 Test: 3–5, 15–17 Beginning/Middle/End-of-Year Test: 12
12.1	Use defining attributes to sort shapes.	Chapter 12 Test: 3, 12, 24
12.2	Describe attributes of two-dimensional shapes.	Chapter 12 Test: 5, 15, 16 Beginning/Middle/End-of-Year Test: 24
12.3	Use objects to compose new two-dimensional shapes.	Chapter 12 Test: 8, 18
12.4	Compose a new shape by combining two-dimensional shapes.	Chapter 12 Test: 11, 22
12.5	Make new shapes from composite two-dimensional shapes using the strategy *act it out*.	Chapter 12 Test: 23
12.6	Decompose combined shapes into shapes.	Chapter 12 Test: 10, 21
12.7	Decompose two-dimensional shapes into parts.	Chapter 12 Test: 4, 14 Beginning/Middle/End-of-Year Test: 25
12.8	Identify equal and unequal parts (or shares) in two-dimensional shapes.	Chapter 12 Test: 1, 2, 13
12.9	Partition circles and rectangles into two equal shares.	Chapter 12 Test: 6, 7, 17
12.10	Partition circles and rectangles into four equal shares.	Chapter 12 Test: 9, 19, 20 Beginning/Middle/End-of-Year Test: 26

Getting Ready Correlations

	Lesson Objectives	Test/Item Numbers
1	Write two-digit numbers in expanded form.	Getting Ready • Lessons 1–11: 3, 17, 21
2	Identify how many hundreds, tens, and ones there are in numbers to 199.	Getting Ready • Lessons 1–11: 1, 10
3	Use <, > and = to compare numbers.	Getting Ready • Lessons 1–11: 7, 24
4	Complete an addition function table.	Getting Ready • Lessons 1–11: 5, 23
5	Complete a subtraction function table.	Getting Ready • Lessons 1–11: 12, 19
6	Complete addition and subtraction function tables.	Getting Ready • Lessons 1–11: 9, 14
7	Choose a strategy to add 3 numbers.	Getting Ready • Lessons 1–11: 4, 13
8	Find the sum of a 1-digit number and a 2-digit number.	Getting Ready • Lessons 1–11: 2, 22
9	Find the sum of two 2-digit numbers.	Getting Ready • Lessons 1–11: 6, 15, 20
10	Use repeated addition to add equal groups.	Getting Ready • Lessons 1–11: 8, 16
11	Use repeated addition to solve real world problems.	Getting Ready • Lessons 1–11: 11, 18
12	Compare and choose non-standard units to measure length.	Getting Ready • Lessons 12–20: 4, 8, 19
13	Measure length with a non-standard ruler.	Getting Ready • Lessons 12–20: 1, 7, 21
14	Compare lengths and measure them with non-standard units.	Getting Ready • Lessons 12–20: 5, 15, 24
15	Tell and write time in hours and half hours using an analog clock.	Getting Ready • Lessons 12–20: 2, 12, 20
16	Read and interpret information displayed on a picture graph.	Getting Ready • Lessons 12–20: 9, 17
17	Read and interpret information displayed on a bar graph.	Getting Ready • Lessons 12–20: 10, 18
18	Take a survey and record the results.	Getting Ready • Lessons 12–20: 6, 13
19	Use attributes, such as number of sides and vertices, to help identify two-dimensional shapes.	Getting Ready • Lessons 12–20: 11, 14, 22
20	Identify halves and fourths in circles, squares, and rectangles.	Getting Ready • Lessons 12–20: 3, 16, 23